JOHN WILLIS'

SCREEN WORLD

1974

Volume 25

CROWN PUBLISHERS, INC.

419 PARK AVENUE SOUTH

NEW YORK, N.Y. 10016

To

JOAN CRAWFORD

whose enduring beauty, meticulous discipline, innate strength, and acknowledged talent, led, not only to an unprecedented long and illustrious career as one of the greatest stars of motion pictures, but also to a career as a respected business executive, and who still remains the object of admiration by millions.

Opposite page center portrait submitted by Miss Crawford for inclusion in this volume. Michaele Vollbracht, artist; Joseph Griffith, photographer.

Jack Lemmon in "Save the Tiger"
1973 Academy Award for Best Actor

CONTENTS

EDITOR: JOHN WILLIS

Assistant Editors: Raymond Frederick, Stanley Reeves

Staff: Joe Baltake, Mark Cohen, Frances Crampon, Miles Kreuger,
Mr. Peanut

ACKNOWLEDGMENTS: We wish to express our gratitude to the following who
helped make this volume possible: Ted Albert, Paul Baise, Mal Barbour, Mike Berman,
Susan Bloch, Philip Castanza, Ed Connor, Jon Davison, Charles Felleman, Barry
Fishel, Larry Forley, Laurence Frank, Claud Hill, Roger Karnbad, Seymour Krawitz,
Don Krim, Ely Landau, John Lee, Ruth Pologe Levinson, Arlene Ludwig, Sam Madell,
Leonard Maltin, Harry Markman, Catherine McDonald, Tom Miller, Misty, Charles
Moses, Eric Naumann, John O'Rourke, Louis Ortiz, Ron Perkins, Kaen Raiman,
Adam Reilly, Bill Schelble, Michael Scrimenti, Lazarus Simon, Ted Spiegel, John
Springer, John Sutherland, Dan Talbot, Ira Teller, Paula Vogel, Sandra Wixon

1. Clint Eastwood

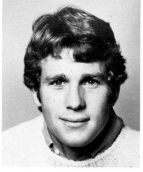
2. Ryan O'Neal

3. Steve McQueen

4. Burt Reynolds

5. Robert Redford

6. Barbra Streisand

7. Paul Newman

8. Charles Bronson

9. John Wayne

10. Marlon Brando

11. Gene Hackman

12. Liza Minnelli

13. Roger Moore

14. Diana Ross

15. Walter Matthau

16. George C. Scott

6

17. Ali MacGraw

18. Woody Allen

19. Dyan Cannon

20. Jane Fonda

1973 RELEASES

21. Glenda Jackson

22. Al Pacino

23. James Coburn

24. Goldie Hawn

25. Dustin Hoffman

Eileen Heckart

Sidney Poitier

Joanne Woodward

SAVE THE TIGER

(PARAMOUNT) Produced and Written by Steve Shagan; Executive Producer, Edward S. Feldman; Director, John G. Avildsen; Photography, Jim Crabe; Editor, David Bretherton; Music, Marvin Hamlisch; Art Director, Jack Collis; Assistant Director, Christopher Seiter; A Filmways production; In Movielab color; Rated R: 100 minutes; January release.

CAST

Harry Stoner	Jack Lemmon
Phil Greene	Jack Guilford
Myra	Laurie Heineman
Fred	Norman Burton
Janet Stoner	Patricia Smith
Charlie Robbins	Thayer David
Meyer	William Hansen
Rico	Harvey Jason
Ula	Liv Von Linden
Margo	Lara Parker
Jackie	Eloise Hardt
Dusty	Janina
Sid	Ned Glass
Cashier	Pearl Shear
Tiger Petitioner	Bliff Elliott
Taxi Driver	Ben Freedman
Receptionist	Madeline Lee

Left: Jack Lemmon

Jack Lemmon received a 1973 Academy Award for Best Actor

Norman Burton, Jack Lemmon, Jack Guilford

Jack Lemmon, Lara Parker, Janina Fischer

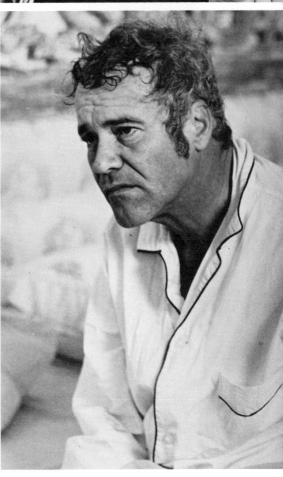

**Harvey Jason, Jack Lemmon Above: Jack Lemmon,
Laurie Heineman Top: Jack Lemmon, Jack Guilford**

**Jack Lemmon
Top: Jack Guilford**

9

THE TRAIN ROBBERS

(WARNER BROS.) Producer, Michael Wayne; Direction and Screenplay, Burt Kennedy; Photography, William H. Clothier; Art Director, Alfred Sweeney; Editor, Frank Santillo; Music, Dominic Frontiere; Assistant Director, Fred Simpson; A Batjac production in Panavision and Technicolor; Rated PG: 92 minutes; January release.

CAST

Lane	John Wayne
Mrs. Lowe	Ann-Margret
Grady	Rod Taylor
Jesse	Ben Johnson
Calhoun	Christopher George
Ben Young	Bobby Vinton
Sam Turner	Jerry Gatlin
Pinkerton Man	Ricardo Montalban

Right: John Wayne, Ann-Margret

John Wayne, Ann-Margret, Ben Johnson, also above with Rod Taylor

Ben Johnson, John Wayne Above: Johnson, Chris George, Taylor, Ann-Margret

CHARLOTTE'S WEB

(PARAMOUNT) Producers, Joseph Barbera, William Hanna; Directors, Charles A. Nichols, Iwao Takamoto; Screenplay, Earl Hamner, Jr.; Based on book by E. B. White; Music and Lyrics, Richard M. and Robert B. Sherman; Art Director, Bob Singer; Editors, Larry Cowan, Pat Foley; Photography, Roy Wade, Dick Blundell, Ralph Migliori, Dennis Weaver, George Epperson; In Movielab color; Rated G; 94 minutes; February release.

CAST

		Voice of:
Charlotte		Debbie Reynolds
Templeton		Paul Lynde
Wilbur		Henry Gibson
Narrator		Rex Allen
Mrs. Arable		Martha Scott
Old Sheep		Dave Madden
Avery		Danny Bonaduce
Geoffrey		Don Messick
Lurvy		Herb Vigran
The Goose		Agnes Moorehead
Fern Arable		Pam Ferdin
Mrs. Zuckerman/Mrs. Fussy		Joan Gerber
Homer Zuckerman		Robert Holt
Arable		John Stephenson
Henry Fussy		William B. White

SHAMUS

(COLUMBIA) Producer, Robert M. Weitman; Director, Buzz Kulik; Screenplay, Barry Beckerman; Associate Producer, Jim Digangi; Photography, Victor J. Kemper; Music, Jerry Goldsmith; Art Director, Philip Rosenberg; Editor, Walter Thompson; Costumes, Frank Thompson; Assistant Director, Ted Zachary; In Panavision and color; Rated PG; 98 minutes; February release.

CAST

McCoy	Burt Reynolds
Alexis	Dyan Cannon
Col. Hardcore	John Ryan
Lt. Promuto	Joe Santos
Dottore	Georgio Tozzi
Hume	Ron Weyand
Springy	Larry Block
Bolton	Beeson Carroll
The Kid	Kevin Conway
Bookstore Girl	Kay Frye
Johnnie	John Glover
Schnook	Merwin Goldsmith
First Woman	Melody Santangelo
Heavy	Irving Selbst
Felix	Alex Wilson
Willie	Tony Amato, Jr.
Rock	Lou Martell
Dealer	Marshall Anker
Doorman	Bert Bertram
Grifter	Jimmy Kelly
Hatcheck Girl	Alisha Fontaine
Pimp	Mickey Freeman
Handler	Capt. Arthur Haggerty
Tait	Tommy Lane
Angie	Ric Mancini
Marvin	Norman Marshall
Big Jake	Fat Thomas Rand
Bookie	Frank Silvero
Knifer	Alex Stevens
Hardnose	Steven Vignari
Detective	Mark Weston
Thugs	Glenn Wilder, Charles Picerni, Tony Amato, Sr.

Top: Burt Reynolds. Bullethead
Left: Beeson Carroll, Burt Reynolds

Dyan Cannon, Burt Reynolds
Above: Ron Weyand, Burt Reynolds

THE WORLD'S GREATEST ATHLETE

(BUENA VISTA) Producer, Bill Walsh; Director, Robert Scheerer;
Screenplay, Gerald Gardner, Dee Caruso; Photography, Frank Phil-
ips; Music, Marvin Hamlisch; Athletic Adviser, Bill Toomey; Art
Directors, John B. Mansbridge, Walter Tyler; Editor, Cotton War-
burton; Assistant Director, Michael Dmytryk; Costumes, Chuck
Keehne, Emily Sundby; A Walt Disney production in Technicolor;
Rated G; 93 minutes; February release.

CAST

Coach Archer	John Amos
Nanu	Jan-Michael Vincent
Gazenga	Roscoe Lee Browne
Milo	Tim Conway
Jane	Dayle Haddon
Landlady	Nancy Walker
Maxwell	Billy DeWolfe
Leopold	Danny Goldman

and Don Pedro Colley, Vito Scotti, Liam Dunn, Ivor Francis, Leon
Askin, Howard Cosell, Frank Gifford, Jim McKay, Bud Palmer, Joe
Kapp, Bill Toomey, Clarence Muse, Virginia Capers, John Lupton,
Russ Conway, Dick Wilson, Jack Griffin, Leigh Christian, Philip
Ahn, Sarah Selby, Al Checco, Dorothy Shay, David Manzy

Right: Jan-Michael Vincent

**Dayle Haddon, Jan-Michael Vincent, also
above with John Amos**

John Amos

WALKING TALL

(CINERAMA) Executive Producer, Charles A. Pratt; Producer, Mort Briskin; Director, Phil Karlson; Screenplay, Mort Briskin; Associate Producer, Joel Briskin; Music, Walter Scharf; Title Song, Don Black, Walter Scharf; Sung by Johnny Mathis; Photography, Jack A. Marta; Designer, Stan Jolley; Editor, Harry Gerstad; Assistant Directors, Ralph Black, David (Buck) Hall; Technical Consultant, Sheriff Buford Pusser; Costumes, Oscar Rodriguez, Phyllis Garr; A BCP production in color; Rated R; 125 minutes; February release.

CAST

Buford Pusser	Joe Don Baker
Pauline Pusser	Elizabeth Hartman
Sheriff Al Thurman	Gene Evans
Grandpa Pusser	Noah Beery
Luan Paxton	Brenda Benet
Prentiss Parley	John Brascia
Grady Coker	Bruce Glover
Buel Jaggers	Arch Johnson
Obra Eaker	Felton Perry
Arno Purdy	Richard X. Slattery
Callie Hacker	Rosemary Murphy
Margie Ann	Lynn Borden
Lutie McVeigh	Ed Call
Sheldon Levine	Sidney Clute
Judge Clarke	Douglas V. Fowley
Dr. Lamar Stivers	Don Keefer
Willie Rae Lockman	Sam Laws
Zolan Dicks	Pepper Martin
Lester Dickens	John Myhers
John Witter	Logan Ramsey
Augie McCullah	Kenneth Tobey
Grandma Pusser	Lurene Tuttle

and Wanea Wes (Singer), Leif Garret (Mike), Dawn Lyn (Dwana), Dominick Mazzie (Bozo), Russell Thorson (Meaks), Gil Perkins, Gene Lebell (Bouncers), Carey Loftin (Dice Player), Warner Venetz (Stickman), Del Monroe (Otie), Lloyd Tatum (Prosecutor), Vaudie Plunk (Foreman), Pearline Wynn (Hassie), Ted Jordan (Virgil), Red West (Tanner), Andrew J. Pirtle (Prisoner).

Right: Joe Don Baker (L), Douglas V. Fowley (R)
Top: Joe Don Baker, Elizabeth Hartman

Rosemary Murphy

Felton Perry, Joe Don Baker, Deputy

14

PAYDAY

(CINERAMA) Producer, Martin Fink; Executive Producer, Ralph J. Gleason; Director, Daryl Duke; Screenplay and Co-Producer, Don Carpenter; Photography, Richard Glouner; Editor, Richard Halsey; Songs, Shel Silverstein, Ian and Sylvia Tyson, Bobb Smith and Tommy McKinney; Assistant Director, Gary B. Grillo; In color by CF; Rated R; 103 minutes; February release.

CAST

Maury Dann	Rip Torn
Mayleen	Ahna Capri
Rosamond	Elayne Heilveil
Clarence	Michael C. Gwynne
Tally	Jeff Morris
Chauffeur	Cliff Emmich
Ted	Henry O. Arnold
Bridgeway	Walter Bamberg
Sandy	Linda Spatz
Galen Dann	Eleanor Fell
Mama Dann	Clara Dunn
Disk Jockey	Earle Trigg
Restaurant Manager	Mike Edwards
Highway Policeman	Winton McNair

Top: Rip Torn, Linda Spatz
Below: Elayne Heilveil, Rip Torn,
Ahna Capri

Rip Torn, also top with Jeff Morris
Above: Michael C. Gwynne

GODSPELL

(COLUMBIA) Producer, Edgar Lansbury; Director, David Greene; Associate Director, John-Michael Tebelak; Screenplay, David Greene, John-Michael Tebelak; Based on stage production by Mr. Tebelak; Music and Lyrics, Stephen Schwartz; Photography, Richard G. Heimann; Editor, Alan Heim; In color; Rated G; 103 minutes; March release.

CAST

Jesus	Victor Garber
John/Judas	David Haskell
Jerry	Jerry Sroka
Lynne	Lynne Thigpen
Katie	Katie Hanley
Robin	Robin Lamont
Gilmer	Gilmer McCormick
Joanne	Joanne Jonas
Merrell	Merrell Jackson
Jeffrey	Jeffrey Mylett

Left: Victor Garber, Joanne Jonas, (center) Merrell Jackson, Lynne Thigpen, Jerry Sroka, Robin Lamont, (back) Jeffrey Mylett, Katie Hanley, David Haskell, Gilmer McCormick

Victor Garber

Front: Lynne Thigpen, Jerry Sroka, David Haskell Back: Katie Hanley, Robin Lamont, Jeffrey Mylett Above: Victor Garber, David Haskell

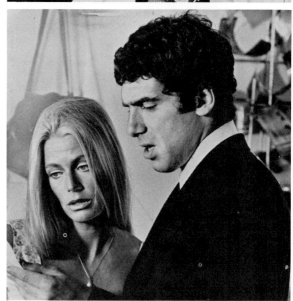

THE LONG GOODBYE

(UNITED ARTISTS) Executive Producer, Elliott Kastner; Producer, Jerry Bick; Director, Robert Altman; Screenplay, Leigh Brackett; Associate Producer, Robert Eggenweiler; Based on novel by Raymond Chandler; Photography, Vilmostz Sigmond; Editor, Lou Lombardo; Music, John Williams; Assistant Director, Tommy Thompson; In Panavision and Technicolor; Rated R; 112 minutes; March release.

CAST

Philip Marlowe	Elliott Gould
Eileen Wade	Nina van Pallandt
Roger Wade	Sterling Hayden
Marty Augustine	Mark Rydell
Dr. Verringer	Henry Gibson
Harry	David Arkin
Terry Lennox	Jim Bouton
Morgan	Warren Berlinger
Jo Ann Eggenweiler	Jo Ann Brody
Hood	Jack Knight
Pepe	Pepe Callahan
Hoods	Vince Palmieri, Arnold Strong
Marlowe's Neighbors	Rutanya Alda, Tammy Shaw
Piano Player	Jack Riley
Colony Guard	Ken Sansom
Bartender	Danny Goldman
Real Estate Lady	Sybil Scotford
Detective Farmer	Steve Coit
Detective	Tracy Harris
Detective Green	Jerry Jones
Clerk	Rodney Moss

Top: Elliott Gould, Nina van Pallandt
Right: Nina van Pallandt, Sterling Hayden

18

Nina van Pallandt, Elliott Gould
Above: Mark Rydell

LOST HORIZON

(COLUMBIA) Producer, Ross Hunter; Director, Charles Jarrott; Screenplay, Larry Kramer; From novel by James Hilton; Music, Burt Bacharach; Lyrics, Hal David; Photography, Robert Surtees; Costumes, Jean Louis; Musical Numbers Staged by Hermes Pan; Title song sung by Shawn Phillips; Designer, Preston Ames; Associate Producer, Jacque Mapes; Assistant Director, Sheldon Schrager; Editor, Maury Winetrobe; In Panavision and color; Rating G; 150 minutes; March release.

CAST

Richard Conway	Peter Finch
Catherine	Liv Ullmann
Sally Hughes	Sally Kellerman
Sam Cornelius	George Kennedy
George Conway	Michael York
Maria	Olivia Hussey
Harry Lovett	Bobby Van
Brother To-Lenn	James Shigeta
High Lama	Charles Boyer
Chang	John Gielgud

Right: John Gielgud, Bobby Van, Sally Kellerman, Peter Finch, Michael York, George Kennedy

Liv Ullmann, Peter Finch Above: John Gielgud, James Shigeta, Michael York, Olivia Hussey, Peter Finch, Liv Ullmann, George Kennedy, Sally Kellerman, Bobby Van, Charles Boyer

Olivia Hussey, Michael York Above: Charles Boyer, Peter Finch

TOM SAWYER

(UNITED ARTISTS) Producer, Arthur P. Jacobs; Director, Don Taylor; Screenplay, Robert B. and Richard M. Sherman; Based on "The Adventures of Tom Sawyer" by Mark Twain; Associate Producer, Frank Capra, Jr.; Executive Producer, Walter Bien; Editor, Marion Rothman; Music and Lyrics, Richard M. and Robert B. Sherman; Photography, Frank Stanley; Designer, Philip Jeffries; Costumes, Donfeld; Choreography, Danny Daniels; Assistant Directors, Newton Arnold, Ron Wright, Neil Machlis; An Apjac International picture; In Panavision and DeLuxe color; Rated G; 103 minutes; March release.

CAST

Tom Sawyer	Johnny Whitaker
Aunt Polly	Celeste Holm
Muff Potter	Warren Oates
Huckleberry Finn	Jeff East
Becky Thatcher	Jodie Foster
Widder Douglas	Lucille Benson
Mister Dobbins	Henry Jones
Judge Thatcher	Noah Keen
Clayton	Dub Taylor
Doc Robinson	Richard Eastham
Constable Clemens	Sandy Kenyon
Cousin Sidney	Joshua Hill Lewis
Cousin Mary	Susan Joyce
Ben Rogers	Steve Hogg
Billy Fisher	Sean Summers
Joe Jefferson	Kevin Jefferson
Saloon Girl	Page Williams
Injun Joe	Kunu Hank
Blacksmith	James A. Kuhn
Prosecuting Attorney	Mark Lynch
Small Boy	Jonathan Taylor
Girl	Anne Voss

Left: Johnny Whitaker, Susan Joyce, Celeste Holm, Joshua Hill Lewis Top: Jeff East, Warren Oates, Johnny Whitaker

Johnny Whitaker, Jodie Foster

Noah Keen, Kunu Hank

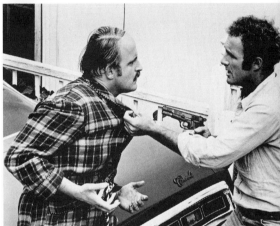

SLITHER

(MGM) Producer, Jack Sher; Director, Howard Zieff; Screenplay, W. D. Richter; Associate Producer, W. D. Richter, Music, Tom McIntosh; Photography, Laszlo Kovacs; Art Director, Dale Hennessy; Editor, David Bretherton; Assistant Director, Les Sheldon; A Talent Associates-Norton Simon production in Metrocolor; Rated PG; 97 minutes; March release.

CAST

Dick Kanipsia	James Caan
Barry Fenaka	Peter Boyle
Kitty Kopetzky	Sally Kellerman
Mary Fenaka	Louise Lasser
Vincent J. Palmer	Allen Garfield
Harry Moss	Richard B. Shull
Man with ice cream	Alex Rocco
Farmer in truck	Seamon Glass
Highway Patrolman	Wayne Storm
Band Singer	Diana Darrin
Buddy	Stuart Nisbet
Bingo Player	Edwina Gough
Man in men's room	Al Dunlap
Short Order Cook	James Joseph
Bingo Caller	Virginia Sale
Man at phone booth	Alex Henteloff
Jogger	Len Lesser
Man with camera	Garry Goodrow

**Top: James Caan, Louise Lasser, Sally Kellerman
Below: James Caan, Richard B. Shull**

James Caan, Peter Boyle, Sally Kellerman

HIGH PLAINS DRIFTER

(UNIVERSAL) Producer, Robert Daley; Director, Clint Eastwood; Executive Producer, Jennings Lang; Screenplay, Ernest Tidyman; Photography, Bruce Surtees; Art Director, Henry Bumstead; Editor, Ferris Webster; Music, Dee Barton; Assistant Director, Jim Fargo; A Malpaso production in Panavision and Technicolor; Rated R; 105 minutes; April release.

CAST

The Stranger	Clint Eastwood
Sarah Belding	Verna Bloom
Callie Travers	Mariana Hill
Dave Drake	Mitchell Ryan
Morgan Allen	Jack Ging
Mayor Jason Hobart	Stefan Gierasch
Lewis Belding	Ted Hartley
Mordecai	Billy Curtis
Stacey Bridges	Geoffrey Lewis
Bill Borders	Scott Walker
Sheriff Sam Shaw	Walter Barnes
Lutie Naylor	Paul Brinegar
Asa Goodwin	Richard Bull
Preacher	Robert Donner
Bootmaker	John Hillerman
Cole Carlin	Anthony James
Barber	William O'Connell
Jake Ross	John Quade
Townswoman	Jane Aull
Dan Carlin	Dan Vadis
Gunsmith	Reid Cruickshanks
Tommy Morris	James Gosa
Saddlemaker	Jack Kosslyn
Fred Short	Russ McCubbin
Mrs. Lake	Belle Mitchell
Warden	John Mitchum
Teamster	Carl C. Pitti
Stableman	Chuck Waters
Marshall Jim Duncan	Buddy Van Horn

**Top: Clint Eastwood, also right
with Mariana Hill**

**Verna Bloom, Clint Eastwood
Above: Billy Curtis, Clint Eastwood**

BOOK OF NUMBERS

(AVCO EMBASSY) Producer-Director, Raymond St. Jacques; Associate Producers, Joe Dennis, Mike Fields; Photography, Gayne Rescher; Screenplay, Larry Spiegel; Based on novel by Robert Deane Phaar; Presented by Joseph E. Levine and Brut Productions; In color; Rated R; 81 minutes; April release.

CAST

Blueboy Harris	Raymond St. Jacques
Kelly Simms	Freda Payne
Dave Greene	Philip Thomas
Pigmeat Goins	Hope Clarke
Makepeace Johnson	Willie Washington, Jr.
Eggy	Doug Finell
Kid Flick	Sterling St. Jacques
Blip Blip	C. L. Williams
Billy Bowlegs	D'Urville Martin
Joe Gaines	Jerry Leon
Luis Antoine	Gilbert Greene
Carlos	Frank De Sal
Sister Clara Goode	Temie Mae Williams
Sister #2	Pauline Herndon
Sister #3	Ethel Marie Crawford
Bus Station Prostitute	Mimi Lee Dodd
Mr. Booker	Charles F. Elyston
Mrs. Booker	Queen Esther Gent
Georgia Brown	Irma Hall
Didi	Chiquita Jackson
Honey	Katie Peters
Becky	Pat Peterson
Goons	Ray McDonald, Charles Lewis

Right: Raymond St. Jacques, Hope Clarke, Freda Payne, Sterling St. Jacques, Philip Thomas

Raymond St. Jacques, Freda Payne
Above: Raymond St. Jacques, Philip Thomas

Freda Payne, Frank DeSal
Above: Freda Payne, Philip Thomas

CHARLEY AND THE ANGEL

(BUENA VISTA) Producer, Bill Anderson; Director, Vincent McEveety; Screenplay, Roswell Rogers; Based on "The Golden Evenings of Summer" by Will Stanton; Photography, Charles F. Wheeler; Music, Buddy Baker; Art Directors, John B. Mansbridge, Al Roelofs; Editors, Ray de Leuw, Bob Bring; Costumes, Shelby Tatum; Assistant Director, Ronald R. Grow; A Walt Disney production in Technicolor; Rated G; 93 minutes; April release.

CAST

Charley Appleby	Fred MacMurray
Nettie Appleby	Cloris Leachman
The Angel	Harry Morgan
Ray Ferris	Kurt Russell
Leonora Appleby	Kathleen Cody
Willie Appleby	Vincent Van Patten
Rupert Appleby	Scott Kolden
Pete	George Lindsey
Banker	Edward Andrews
Buggs	Richard Bakalyan
Sadie	Barbara Nichols
Policeman	Kelly Thordsen
Dr. Sprague	Liam Dunn
Felix	Larry D. Mann
Police Chief	George O'Hanlon
Miss Partridge	Susan Tolsky
Frankie Zuto	Mills Watson
Derwood Moseby	Ed Begley, Jr.
Susie	Christina Anderson
Driver	Roy Engel
Girl in Sadie's Palace	Pat Delany
News Reporter	Bob Hastings
Policeman #2	Jack Griffin

Left: Fred MacMurray, Harry Morgan Top: Fred MacMurray, Vincent Van Patten, Cloris Leachman, Scott Kolden

Kurt Russell, Kathleen Cody

Richard Bakalyan, Scott Kolden, Mills Watson, Vincent Van Patten Above: Fred MacMurray, Pat Delaney

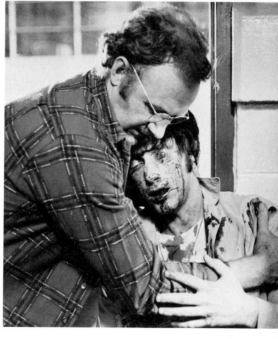

SCARECROW

(WARNER BROS.) Producer, Robert M. Sherman; Director, Jerry Schatzberg; Screenplay, Garry Michael White; Photography, Vilmos Zsigmond; Designer, Al Brenner; Editor, Evan Lottman; Music, Fred Myrow; Costumes, Jo Ynocencio; Assistant Directors, Tom Shaw, Charles Bonniwell; In Panavision and Technicolor; Rated R; 112 minutes; April release.

CAST

Max	Gene Hackman
Lion	Al Pacino
Coley	Dorothy Tristan
Frenchy	Ann Wedgeworth
Riley	Richard Lynch
Darlene	Eileen Brennan
Annie	Penny Allen
Mickey	Richard Hackman
Skipper	Al Cingolani
Woman in camper	Rutanya Alda

**Top: Gene Hackman, Al Pacino,
also below, and top left**

**Al Pacino, Gene Hackman, and above with
Anne Wedgeworth, Dorothy Tristan**

CLASS OF '44

(WARNER BROS.) Executive Producer, Harry Keller; Producer-Director, Paul Bogart; Screenplay, Herman Raucher; Photography, Andrew Laszlo; Designer, Ben Edwards; Editor, Michael A. Hoey; Music, David Shire; Assistant Director, Peter Bogart; In Panavision and Technicolor; Rated PG; 95 minutes; April release.

CAST

Hermie	Gary Grimes
Oscy	Jerry Houser
Benjie	Oliver Conant
Fraternity President	William Atherton
Marty	Sam Bottoms
Julie	Deborah Winters
Professor	Joe Ponazecki
Principal	Murray Westgate
Grade Adviser	Marion Waldman
Valedictorian	Mary Long
Mrs. Gilhuly	Marcia Diamond
Editor	Jeffrey Cohen
Assistant Editor	Susan Marcus
First Proctor	Lamar Criss
Second Proctor	Michael A. Hoey
Father	Dan McDonald
Mother	Jan Campbell

Right: Gary Grimes, Deborah Winters

Jerry Houser, Gary Grimes also center above

Deborah Winters, Gary Grimes Above: Gary Grimes, Oliver Conant, Jerry Houser

26

THE MACK

(CINERAMA) Producer, Harvey Bernhard; Director, Michael Campus; Screenplay, Robert J. Poole; Music, Willie Hutch; Photography, Ralph Woolsey; Editor, Frank C. Decot; Associate Producer, R. Hansel Brown; Rated R; 110 minutes; April release.

CAST

Goldie	Max Julien
Hank	Don Gordon
Slim	Richard Pryor
Lulu	Carol Speed
Olinga	Roger E. Mosley
Pretty Tony	Dick Williams
Jed	William C. Watson
Fatman	George Murdock
Mother	Juanita Moore
Blind Man	Paul Harris
Chico	Kai Hernandez
China Doll	Annazette Chase
Baltimore Bob	Junero Jennings
Sgt. Duncan	Lee Duncan
Announcer	Stu Gulliam
Diane	Sandra Brown
Jesus Christ	Christopher Brooks
Desk Sergeant	Fritz Ford
Hotel Trick	John Vick
Big Woman	Norma McClure
Laughing David	David Mauro

and Allen Van, Willie Redman, Frank Ward, Ted Ward, Willie Ward, Andrew Ward, Roosevelt Taylor, Jay Payton, Terrible Tom, Bill Barnes, Jack Hunter

**Right: Max Julien, Sandra Brown
Top: Max Julien, Richard Pryor**

**Dick Williams Above: Max Julien,
George Murdock**

Annazette Chase, Richard Pryor

ACE ELI AND RODGER OF THE SKIES

(20th CENTURY-FOX) Producer, Boris Wilson; Director, Bill Sampson; Screenplay, Chips Rosen; Story, Steven Spielberg; Photography, David M. Walsh; Music, Jerry Goldsmith; Song written and sung by Jim Grady; Editors, Louis Lombardo, Robert Belcher; Costumes, Theadora Van Runkle; Assistant Director, David Hall; Art Directors, Jack Martin Smith, Joel Schiller; In Panavision and DeLuxe color; Rated PG; 92 minutes; April release.

CAST

Eli	Cliff Robertson
Rodger	Eric Shea
Shelby	Pamela Franklin
Hannah	Rosemary Murphy
Allison	Bernadette Peters
Sister Lite	Alice Ghostley
Rachel	Kelly Jean Peters
Mr. Parsons	Don Keefer
Wilma	Patricia Smith
Jake	Royal Dano
Dumb Dickie	Robert Hamm
Frank Savage	Herb Gatlin
Brother Watson	Arthur Malet
Betty Jo	Ariane Munker
Laura	Hope Summers
Abraham	Jim Boles
Harrison	Lew Brown
Jeffrey	Brent Hurst
Mrs. Parsons	Jan Simms
Leroy	Rodger Peck
Ann	Claudia Bryar
Mrs. Harrison	Dixie Lee
Linette	Felicity Van Runkle
Brother Foster	Pat O'Connor
Mortician	Bill Quinn
Gambler	Jerry Ayres
Sheriff	Hubert Brotten
Charlie	Gary L. Clothier
Bride	Penny Metropulos
Groom	John O'Connell

Top: Pamela Franklin Left: Alice Ghostley, Eric Shea, Cliff Robertson

**Cliff Robertson, Patricia Smith
Above: Eric Shea, Bernadette Peters**

LET THE GOOD TIMES ROLL

(COLUMBIA) Executive Producer, Charles Fries; Producer, Gerald I. Isenberg; Directors, Sid Levin, Robert Abel; Photography, Robert Thomas; Editors, Sid Levin, Hyman Kaufman, Bud Friedgen, Yeu-Bun-Yee; A Metromedia Producers Corp., and Richard Nader production; A Cinema Associates Film in color; Rated PG; 99 minutes; May release.

CAST
Chuck Berry
Little Richard
Fats Domino
Chubby Checker
Bo Diddley
The Shirelles
The Five Satins
The Coasters
Danny and the Juniors
Bobby Comstock Rock and Roll Band
Bill Haley and the Comets
Richard Nader, MC

Right: Richard Nader

Fats Domino Above: Bill Haley
and the Comets

The Shirelles
Above: The Five Satins

29

Dennis Hopper, Lee Purcell
Top: Dennis Hopper, Janice Rule

KID BLUE

(20th CENTURY-FOX) Producer, Marvin Schwartz; Director, James Frawley; Screenplay, Edwin Shrake; Photography, Billy Williams; Designer, Joel Schiller; Costumes, Theadora Van Runkle; Editor, Stefan Arnsten; Assistant Director, Tony Ray; Music, Tim McIntire, John Rubinstein; In Panavision and Deluxe color; Rated PG; 108 minutes; May release.

CAST

Bickford Waner	Dennis Hopper
Reese Ford	Warren Oates
Preacher Bob	Peter Boyle
Sheriff "Mean John" Simpson	Ben Johnson
Molly Ford	Lee Purcell
Janet Conforto	Janice Rule
Drummer	Ralph Waite
Mr. Hendricks	Clifton James
Old Coyote	Jose Torvay
Mrs. Evans	Mary Jackson
Mendoza	Jay Varela
Tough Guy	Claude Ennis Starrett, Jr.
Wills	Warren Finnerty
Confectionery man	Howard Hessman
Barber	M. Emmet Walsh
Joe Cloudmaker	Henry Smith
Bartender	Bobby Hall
Blackman	Melvin Stewart
Huey	Eddy Donno
Train Robbers	Owen Orr, Richard Rust

Top: Jay Varela, Dennis Hopper, Jose Torvay
Below: Warren Oates, Dennis Hopper

30

THE SOUL OF NIGGER CHARLEY

(PARAMOUNT) Produced, Directed, and Story by Larry G. Spangler; Screenplay, Harold Stone; Photography, Richard C. Glouner; Music, Don Costa; Editor, Howard Kuperman; Art Director, Gene Rudolph; Assistant Director, Angelo Laiacona; In Movielab color; Rated R; 110 minutes; May release.

CAST

Charley	Fred Williamson
Toby	D'Urville Martin
Elena	Denise Nicholas
Sandoval	Pedro Armendariz, Jr.
Marcellus	Kirk Calloway
Ode	George Allen
Colonel Blanchard	Kevin Hagen
Sergeant Foss	Michael Cameron
Roy	Johnny Greenwood
Collins	James Garbo
Anita	Nai Bonet
Fred	Robert Minor
Woods	Fred Lerner
Lee	Joe Henderson
Walker	Dick Farnsworth
Aben	Tony Brubaker
Donovan	Boyd Red Morgan
Vet	Al Hassan
Mexicans	Ed Hice, Henry Wills
Pedro	Phil Avenetti

Top: Fred Williamson, also right, and
below with Pedro Armendariz, Jr.,
D'Urville Martin (R)

George Allen, Fred Williamson, Denise Nicholas,
Kirk Calloway, D'Urville Martin, also above

Ryan O'Neal, Tatum O'Neal, also
above, and top

PAPER MOON

(**PARAMOUNT**) Producer-Director, Peter Bogdanovich; Screenplay, Alvin Sargent; Based on novel "Addie Pray" by Joe David Brown; Photography, Laszlo Kovacs; Editor, Verna Fields; Designer, Polly Platt; Assistant Director, Ray Gosnell; A Directors Company presentation; In black and white; Rated PG; 102 minutes; May release.

CAST

Moses Pray	Ryan O'Neal
Addie Loggins	Tatum O'Neal
Trixie Delight	Madeline Kahn
Deputy Hardin	John Hillerman
Imogene	P. J. Johnson
Floyd	Burton Gilliam
Leroy	Randy Quade
Widow Huff	Dorothy Forster
Miss Ollie	Jessie Lee Fulton
Minister	Jim Harrell
Minister's Wife	Lila Waters
Robertson	Noble Willingham
Gas Station Attendant	Bob Young
Station Master	Jack Saunders
Widow Pearl Morgan	Liz Ross
Widow Marie Bates	Yvonne Harrison
Lawman	Ed Reed

and Dorothy Price, Eleanor Bogart, Lana Daniel, Herschel Morris, Dejah Moore, Ralph Coder, Harriet Ketchum, Desmond Dhooge, Kenneth Hughes, George Lillie, Floyd Mahaney, Randy Arnold, Vernon Schwanke, Dennis Beden, Hugh Gillin, Art Ellison, Rosemary Rumbley

Top: Tatum O'Neal, Ryan O'Neal
Below: Ryan O'Neal, Madeline Kahn, P. J. Johnson

*Tatum O'Neal won 1973 Academy Award
for Best Supporting Actress*

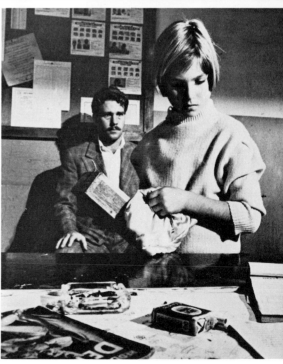

Tatum O'Neal, P. J. Johnson Above: Dorothy Price, Tatum O'Neal, Ryan O'Neal

Ryan O'Neal, Tatum O'Neal Above: Madeline Kahn, Tatum O'Neal

SOYLENT GREEN

(MGM) Producers, Walter Seltzer, Russell Thacher; Director, Richard Fleischer; Screenplay, Stanley R. Greenberg; Based on novel by Harry Harrison; Music, Fred Myrow; Photography, Richard H. Kline; Art Director, Edward C. Carfagno; Editor, Samuel E. Beetley; Assistant Directors, Daniel S. McCauley, Gene Marum; Costumes, Pat Barto; In Metrocolor and Panavision; Rated PG; 97 minutes; May release.

CAST

Thorn	Charlton Heston
Shirl	Leigh Taylor-Young
Tab	Chuck Connors
Simonson	Joseph Cotten
Hatcher	Brock Peters
Martha	Paula Kelly
Sol Roth	Edward G. Robinson
Gilbert	Stephen Young
Kulozik	Mike Henry
Priest	Lincoln Kilpatrick
Donovan	Roy Jenson
Charles	Leonard Stone
Santini	Whit Bissell
Exchange Leader	Celia Lovsky
Mrs. Santini	Jane Dulo
Usher	Dick Van Patten
Brady	Tim Herbert
Wagner	John Dennis
Bandana Woman	Jan Bradley
New Tenant	Carlos Romero
Fat Guard	Pat Houtchens

and Morgan Farley (Book 1), John Barclay (Book 2), Belle Mitchell (Book 3), Cyril Delevanti (Book 4), Forrest Wood, Faith Quabius (Attendants), Joyce Williams, Beverly Gill, Cheri Howell, Jennifer King, Erica Hagen, Suesie Eejima, Kathy Silva, Marion Charles (Furniture Girls)

Left: Chuck Connors, Charlton Heston
Top: Leigh Taylor-Young, Charlton Heston

Edward G. Robinson, Charlton Heston

Brock Peters, Charlton Heston
Above: Joseph Cotten, Stephen Young

BATTLE FOR THE PLANET OF THE APES

(20th CENTURY-FOX) Producer, Arthur P. Jacobs; Director, J. Lee Thompson; Associate Producer, Frank Capra, Jr.; Story, Paul Dehn; Based on characters by Pierre Boulle; Screenplay, John William Corrington, Joyce Hooper Corrington; Music, Leonard Rosenman; Photography, Richard H. Kline; Editors, Ala L. Jaggs, John C. Horger; Art Director, Dale Hennesy; Assistant Directors, Ric Rondell, Barry Stern; An Apjac International production in Panavision and DeLuxe color; Rated G; 86 minutes; June release.

CAST

Caesar	Roddy McDowall
Aldo	Claude Akins
Lawgiver	John Huston
Lisa	Natalie Trundy
Kolp	Severn Darden
Mandemus	Lew Ayres
Virgil	Paul Williams
MacDonald	Austin Stoker
Teacher	Noah Keen
Mutant Captain	Richard Eastham
Alma	France Nuyen
Mendez	Paul Stevens
Doctor	Heather Lowe
Cornelius	Bobby Porter
Jake	Michael Stearns
Soldier	Cal Wilson
Young Chimp	Pat Cardi
Jake's Friend	John Landis
Mutant on motorcycle	Andy Knight

Top: (L) Austin Stoker, Paul Williams, Noah Keen
(R) Severn Darden (C) Center: (L) John Huston
(R) Paul Williams, Roddy McDowall, Austin Stoker

Roddy McDowall, Bobby Porter, Natalie Trundy

37

THE LEGEND OF HELL HOUSE

(20th CENTURY-FOX) Executive Producer, James H. Nicholson; Director, John Hough; Producers, Albert Fennell, Norman T. Herman; Screenplay, Richard Matheson; Based on his novel "Hell House"; Photography, Alan Hume; Designer, Ron Fry; Editor, Geoffrey Foot; Music and Electronic Score, Brian Hodgson, Delia Derbyshire; Assistant Director, Bert Batt; An Academy Pictures production in DeLuxe color; Rated PG; 90 minutes; June release.

CAST

Florence Tanner	Pamela Franklin
Ben Fischer	Roddy McDowall
Dr. Chris Barrett	Clive Revill
Ann Barrett	Gayle Hunnicutt
Rudolph Deutsch	Roland Culver
Hanley	Peter Bowles

Right: Pamela Franklin

Roddy McDowall, Gayle Hunnicutt, Clive Revill

THE MAN WHO LOVED CAT DANCING

(MGM) Producers, Martin Poll, Eleanor Perry; Director, Richard C. Sarafian; Screenplay, Eleanor Perry; Based on novel by Marilyn Durham; Music, John Williams; Photography, Harry Stradling, Jr.; Art Director, Edward C. Carfagno; Editor, Tom Rolf; Associate Producer, T. W. Sewell; Costumes, Frank Thompson; Assistant Director, Les Sheldon; In Panavision and Metrocolor; Rated PG; 114 minutes; June release.

CAST

Jay	Burt Reynolds
Catherine	Sarah Miles
Lapchance	Lee J. Cobb
Dawes	Jack Warden
Crocker	George Hamilton
Billy	Bo Hopkins
Dub	Robert Donner
Ben	Sandy Kevin
Iron Knife	Larry Littlebird
Sudie	Nancy Malone
The Chief	Jay Silverheels
Charlie	Jay Varela
Conductor	Owen Bush
Bartender	Larry Finley
Dream Speaker	Sutero Garcia, Jr.

Right: Sarah Miles, Burt Reynolds

Bo Hopkins, Sarah Miles, Burt Reynolds, Jack Warden Above: Reynolds, Hopkins, Miles, Nancy Malone

Sarah Miles, Burt Reynolds Above: Lee J. Cobb, George Hamilton

CAHILL, UNITED STATES MARSHALL

(WARNER BROS.) Producer, Michael Wayne; Director, Andrew V. McLaglen; Screenplay, Harry Julian Fink, Rita M. Fink; Story, Barney Slater; Photography, Joseph Biroc; Designer, Walter Simonds; Music, Elmer Bernstein; Editor, Robert L. Simpson; Assistant Directors, Joe Florence, Fred R. Simpson; A Batjac production; In Panavision and Technicolor; Rated PG; 103 minutes; June release.

CAST

Cahill	John Wayne
Fraser	George Kennedy
Danny Cahill	Gary Grimes
Lightfoot	Neville Brand
Billy Joe Cahill	Clay O'Brien
Mrs. Green	Marie Windsor
Struther	Morgan Paull
Brownie	Dan Vadis
MacDonald	Royal Dano
Ben Tildy	Scott Walker
Denver	Denver Pyle
Charlie Smith	Jackie Coogan
Pee Wee Simser	Rayford Barnes
Joe Meehan	Dan Kemp
Hank	Harry Carey, Jr.
Sheriff Grady	Walter Barnes
Old Man	Paul Fix
Hard Case	Pepper Martin
Negro	Vance Davis
Boy	Ken Wolger
Undertaker	Hank Worden
Doctor	James Nusser
Deputy Gordine	Murray MacLeod
Deputy Jim Kane	Hunter von Leer

Left: Gary Grimes, John Wayne
Top: Marie Windsor, John Wayne

Neville Brand, John Wayne

John Wayne, George Kennedy, Gary Grimes

40 CARATS

(COLUMBIA) Producer, M. J. Frankovich; Director, Milton Katselas; Screenplay, Leonard Gershe; Based on play adapted by Jay Allen from Barillet and Gredy; Photography, Charles B. Lang; Costumes, Jean Louis; Editor, David Blewitt; Designer, Robert Clatworthy; Music, Michel Legrand; Assistant Directors, Dick Moder, David Hawks; In color; Rated PG; 108 minutes; June release.

CAST

Ann Stanley	Liv Ullmann
Peter Latham	Edward Albert
Billy Boylan	Gene Kelly
Maud Ericson	Binnie Barnes
Trina Stanley	Deborah Raffin
J. D. Rogers	Billy Green Bush
Mrs. Margolin	Nancy Walker
Mr. Latham	Don Porter
Mrs. Latham	Rosemary Murphy
Mrs. Adams	Natalie Schafer
Arthur Forbes	Sam Chew, Jr.
Gabriella	Claudia Jennings
Polly	Brooke Palance

Top: (L) Liv Ullmann, Deborah Raffin
(R) Edward Albert, Liv Ullmann Center:
(L) Edward Albert, Deborah Raffin, Binnie
Barnes, Liv Ullmann (R) Gene Kelly, Liv
Ullmann

Edward Albert, Liv Ullmann

41

SUPER FLY T.N.T.

(PARAMOUNT) Producer, Sig Shore; Director, Ron O'Neal; Screenplay, Alex Haley; Story, Ron O'Neal, Sig Shore; Photography, Robert Gaffney; Music, Osibisa; Editor, Bob Brady; Designer, Giuseppe Bassan; In Movielab color; Rated R; 87 minutes; June release.

CAST

Priest	Ron O'Neal
Dr. Lamine Sonko	Roscoe Lee Browne
Georgia	Sheila Frazier
Jordan Gaines	Robert Guillaume
Matty Smith	Jacques Sernas
Lefevre	William Berger
Customs Man	Roy Bosler
George	Silvio Nardo
Lisa	Olga Bisera
Rik	Rik Boyd
Rand	Dominic Barto
General	Minister Dem
Riding Instructress	Jeannie McNeill
Pilot	Dan Davis
Crew Chief	Luigi Orso
Photographer	Ennio Catalfamo
Warehouse Custodian	Francesco Rachini
Poker Players	George Wang, Fernando Piazza, Ferrucio Brusarosco

**Top: Ron O'Neal, Sheila Frazier, Roscoe
Lee Browne Below: Robert Guillaume,
Ron O'Neal**

Ron O'Neal, Sheila Frazier, also top

THE LAST OF SHEILA

(WARNER BROTHERS) Executive Producer, Stanley O'Toole; Producer-Director, Herbert Ross; Screenplay, Anthony Perkins, Stephen Sondheim; Photography, Gerry Turpin; Designer, Ken Adam; Editor, Edward Warschilka; Art Director, Tony Roman; Music, Billy Goldenberg; In Technicolor; Rated PG; 120 minutes; June release.

CAST

Tom	Richard Benjamin
Christine	Dyan Cannon
Clinton	James Coburn
Lee	Joan Hackett
Philip	James Mason
Antony	Ian McShane
Alice	Raquel Welch
Sheila	Yvonne Romain
Vittorio	Pierro Rosso

and Serge Citon, Robert Rossi, Elaine Geisinger, Elliot Geisinger, Jack Pugeat, Maurice Crosnier

Right: James Mason, James Coburn, and below (L) with Raquel Welch, Joan Hackett, Ian McShane, Dyan Cannon, Richard Benjamin

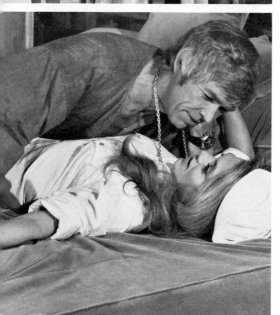

James Coburn, Dyan Cannon

Richard Benjamin, Raquel Welch
Above: Richard Benjamin

THE FRIENDS OF EDDIE COYLE

(PARAMOUNT) Produced and Written by Paul Manash; Director Peter Yates; Based on novel by George V. Higgins; Photography Victor J. Kemper; Editor, Patricia Lewis Jaffe; Music, Dave Grusin Designer, Gene Callahan; Assistant Director, Peter Scoppa; In Technicolor; Rated R; 102 minutes; June release.

CAST

Eddie Coyle	Robert Mitchum
Dillon	Peter Boyle
Foley	Richard Jordan
Jackie Brown	Steven Keats
Scalise	Alex Rocco
Artie Van	Joe Santos
Waters	Mitchell Ryan
Coyle's Wife	Helena Carroll
Bank Managers	Peter MacLean, Kevin O'Morrison
Nancy	Carolyn Pickman
Vernon	Marvin Lichterman
Contact Man	James Tolkan
Pete	Matthew Cowles
Andrea	Margaret Ladd
Wanda	Jane House
The Kid	Michael McCleery
Phil	Alan Koss
Webber	Dennis McMullen
Mrs. Partridge	Judith Ogden Cabot
Pale Kid	Jan Egleson
The Beard	Jack Kehoe
Moran	Robert Anthony
Ames	Gus Johnson
Sauter	Ted Maynard
Ferris	Sheldon Feldner

Left: Michael McCreery, Robert Mitchum, Peter Boyle Top: Jane House, Robert Mitchum

Robert Mitchum

Richard Jordan, Robert Mitchum

SHAFT IN AFRICA

(MGM) Producer, Roger Lewis; Director, John Guillermin; Screenplay, Stirling Silliphant; Based on characters by Ernest Tidyman; Associate Producer, Rene Dupont; Music, Johnny Pate; Photography, Marcel Grignon; Designer, John Stoll; Editor, Max Benedict; Assistant Director, Miguel Angel Gil, Jr.; In Panavision and Metrocolor; Rated R; 112 minutes; June release.

CAST

John Shaft	Richard Roundtree
Amafi	Frank Finlay
Aleme	Vonetta McGee
Jazar	Neda Arneric
Wassa	Debebe Eshetu
Sassari	Spiros Focas
Perreau	Jacques Herlin
Ziba	Jho Jhenkins
Oyo	Willie Jonah
Piro	Adolfo Lastretti
Colonel Gondar	Marne Maitland
Osiat	Frank McRae
Prostitute	Zenebech Tadesse
Ramila's son	A. V. Falana
Williams	James E. Myers
Zubair	Nadim Sawalha
Kopo	Thomas Baptiste
Shimba	Jon Chevron
Vanden	Glynn Edwards
Emir Ramila	Cy Grant
Cusset	Jacques Marin
Sadi	Nick Zaran
Angelo	Aldo Sambrell

Top: Thomas Baptiste, Richard Roundtree, Spiro Focas Below: Frank Finlay, Neda Arneric

Vonetta McGee, Richard Roundtree, also top Above: Neda Arneric, Richard Roundtree

45

WHITE LIGHTNING

(UNITED ARTISTS) Producers, Arthur Gardner, Jules V. Levy; Director, Joseph Sargent; Screenplay, William Norton; Music, Charles Bernstein; Photography, Edward Rosson; Editor, George Nicholson; Assistant Director, Edward Teets; In color; Rated PG; 101 minutes; July release.

CAST

Gator McKlusky	Burt Reynolds
Lou	Jennifer Billingsley
Sheriff Connors	Ned Beatty
Roy Boone	Bo Hopkins
Dude Watson	Matt Clark
Martha Culpepper	Louise Latham
Maggie	Diane Ladd
Big Bear	R. G. Armstrong
Deputy	Conlan Carter
Pa McKluskey	Dabbs Greer
Superintendent Simms	Lincoln Demyan
Skeeter	John Steadman
Ma McKluskey	Iris Korn
Jenny	Stephanie Burchfield
Louella	Barbara Muller
Harvey	Robert Ginnaven
Sister Linda Fay	Fay Martin
Treasury Agents	Richard Allin, Bill Bond
Junior	Glenn Wilder
Student	Kathy Finley
Highway Patrolmen	Dick Ziker, Buddy Joe Hooker

**Right: Jennifer Billingsley, Bo Hopkins
Top: Burt Reynolds, Iris Korn**

Burt Reynolds

Burt Reynolds, Jennifer Billingsley

BADGE 373

(PARAMOUNT) Producer-Director, Howard W. Koch; Screenplay, Pete Hamill; Photography, Arthur J. Ornitz; Editor, John Woodcock; Music, J. J. Jackson; Art Director, Philip Rosenberg; Assistant Director, Michael P. Petrone; In Technicolor; Rated R; 116 minutes; July release.

CAST

Eddie Ryan	Robert Duvall
Maureen	Verna Bloom
Sweet William	Henry Darrow
Scanlon	Eddie Egan
Ruben	Felipe Luciano
Mrs. Caputo	Tina Cristiani
Rita Garcia	Marina Durell
Frankie Diaz	Chico Martinez
Ferrer	Jose Duval
Gigi Caputo	Louis Cosentino
Chico	Luis Avalos
Mrs. Diaz	Nubia Olivero
Assistant D. A.	Sam Schact
Commissioner	Edward F. Carey
Superintendent	John Marriott
Reporter	Pete Hamill
Manuel	Joel Veiga
Bouncer	Mark Tendler
Hans	Robert Weil
Rose Ann	Rose Ann Scamardella
Cop	Larry Appelbaum
Bus Driver	John McCurry
Patrolman	Bob Farley
Delivery Boy	Tracy Walter
Tugboat Crew	John Scanlon, Jimmy Archer, Ric Mancini, Mike O'Dowd
Sweet William's Hoods	Robert Miano, Pompie Pomposello, Hector Troy

Right: Robert Duvall, Verna Bloom
Top: Robert Duvall, Eddie Egan

Robert Duvall

Robert Duvall, Chico Martinez, Marina Durell

AMERICAN GRAFFITI

(UNIVERSAL) Producer, Francis Ford Coppola; Co-Producer, Gary Kurtz; Director, George Lucas; Screenplay, George Lucas, Gloria Katz, Willard Huyck; Editors, Verna Fields, Marcia Lucas; Photography, Ron Eveslage, Jan D'Alquen; Art Director, Dennis Clark; Costumes, Aggie Guerard Rodgers; Assistant Directors, Ned Kopp, Charles Myers; Choreographer, Toni Basil; In Technicolor; Rated PG; 110 minutes; July release.

CAST

Curt	Richard Dreyfuss
Steve	Ronny Howard
John	Paul LeMat
Terry	Charlie Martin Smith
Laurie	Cindy Williams
Debbie	Candy Clark
Carol	Mackenzie Phillips
Disc Jockey	Wolfman Jack
Bob	Harrison Ford
Joe	Bo Hopkins
Carlos	Manuel Padilla, Jr.
Ants	Beau Gentry

At the Sock Hop:

Herby and the Heartbeats	Flash Cadillac and the Continental Kids
Peg	Kathy Quinlan
Eddie	Tim Crowley
Mr. Wolfe	Terry McGovern
Girl	Jan Wilson
Announcer	Caprice Schmidt

At Mel's Burger City:

Budda	Jana Bellan
Vic	Joe Spano
Al	Chris Pray
Judy	Susan Richardson
Carhop 2	Donna Wehr

On the streets with John:

Policeman Holstein	Jim Bohan
Jeff Pazzuto	Ron Vincent
Ferber	Fred Ross
Girl in Studebaker	Jody Carlson
Balloon girl	Cam Whitman
Gas station attendant	John Bracci

On the streets with Curt:

Wendy	Debbie Celiz
Bobbie	Lynn Marie Stewart
Kip Pullman	Ed Greenberg
Blond in T-Bird	Suzanne Somers

On the streets with Terry:

Bozo	Gordon Analla
Girl in Dodge	Lisa Herman
Falfa's girl	Debralee Scott
Man at accident	Charles Dorsett
Kid at accident	Stephen Knox

On the streets with Steve:

Dale	Bob Pasaak

At the liquor store:

Man	Joseph Miksak
Bum	George Meyer
Clerk	William Niven
Thief	James Cranna

In the alley:

Man	Del Close
Old Man	Charlie Murphy
Old Woman	Jan Dunn
Badass 1	Johnny Weissmuller, Jr.

At the amusement arcade:

Mr. Gordon	Scott Beach
Hank	Al Nalbandian

Charlie Martin Smith, Candy Clark

Top Left: Ronny Howard, Cindy Williams
Below: (C) Richard Dreyfuss

Candy Clark, Charlie Martin Smith, also above
with Ronny Howard Top: Paul LeMat

Ronny Howard, Cindy Williams

THE LAST AMERICAN HERO

(20th CENTURY-FOX) Executive Producer, Joe Wizen; Producers, William Roberts, John Cutts; Director, Lamont Johnson; Screenplay, William Roberts; Based on articles by Tom Wolfe; Photography, George Silano; Art Director, Lawrence Paull; Editor, Robbe Roberts; Assistant Director, Fred Brost; Music, Charles Fox; "I Got a Name" sung by Jim Croce; In DeLuxe color; Rated PG; 95 minutes; July release.

CAST

Elroy Jackson, Jr.	Jeff Bridges
Marge	Valerie Perrine
Mrs. Jackson	Geraldine Fitzgerald
Hackel	Ned Beatty
Wayne Jackson	Gary Busey
Elroy Jackson, Sr.	Art Lund
Burton Colt	Ed Lauter
Kyle Kingman	William Smith II
Morley	Gregory Walcott
Lamar	Tom Ligon
Davie Baer	Ernie Orsatti
Trina	Erica Hagen
Spud	James Murphy
Rick Penny	Lane Smith

Top: Jeff Bridges, Gary Busey, Geraldine
Fitzgerald, Art Lund

Jeff Bridges, Art Lund

Valerie Perrine, Jeff Bridges
Top: Jeff Bridges, Ed Lauter

Jeff Bridges, also top with
Valerie Perrine

OKLAHOMA CRUDE

(COLUMBIA) Producer-Director, Stanley Kramer; Screenplay, Marc Norman; Photography, Robert Surtees; Designer, Alfred Sweeney; Costumes, Bill Thomas; Music, Henry Mancini; Song, Henry Mancini, Hal David; Sung by Anne Murray; Editor, Folmar Blangsted; Associate Producer, Ivan Volkman; In Panavision and color; Rated PG; 108 minutes; July release.

CAST

Mase	George C. Scott
Lena	Faye Dunaway
Cleon	John Mills
Hellman	Jack Palance
Marion	William Lucking
Wilcox	Harvey Jason
Wobbly	Ted Gehring
Massive Man	Cliff Osmond
Jimmy	Rafael Campos
Lawyer	Woodrow Parfrey
Bloom	John Hudkins
Bliss	Harvey Parry
Dulling	Bob Herron
Rucker	Jerry Brown
Moody	Jim Burk
Walker	Henry Wills
C. R. Miller	Hal Smith
Indian	Cody Bearpaw
Stapp	James Jeter
Deke Watson	Larry D. Mann
Farmer	John Dierkes
Hobo 1	Karl Lukas
Hobo 2	Wayne Storm
Cook	Billy Varga

Left: George C. Scott, John Mills, Faye Dunaway
Top: George C. Scott, Faye Dunaway

George C. Scott, Jack Palance

George C. Scott, Faye Dunaway

GORDON'S WAR

(20th CENTURY-FOX) Executive Producer, Edgar J. Scherick; Producer, Robert L. Schaffel; Director, Ossie Davis; Screenplay, Howard Friedlander, Ed Spielman; Photography, Victor J. Kemper; Assistant Directors, Dwight Williams, Neil Machlis; Art Director, Perry Watkins; Editor, Eric Albertson; Costumes, Anna Hill Johnstone; Music and Songs, Andy Badale, Al Elias; Sung by Barbara Mason, New Birth; A Palomar Picture; In Panavision and DeLuxe color; Rated R; 89 minutes; August release.

CAST

Gordon	Paul Winfield
Bee	Carl Lee
Otis	David Downing
Roy	Tony King
Spanish Harry	Gilbert Lewis
Luther the Pimp	Carl Gordon
Big Pink	Nathan C. Heard
Mary	Grace Jones
Bedroom Girl	Jackie Page
Caucasian	Charles Bergansky
Hustler	Adam Wade
Dog salesman	Hansford Rowe
Goose	Warren Taurien
Black Hit Man	Ralph Wilcox
Hotel proprietor	David Connell
Gordon's wife	Richelle LeNoir
Gray-haired executive	Michael Galloway

**Top: (L) Paul Winfield (R) Gilbert Lewis
Center: (L) David Downing, Paul Winfield, Tony
E. King, Carl Lee (R) Downing, Joseph Lacosta,
Lee, Winfield**

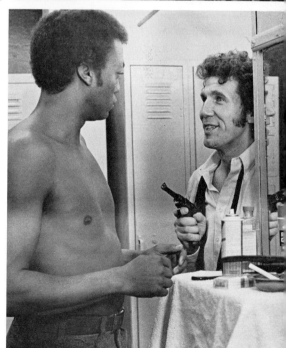

Paul Winfield, Charles Bergansky

HEAVY TRAFFIC

(AMERICAN INTERNATIONAL) Producer, Steve Krantz; Directed and Written by Ralph Bakshi; Photography, Ted C. Bemiller, Gregg Heschong; Editor, Donald W. Ernst; Music, Ray Shanklin, Ed Bogas; In color; Rated X; 77 minutes; August release.

CAST

Michael .... Joseph Kaufman
Carole .... Beverly Hope Atkinson
Angie .... Frank DeKova
Ida .... Terri Haven
Molly .... Mary Dean Lauria
Rosalyn .... Jacqueline Mills
Rosa .... Lillian Adams
and the voices of Jim Bates, Jamie Farr, Robert Easton, Charles Gordone, Michael Brandon, Morton Lewis, Bill Strigolis, Jay Lawrence, Lee Weaver, Phyllis Thompson, Kim Hamilton, Carol Graham, Candy Candido, Helene Winston, William Keene, Peter Hobbs, John Bleifer.

Right: Beverly Hope Atkinson, Joseph Kaufman

ENTER THE DRAGON

(WARNER BROTHERS) Producers, Fred Weintraub, Paul Heller; Associate Producer, Raymond Chow; Director, Robert Clouse; Screenplay, Michael Allin; Photography, Gilbert Hubbs; Music, Lalo Schifrin; Editors, Kurt Hirshler, George Watters; Art Director, James Wong Sun; A Concord production; In Technicolor; Rated R; 98 minutes; August release.

CAST

Lee	Bruce Lee
Roper	John Saxon
Williams	Jim Kelly
Han	Shih Kien
Oharra	Bob Wall
Tania	Ahna Capri
Su-Lin	Angela Mao Ying
Mei Ling	Betty Chung
Braithwaite	Geoffrey Weeks
Bolo	Yang Sze
Parsons	Peter Archer

Right: Ahna Capri, John Saxon

Bruce Lee

Bruce Lee

BANG THE DRUM SLOWLY

(PARAMOUNT) Producers, Maurice and Lois Rosenfield; Director, John Hancock; Screenplay, Mark Harris; Based on his novel; Photography, Richard Shore; Editor, Richard Marks; Music, Stephen Lawrence; Designer, Robert Gundlach; Assistant Director, Allan Wertheim; In Movielab color; Rated PG; 98 minutes; August release.

CAST

Henry Wiggen	Michael Moriarty
Bruce Pearson	Robert De Niro
Dutch Schnell	Vincent Gardenia
Joe Jaros	Phil Foster
Katie	Ann Wedgeworth
Mr. Pearson	Patrick McVey
Piney Woods	Tom Ligon
Holly Wiggen	Heather Macrae
Tootsie	Selma Diamond
Team Owners	Barbara Babcock, Maurice Rosenfield
Ugly Jones	Andy Jarrell
Bradley Lord	Marshall Efron
Red Traphagen	Barton Heyman
Perry	Donny Burks
Diego	Hector Elias
Goose Williams	Tom Signorelli
Canada Smith	Jim Donahue
Aleck Olson	Nicolas Surovy
Horse	Danny Aiello
George	Hector Troy
Jonah	Tony Major
Dr. Loftus	Alan Manaon
Dr. Chambers	Ernesto Gonzales
Tegwar Players	Jack Hollander, Lou Girolami
Detective	Arnold Kapnick
Dutch's Wife	Jean David
Joe's Wife	Bea Blau
Keith Crane	Herb Henry
Bruce's Mother	Dorothy Nuebert
Sid Goldman	Pierrino Mascarino
Gem	Kaydette Grant
Third Base Coach	Dell Bethel
Bat Boy	Forrest Wynn
Baseball Players	Vince Camuto, Jeff Sartorius, Willie Lemmey, Doug Major

Robert De Niro, also top

Top: Michael Moriarty

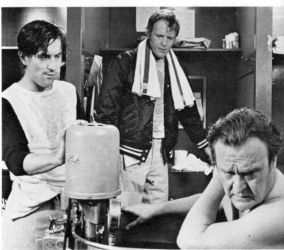

Vincent Gardenia, Dell Bethel, Phil Foster
Above: Hector Troy, Tom Ligon, Robert De Niro,
Michael Moriarty, Phil Foster Top: De Niro,
Heather MacRae, Moriarty

Robert De Niro, Michael Moriarty, Vincent Gardenia
Above: Anne Wedgeworth, Robert De Niro

JEREMY

(UNITED ARTISTS) Producer, George Pappas; Direction and Screenplay, Arthur Barron; Executive Producer, Elliott Kastner; Music, Lee Holdridge; Photography, Paul Goldsmith; Editor, Zina Voynow; Associate Producer, Norman Schwartz; Art Director, Peter Bocour; Title Song, Lee Holdridge, Dorothea Joyce; Sung by Glynnis O'Connor; A Kenasset production; In color; Rated PG; 90 minutes; August release.

CAST

Jeremy Jones	Robby Benson
Susan Rollins	Glynnis O'Connor
Ralph Manzoni	Len Bari
Cello Teacher	Leonardo Cimino
Susan's Father	Ned Wilson
Jeremy's Father	Chris Bohn
Jeremy's Mother	Pat Wheel
Music Class Teacher	Ted Sorel
Candy Store Owner	Bruce Friedman
Susan's Aunt	Eunice Anderson

Left: Glynnis O'Connor, Robby Benson

Robby Benson, Glynnis O'Connor

Glynnis O'Connor, Robby Benson

HARRY IN YOUR POCKET

(UNITED ARTISTS) Executive Producer, Alden Schwimmer; Producer-Director, Bruce Geller; Screenplay, James David Buchanan, Ron Austin; Associate Producer, Alan Godfrey; Photography, Fred Koenekamp; Music, Lalo Schifrin; Assistant Director, Ric Rondell; Editor, Arthur L. Hilton; In color; Rated PG; 103 minutes; August release.

CAST

Harry	James Coburn
Ray	Michael Sarrazin
Sandy	Trish Van Devere
Casey	Walter Pidgeon
Fence	Michael C. Gwynne
First Detective	Tony Giorgio
Second Detective	Michael Stearns
Francine	Sue Mullen
Salesman	Duane Bennet
Mr. Bates	Stanley Bolt
Bellboy	Barry Grimshaw

Top: Michael Sarrazin, James Coburn

James Coburn, Trish Van Devere

ELECTRA GLIDE IN BLUE

(UNITED ARTISTS) Producer-Director, James William Guercio; Screenplay, Robert Boris; Story, Robert Boris, Rupert Hitzig; Photography, Conrad Hall; Assistant Director, Tom Shaw; Music, James William Guercio; Editors, Jim Benson, John F. Link III, Jerry Greenberg; Costumes, Rita Riggs; In Panavision and color; Rated PG; 106 minutes; August release.

CAST

John Wintergreen	Robert Blake
Zipper Davis	Billy "Green" Bush
Harve Poole	Mitchell Ryan
Jolene	Jeannine Riley
Willie	Elisha Cook
Coroner	Royal Dano
Bus Driver	David Wolinski
Bob Zemko	Peter Cetera
Killer	Terry Kath
Pig Man	Lee Loughnane
Loose Lips	Walter Parazaider
Sgt. Ryker	Joe Samsil
L. A. Detective	Jason Clark
Truck Driver	Michael Butler
Ice Cream Girls	Susan Forristal, Lucy Angle Guercio
Zemko's Girlfriend	Melissa Green
Detective	Jim Gilmore
The Beard	Bob Zemko

Right: Jeannine Riley, Robert Blake

Robert Blake, David Wolinski
Above: Elisha Cook, Robert Blake

Royal Dano, Robert Blake
Above: Robert Blake

COPS AND ROBBERS

(UNITED ARTISTS) Producer, Elliott Kastner; Director, Aram Avakian; Screenplay, Donald E. Westlake; Music, Michel Legrand; Assistant Directors, Alan Hopkins, Mike Haley; Art Director, Gene Rudolf; Photography, David Quaid; Costumes, John Boyt; Editor, Barry Malkin; In color; Rated PG; 89 minutes; August release.

CAST

Tom	Cliff Gorman
Joe	Joe Bologna
Paul Jones	Dick Ward
Eastpoole	Shepperd Strudwick
Secretary	Ellen Holly
Patsy	John Ryan
Bandell	Nino Ruggeri
Mary	Gayle Gorman
Grace	Lucy Martin
Hardware Store Owner	Lee Steel
Black Lady	Frances Foster
Thief	Jacob Weiner
Attendants	Arthur Pierce, Martin Cove
Clerk	Jim Ferguson
Wino	Walter Gorney
Rocco	Frank Gio
Ed	Jeff Ossuno
Marty	Joseph Spinell
Harry	George Harris II

Right: Joseph Bologna (R)

Joseph Bologna, Cliff Gorman, Shepperd Strudwick

YOUR THREE MINUTES ARE UP

(CINERAMA) Producers, Jerry Gershwin, Mark C. Levy; Director, Douglas N. Schwartz; Screenplay, James Dixon; Editor, Aaron Stell; Photography, Stephen M. Katz; Music, Perry Botkin, Jr.; Art Director, Joseph Crowingham; Assistant Director, Peter Cornberg; Costumes, Jac McAnelly; "It's Only Me" (Dennis Lambert, Brian Potter, Perry Botkin, Jr.) sung by Mark Lindsay; In DeLuxe color; Rated R; 93 minutes; August release.

CAST

Charlie	Beau Bridges
Mike	Ron Leibman
Betty	Janet Margolin
Mrs. Wilk	Kathleen Freeman
Mr. Kellogg	David Ketchum
Dr. Claymore	Stu Nisbet
Eddie Abruzzi	Read Morgan
Teenage driver	Jennifer Ashley
Sugar	Sherry Bain
Gas station operator	Paul Barselou
Susan	Kitty Carl
Operator's wife	Rhodie Cogan
Sherry	Ronda Copland
Howard	James Dixon
Pickup truck driver	James Driskill
Bun warmer girl	Barbara Douglas
Sandi	June Fairchild
Clothing salesman	Lester Fletcher
Policeman	Robert Funk
Repossession man	Don Gazzaniga
Mr. Roberts	Larry Gelman
Massage receptionist	Suzi Goei
Josie	Elizabeth Harding
Elsie	Sylvia Hayes
Pharmacist	Leigh Heine

and Pat Houtchens (Catto), Candace Howerton (1st nurse), Sharon Johansen (Ilsa), Raymond Kark (Western Union messenger), Carol Kristy (Bank teller), Myrna La Bow (2nd nurse), Paul Lichtman (Chef), Sherry Miles (Debbie), Tom Moses (Gas station attendant), Sam Nudell (Tailor), Michael Perrotta (Waiter), Barbara Sammeth (Cindy), Patti Shayne (Waitress), Orville Sherman (Mr. Sherman), Lynne Marie Stewart (Ibis lady), Nedra Volz (Free Press lady), Patricia Walker (Unemployment clerk).

Left: Beau Bridges, Myrna LaBow, Ron Leibman
Top: Kitty Carl, Ron Leibman

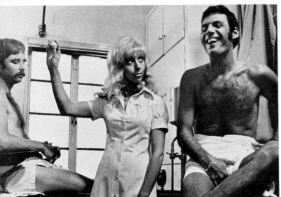

Ron Leibman, Beau Bridges, Paul Lichtman

Cashier, Lester Fletcher, Ron Leibman,
Beau Bridges

THE STONE KILLER

(COLUMBIA) Producer—Director, Michael Winner; Screenplay, Gerald Wilson; From "A Complete State of Death" by John Gardner; Music, Roy Budd; Photography, Richard Moore; Art Director, Ward Preston; Assistant Directors, Joe Ellis, Mel Efros; A Dino De Laurentiis presentation; In Technicolor; Rated R; 95 minutes; August release.

CAST

Torrey	Charles Bronson
Vescari	Martin Balsam
Lorenz	David Sheiner
Daniels	Norman Fell
Mathews	Ralph Waite
Armitage	Eddie Firestone
J. D.	Walter Burke
Lipper	David Moody
Psychiatrist	Charles Tyner
Langley	Paul Koslo
Lawrence	Stuart Margolin
Hart	John Ritter
Police Chief	Byron Morrow
Jumper	Jack Colvin
Calabriese	Frank Campanella
Champion	Alfred Ryder
Paul Long	Gene Woodbury
Mossman	Harry Basch
Vechetti	Jan Arvan
Helen	Lisabeth Hush
Waitress	Mary Cross
Gerry Wexton	Kelly Miles
Fussy Man	Robert Emhardt

Top: Charles Bronson, Ralph Waite
Below: Ralph Waite, Norman Fell, Charles Bronson

Charles Bronson, also above, and top with Kelly Miles

Ted Neeley, and top center

JESUS CHRIST SUPERSTAR

(UNIVERSAL) Producers, Norman Jewison, Robert Stigwood; Director, Norman Jewison; Screenplay, Melvyn Bragg, Norman Jewison; Based on rock opera with book and lyrics by Tim Rice, and Music by Andrew Lloyd Webber; Associate Producer, Patrick Palmer; Photography, Douglas Slocombe; Designer, Richard Macdonald; Editor, Anthony Gibbs; Choreography, Rob Iscove; Costumes, Yvonne Blake; Art Director, John Clark; Assistant Directors, Jack N. Reddish, Dusty Symonds; In Technicolor; Rated G; 108 minutes; August release.

CAST

Jesus Christ	Ted Neeley
Judas Iscariot	Carl Anderson
Mary Magdalene	Yvonne Elliman
Pontius Pilate	Barry Dennen
Caiaphas	Bob Bingham
Simon Zealotes	Larry T. Marshall
King Herod	Joshua Mostel
Annas	Kurt Yahgjian
Peter	Philip Toubus

APOSTLES: Pi Douglass, Jonathan Wynne, Richard Molinare, Jeffrey Hyslop, Robert LuPone, Thommie Walsh, David Devir, Richard Orbach, Shooki Wagner
WOMEN: Darcel Wynne, Sally Neal, Vera Biloshisky, Wendy Maltby, Baayork Lee, Susan Allanson, Ellen Hoffman, Judith Daby, Adaya Pilo, Marcia McBroom, Leeyan Granger, Kathryn Wright, Denise Pence, Wyetta Turner, Tamar Zafria, Riki Oren, Lea Kestin
PRIESTS: Zvulun Cohen, Meir Israel, Itzhak Sidranski, David Rfjwan, Amity Razi, Avi Ben-Haim, Haim Bashi, David Duack
ROMAN SOLDIERS: Steve Boockvor, Peter Luria, David Barkan, Danny Basevitch, Cliff Michaelevski, Tom Guest, Stephen Denenberg, Didi Liekov
TEMPLE GUARDS: Doron Gaash, Noam Cohen, Zvi Lehat, Moshe Uziel

Top: Sally Neal

Ted Neeley Above: Ted Neeley, Carl
Anderson Top: Joshua Mostel

HIT!

(PARAMOUNT) Producer, Harry Korshak; Executive Producer Gray Frederickson; Director, Sidney J. Furie; Screenplay, Alan R Trustman, David M. Wolf; Photography, John A. Alonzo; Editor Argyle Nelson; Music, Lalo Schifrin; In Technicolor; Rated R; 134 minutes; September release.

CAST

Nick Allen	Billy Dee Williams
Mike Willmer	Richard Pryor
Barry Strong	Paul Hampton
Sherry Nielson	Gwen Welles
Dutch Schiller	Warren Kemmerling
Ida	Janet Brandt
Herman	Sid Melton
Carlin	David Hall
Crosby	Todd Martin
Director	Norman Burton
Madame Frelou	Jenny Astruc
Romain	Yves Barsacq
Jean-Baptiste	Jean-Claude Bercq
Bornou	Henri Cogan
Zero	Pierre Collet
Mr. Frelou	Robert Lombard
Jyras	Paul Mercy
Madame Orissa	Malka Ribovska
Monteca	Richard Saint-Bris
Jeannie Allen	Tina Andrews
Judge	Frank Christi
Boyfriend	Mwako Cumbuka
Pusher	Lee Duncan
Esther	Janear Hines
Weasel	Jerry Jones

Left: Gwen Welles, Billy Dee Williams

Billy Dee Williams, Paul Hampton Above: Sid Melton, Janet Brandt, Billy Dee Williams

Billy Dee Williams, Richard Pryor Above: Billy Dee Williams, Warren Kemmerling

SAVE THE CHILDREN

(PARAMOUNT) Producer, Matt Robinson; Executive Producer, Clarence Avant; Director, Stan Lathan; Narration written and spoken by Matt Robinson; Photography, Charles Blackwell, Bob Fletcher, Robert Grant, Doug Harris, Rufus Hinton, Roy Lewis, Leroy Lucas, David Myers; Editors, George Bowers, Paul Evans; Art Director, Charles Rosen; Assistant Director, Dwight Williams; Rated G; In Eastmancolor; 123 minutes; September release.

CAST

Marvin Gaye, The Staple Singers, The Temptations, The Chilites, The Main Ingredient, The O'Jays, Issac Hayes, Zulema, Cannonball Adderly Quintet, Albertina Walker, Push Mass Choir, Loretta Oliver, James Cleveland, Bill Withers, Curtis Mayfield, Sammy Davis, Jr., Roberta Flack, Quincy Jones, Gladys Knight and the Pips, Jerry Butler, Brenda Lee Eager, Ramsey Lewis, Nancy Wilson, The Jackson Five, Jackie Verdell, Jesse Jackson

Top: Roberta Flack
Below: The Jackson Five

Isaac Hayes
Top: Sammy Davis, Jr.

SISTERS

(AMERICAN INTERNATIONAL) Producer, Edward R. Pressman; Director, Brian De Palma; Screenplay, Brian De Palma, Louisa Rose; Story, Brian De Palma; Associate Producers, Lynn Pressman, Robert Rohdie; Music, Bernard Herrmann; Photography, Gregory Sandor; Editor, Paul Hirsch; Designer, Gary Weist; Assistant Director, Alan Hopkins; A Pressman-Williams Enterprises production; In color; Rated R; 92 minutes; September release.

CAST

Danielle Breton	Margot Kidder
Grace Collier	Jennifer Salt
Joseph Larch	Charles Durning
Emil Breton	Bill Finley
Philip Woode	Lisle Wilson
Mr. McLennen	Barnard Hughes
Mrs. Collier	Mary Davenport
Detective Kelley	Dolph Sweet

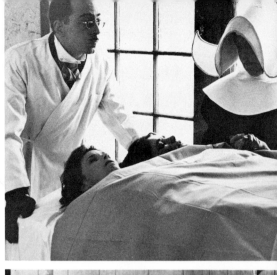

Right: Bill Finley, Margot Kidder, Jennifer Salt

Bill Finley, Margot Kidder
Above: Jennifer Salt, Charles Durning

Lisle Wilson, Margot Kidder

FROM THE MIXED-UP FILES OF MRS. BASIL E. FRANKWEILER

(CINEMA 5) Producer, Charles G. Mortimer, Jr.; Director, Fielder Cook; Screenplay, Blanche Hanalis; Based on novel by E. L. Konigsburg; Photography, Victor J. Kemper; Editor, Eric Albertson; Music, Donald Devor; A Westfall production; Rated G; 105 minutes; September release.

CAST

Mrs. Frankweiler	Ingrid Bergman
Claudia	Sally Prager
Jamie	Johnny Doran
Saxonburg	George Rose
Mr. Kincaid	Richard Mulligan
Mrs. Kincaid	Georgann Johnson
Schoolteacher	Madeline Kahn

Right: Sally Prager, Johnny Doran

Sally Prager, Johnny Doran, Ingrid Bergman

SUMMER WISHES, WINTER DREAMS

(COLUMBIA) Producer, Jack Brodsky; Director, Gilbert Cates; Screenplay, Stewart Stern; Photography, Gerald Hirschfeld; Designer, Peter Dohanos; Costumes, Anna Hill Johnstone; Editor, Sidney Katz; Assistant Directors, Michael Hertzberg, Neil Machlis; A Rastar production in color; Rated PG; 93 minutes; October release.

CAST

Rita Walden	Joanne Woodward
Harry Walden	Martin Balsam
Mrs. Pritchett	Sylvia Sidney
Anna	Dori Brenner
Fred Goody	Win Forman
Betty Goody	Tresa Hughes
Joel	Peter Marklin
Bobby Walden	Ron Rickards
Waitress	Charlotte Oberley
Mrs. Bimberg	Minerva Pious
Grandmother	Helen Ludlam
Grandfather	Grant Code
Mr. Goldblatt	Sol Frieder
Student in theatre	Gaetano Lisi
Mrs. Pat Hungerford	Nancy Andrews
Carl Hurlbutt	Lee Jackson
Chauffeur	David Thomas
Nurse	Marian Swan
Dancer in dream	Dennis Wayne

Left: Joanne Woodward

Martin Balsam, Joanne Woodward

Sylvia Sidney
Top: Dori Brenner, Joanne Woodward

Joanne Woodward, Martin Balsam

PAPER CHASE

(20TH CENTURY-FOX) Producers, Robert C. Thompson, Rodrick Paul; Direction and Screenplay, James Bridges; Based on novel by John Jay Osborn, Jr.; Photography, Gordon Willis; Assistant Directors, Christopher Seitz, Gordon McDonald; Art Director, George Jenkins; Editor, Walter Thompson; In Deluxe color; Rated PG; 112 minutes; October release.

CAST

Hart	Timothy Bottoms
Susan	Lindsay Wagner
Kingsfield	John Houseman
Ford	Graham Beckel
Anderson	Edward Herrmann
O'Connor	Bob Lydiard
Bell	Craig Richard Nelson
Kevin	James Naughton
Asheley	Regina Baff
Toombs	David Clennon
Moss	Lenny Baker

Top: Timothy Bottoms, Lindsay Wagner

John Houseman—*1973 Academy Award winner for Best Supporting Actor*

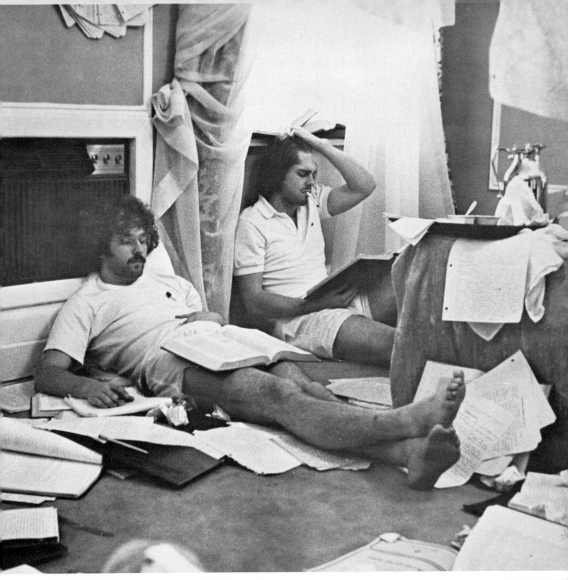

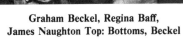

Graham Beckel, Regina Baff,
James Naughton Top: Bottoms, Beckel

Timothy Bottoms, Lindsay Wagner

CHARLEY VARRICK

(UNIVERSAL)Executive Producer, Jennings Lang; Producer-Director, John Vernon; Screenplay, Howard Rodman, Dean Riesner; From novel "The Looters" by John Reese; Photography, Michael Butler; Art Director, Fernando Carrere; Music, Lalo Schifrin; Editor, Frank Morriss; Assistant Directors, Joe Cavalier, Ron Satlof; Costumes, Helen Colvig; In Panavision and Technicolor; Rated PG; 111 minutes; October release.

CAST

Charley Varrick	Walter Matthau
Molly	Joe Don Baker
Sybil Fort	Felicia Farr
Harman Sullivan	Andy Robinson
Maynard Boyle	John Vernon
Jewell Everett	Sheree North
Mr. Garfinkle	Norman Fell
Honest John	Benson Fong
Howard Young	Woodrow Parfrey
Sheriff Bill Horton	William Schallert
Nadine Varrick	Jacqueline Scott
Mrs. Taff	Marjorie Bennett
Rudy Sanchez	Rudy Diaz
Steele	Colby Chester
Highway Deputy	Charlie Briggs
Miss Ambar	Priscilla Garcia
Mr. Scott	Scott Hale
Boy	Charles Matthau
Miss Vesta	Hope Summers
Beverly	Monica Lewis

and Jim Nolan (Clerk), Tom Tully (Tom), Albert Popwell (Randolph), Kathleen O'Malley (Jessie), Christina Hart (Jana), Craig Baxley (Van Sickle), Al Dunlap (Taxi Driver), Virginia Wing (Chinese Hostess), Donald Siegel (Murph).

Left: Walter Matthau

Joe Don Baker and girls

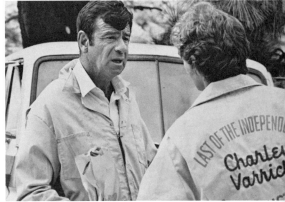

Joe Don Baker Above: John Vernon, Walter
Matthau Top: Sheree North, Walter Matthau

Walter Matthau, Andy Robinson
Above: Matthau, Felicia Farr

THE ICEMAN COMETH

(AMERICAN FILM THEATRE) Producer, Ely A. Landau; Director, John Frankenheimer; Based on play by Eugene O'Neill; Executive Producer, Edward Lewis; Assistant Directors, Kurt Neumann, Barry Steinberg; Photography, Ralph Woolsey; Editor, Harold Kress; Designer, Jack Martin Smith; Costumes, Dorothy Jeakins; In color; 239 minutes; October limited release.

CAST

Hickey	Lee Marvin
Harry Hope	Fredric March
Larry Slade	Robert Ryan
Don Parritt	Jeff Bridges
Willie Oban	Bradford Dillman
Hugo Kalmar	Sorrell Booke
Margie	Hildy Brooks
Pearl	Nancy Juno Dawson
Cora	Evans Evans
Captain (Cecil Lewis)	Martyn Green
Joe Mott	Moses Gunn
Pat McGloin	Clifton James
Jimmy Tomorrow	John McLiam
Chuck Morello	Stephen Pearlman
Rocky Pioggi	Tom Pedi
General (Piet Wetjoen)	George Voskovec
Moran	Bart Burns
Lieb	Don McGovern

Fredric March, Robert Ryan

Top: Hildy Brooks, Lee Marvin, Evans
Evans, Nancy Juno Dawson

George Voskovec, Moses Gunn
Top: Stephen Pearlman, Martyn Green

Robert Ryan, Jeff Bridges
Top: Fredric March, Lee Marvin

THE HOMECOMING

(AMERICAN FILM THEATRE) Producer, Ely A. Landau; Director, Peter Hall; Screenplay, Harold Pinter; Based on his play; Executive Producer, Otto Plaschkes; Assistant Director, Christopher Dryhurst; Photography, David Watkin; Editor, Rex Pike; Designer, John Bury; Art Director, Jack Stevens; Costumes, Elizabeth Haffenden, Joan Bridge; In color; 116 minutes; October limited release.

CAST

Sam	Cyril Cusack
Lenny	Ian Holm
Teddy	Michael Jayston
Ruth	Vivien Merchant
Joey	Terence Rigby
Max	Paul Rogers

Left: Michael Jayston, Vivien Merchant

Paul Rogers, Terence Rigby, Cyril Cusack, Vivien Merchant

Paul Rogers, Vivien Merchant, Michael Jayston,
Cyril Cusack Above: Merchant, Ian Holm

Paul Rogers, Ian Holm Above: Terence Rigby,
Cyril Cusack, Paul Rogers

FIVE ON THE BLACK HAND SIDE

(UNITED ARTISTS) Producers, Brock Peters, Michael Tolan; Director, Oscar Williams; Screenplay, Charlie L. Russell; Based on his play of the same title; Photography, Gene Polito; Editor, Michael Economou; Music, H. B. Barnum; In color; Rated PG; 96 minutes; October release.

CAST

Mrs. Brooks	Clarice Taylor
Mr. Brooks	Leonard Jackson
Ruby	Virginia Capers
Gideon	Glynn Turman
Booker T.	D'Urville Martin
Gail	Bonnie Banfield
Preston	Richard Williams
Sweetmeat	Sonny Jim
Stormy Monday	Ja'Net Dubois
Marvin	Carl Mikal Franklin

Right: Carl Mikal Franklin, Bonnie Banfield

Sonny Jim, Leonard Jackson Above: Virginia Capers, Richard Williams, Clarice Taylor

D'Urville Martin, Clarice Taylor, Carl Mikal Franklin Above: Virginia Capers, Taylor, Ja'Net Dubois

THE ALL-AMERICAN BOY

(WARNER BROS.) Producers, Joseph T. Naar, Saul J. Krugman; Direction and Screenplay, Charles Eastman; Photography, Philip Lathrop; Art Director, Carey O'Dell; Editor, Christopher Holmes; Associate Editor, William Neel; Assistant Director, Terry Morse; A My Shoes production; In Panavision and Technicolor; Rated R; 118 minutes; October release.

CAST

Vic Bealer	Jon Voight
Rodine	Carol Androsky
Drenna Valentine	Anne Archer
Rockoff	Gene Borkan
Larkin	Ron Burns
Poppy	Rosalind Cash
Nola Bealer	Jeanne Cooper
Bett Van Daumee	Peggy Cowles
Lovette	Leigh French
Arty	Ned Glass
Ariel Van Daumee	Bob Hastings
Shereen Bealer	Kathy Mahoney
Jay David Swooze	Art Metrano
Magda	Jaye P. Morgan
Parker	Harry Northup
Connie Swooze	Nancie Phillips
High Valentine	Jeff Thompson

Right: Stoney Land, Jon Voight

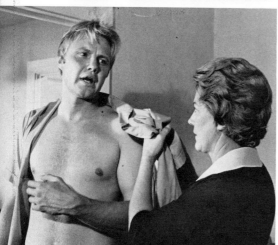

Jon Voight, Jeanne Cooper
Above: E. J. Peaker, Jon Voight

Rosalind Cash, Jon Voight
Above: Jon Voight, Anne Archer

THE WAY WE WERE

(COLUMBIA) Producer, Ray Stark; Director, Sydney Pollack; Screenplay, Arthur Laurents; Photography, Harry Stradling, Jr.; Designer, Stephen Grimes; Editor, Margaret Booth; Associate Producer, Richard Roth; Music, Marvin Hamlisch; Title song, Marvin Hamlisch, Marilyn and Alan Bergman; Sung by Barbra Streisand; Costumes, Dorothy Jeakins, Moss Mabry; Assistant Directors, Howard Koch, Jr., Jerry Ziesmer; A Rastar production; In Panavision and color; Rated PG; 118 minutes; October release

CAST

Katie	Barbra Streisand
Hubbell	Robert Redford
J. J.	Bradford Dillman
Carol Ann	Lois Chiles
George Bissinger	Patrick O'Neal
Paula Reisner	Viveca Lindfors
Rhea Edwards	Allyn Ann McLerie
Brooks Carpenter	Murray Hamilton
Bill Verso	Herb Edelman
Vicki Bissinger	Diana Ewing
Pony Dunbar	Sally Kirkland
Peggy Vanderbilt	Marcia Mae Jones
Actor	Don Keefer
El Morocco captain	George Gaynes
Army corporal	Eric Boles
Ashe blond	Barbara Peterson
Army captain	Roy Jenson
Rally speaker	Brenda Kelly
Frankie McVeigh	James Woods
Jenny	Connie Forslund
Dr. Short	Robert Gerringer
Judianne	Susie Blakely
Airforce	Ed Power
Dumb blonde	Suzanne Zenor
Guest	Dan Seymour

Left: Robert Redford, Barbra Streisand
1973 Academy Award winner for Best Song and Best Scoring

Robert Redford, Barbra Streisand, Patrick O'Neal, Bradford Dillman, Viveca Lindfors, (back row) Murray Hamilton, Diana Ewing, Dan Seymour

Robert Redford, Barbra Streisand, also above with
Lois Chiles, Bradford Dillman, Allyn Ann McLerie
Top: Lois Chiles, Robert Redford

Barbra Streisand, Robert Redford, also
above, and top

MEAN STREETS

(WARNER BROS.) Executive Producer, E. Lee Perry; Producer, Jonathan T. Taplin; Director, Martin Scorsese; Screenplay, Martin Scorsese, Mardik Martin; Photography, Kent Wakeford; Editor, Sid Levin; Assistant Directors, Russell Vreeland, Ron Satloff; In Technicolor; Rated R; 110 minutes; October release.

CAST

Johnny Boy	Robert De Niro
Charlie	Harvey Keitel
Tony	David Proval
Teresa	Amy Robinson
Michael	Richard Romanus
Giovanni	Cesare Danova
Mario	Vic Argo
Boy with gun	Robert Carradine
Diane	Jeannie Bell
Cop	D'Mitch Davis
Drunk	David Carradine
Joey	George Memmoli
Oscar	Murray Mosten
Sammy	Ken Sinclair
Soldier	Harry Northup
Jewish Girl	Lois Waldon
Jimmy	Lenny Scaletta
Benton	Robert Wilder

Harvey Keitel, Richard Romanus

Top: Robert DeNiro, Harvey Keitel

Robert DeNiro, Amy Robinson, Harvey Keitel
Above: Cesare Danova, Keitel Top: Lois
Walden, Keitel

Harvey Keitel, Amy Robinson Above: David
Proval, Robert DeNiro Top: Richard Romanus

EXECUTIVE ACTION

(NATIONAL GENERAL) Producer, Edward Lewis; Co-Producers, Dan Bessie, Gary Horowitz; Director, David Miller; Screenplay, Dalton Trumbo; Story by Donald Freed, Mark Lane; Photography, Robert Steadman; Editors, George Grenville, Irving Lerner; Art Director, Kirk Axtell; Music, Randy Edelman; In color; Rated PG; 91 minutes; November release.

CAST

Farrington	Burt Lancaster
Foster	Robert Ryan
Ferguson	Will Geer
Paulitz	Gilbert Green
Halliday	John Anderson
Gunman Chris	Paul Carr
Tim	Colby Chester
Operation Chief Team A	Ed Lauter
Smythe	Walter Brooke
Depository Clerk	Sidney Clute
Stripper	Deanna Darrin
McCadden	Lloyd Gough
Used Car Salesman	Richard Hurst
Man at rifle range	Robert Karnes
Oswald Imposter	James MacColl
Art Mendoza	Joaquin Martinez
Riflemen Team B.	Dick Miller, Hunter Von Leer, John Brascia
Jack Ruby	Oscar Oncidi
Sergeant	Tom Peters
Officer Brown	Paul Sorenson
Policeman	Sandy Ward
Technician Team B	William Watson
Gunmen Team A	Richard Bull, Lee Delano

Robert Ryan, Burt Lancaster,
also top left

Burt Lancaster
Top: Assassination of President Kennedy

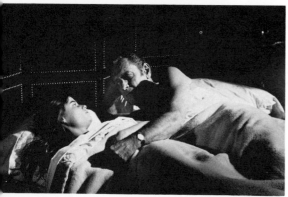

BREEZY

(UNIVERSAL) Producer, Robert Daley; Director, Clint Eastwood; Associate Producer, Jo Heims; Executive Producer, Jennings Lang; Screenplay, Jo Heims; Photography, Frank Stanley; Art Director, Alexander Golitzen; Music, Michel Legrand; Title Song, Mr. Legrand, Marilyn and Alan Bergman; Sung by Shelby Flint; Editor, Ferris Webster; Assistant Directors, Jim Fargo, Tom Joyner; A Universal-Malpaso production; In Technicolor; Rated R; 108 Minutes; November release.

CAST

Frank Harmon	William Holden
Breezy	Kay Lenz
Bob Henderson	Roger C. Carmel
Betty	Marj Dusay
Paula	Joan Hotchkis
Marcy	Jamie Smith Jackson
Man in car	Norman Bartold
Overnight date	Lynn Borden
Nancy	Shelley Morrison
Bruno	Dennis Olivieri
Charlie	Eugene Peterson
Police Officer	Lew Brown
Doctor	Richard Bull
Norman	Johnnie Collins III
Maitre 'd	Don Diamond
Veterinarian	Scott Holden
Real Estate Agent	Sandy Kenyon
Driver	Jack Kosslyn
Waitress	Mary Munday
Saleswoman	Frances Stevenson
Paula's escort	Buck Young
Dress customer	Priscilla Morrill
Sir Love-a-Lot	Earle

William Holden, Lynn Borden
Above: Kay Lenz, William Holden

Top and Below: Kay Lenz, William Holden
Top Left: Holden, Eaugene Peterson,
Marj Dusay

WESTWORLD

(MGM) Producer, Paul N. Lazarus III; Associate Producer, Michael I. Rachmil; Direction and Screenplay, Michael Crichton; Music, Fred Karlin; Photography, Gene Polito; Art Director, Herman Blumenthal; Editor, David Bretherton; Assistant Directors, Claude Binyon, Jr., James Boyle; In MetroColor and Panavision; Rated PG; 91 minutes; November release.

CAST

Gunslinger	Yul Brynner
Peter Martin	Richard Benjamin
John Blane	James Brolin
Medieval Knight	Norman Bartold
Chief Supervisor	Alan Oppenheimer
Medieval Queen	Victoria Shaw
Banker	Dick Van Patten
Arlette	Linda Scott
Technician	Steve Franken
Black Knight	Michael Mikler
Sheriff	Terry Wilson
Miss Carrie	Majel Barrett
Servant girl	Anne Randall
Girl in dungeon	Julie Marcus
Apache girl	Sharyn Wynters
Middle-aged woman	Anne Bellamy
Stewardess	Chris Holter
Bellhop	Charles Seel
Bartender	Wade Crosby
Hostess	Nora Marlowe
Workmen	Will J. White, Ben Young, Tom Falk
Supervisors	Orville Sherman, Lindsay Workman, Lauren Gilbert, Davis Roberts, Howard Platt
Technicians	Jared Martin, Richard Roat, Kenneth Washington, Robert Patten, David Frank, Kip King, David Man, Larry Delaney

**Right: Richard Benjamin, James Brolin
Top: Richard Benjamin, Linda Scott,
James Brolin, Kevin Dignam**

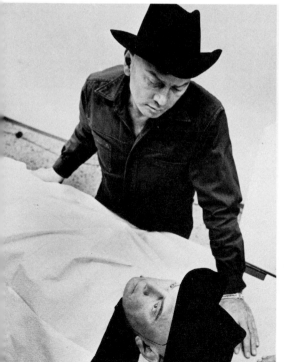

Yul Brynner

Richard Benjamin, Yul Brynner

A DELICATE BALANCE

(AMERICAN FILM THEATRE) Producer, Ely A. Landau; Director, Tony Richardson; Screenplay, Edward Albee from his play; Executive Producer, Neil Hartley; Assistant Director, Andrew Grieve; Photography, David Watkin; Art Director, David Brockhurst; Costumes, Margaret Furse; In color; Rated PG; 132 minutes; November release

CAST

Agnes	Katharine Hepburn
Tobias	Paul Scofield
Julia	Lee Remick
Claire	Kate Reid
Harry	Joseph Cotten
Edna	Betsy Blair

Left: Katharine Hepburn, Lee Remick

Katharine Hepburn, Paul Scofield

Lee Remick, Katharine Hepburn

Katharine Hepburn, Paul Scofield Top: Betsy Blair, Paul Scofield, Joseph Cotten, Kate Reid Center: (L) Lee Remick, Paul Scofield (R) Paul Scofield, Kate Reid

HURRY UP, OR I'LL BE 30

(AVCO EMBASSY) Director-Producer, Joseph Jacoby; Screenplay, David Wiltse, Joseph Jacoby; Music, Stephen Lawrence; Lyrics, Bruce Hart; Photography, Burleigh Wartes; Editor, Stan Warnow; Songs sung by Dennis Cooley; In color; Rated R; 88 minutes; November release.

CAST

George Trapani	John Lefkowitz
Jackie Tice	Linda De Coff
Vince Trapani	Ronald Anton
Flo	Maureen Byrnes
Petey	Danny DeVito
Mr. Trapani	David Kirk
Mark Lossier	Frank Quinn
Mrs. Trapani	Selma Rogoff
Ken Harris	George Welbes
Tony	Steve Inwood
Gypsy Girl/Bar Girl	Faith Langford
Audition Girl #1	Samantha Lynche
Miss Walsh	Susan Peretz
Bartender	Bob O'Connell
Gas Station Attendant	Bill Nunnery

Frank Quinn, Linda DeCoff Above: Danny DeVito, Steve Inwood, John Lefkowitz

Top: John Lefkowitz, Selma Rogoff Below: Lefkowitz, Linda DeCoff, George Welbes Top Left: Lefkowitz, Maureen Byrnes

ARNOLD

(CINERAMA) Producer, Andrew J. Fenady; Director, Georg Fenady; Executive Producer, Charles A. Pratt; Screenplay, Jameson Brewer, John Fenton Murray; Music, George Duning; Lyrics, Andrew J. Fenady; Title Song sung by Shani Wallace; Photography, William Jurgenson; Art Director, Monty Elliott; Editor, Melvin Shapiro; Assistant Director, Daniel S. McCauley; Costumes, Oscar Rodriguez, Vou Le Giokaris; A BCP presentation; In color; Rated PG; 94 minutes; November release.

CAST

Karen	Stella Stevens
Robert	Roddy McDowall
Hester	Elsa Lanchester
Jocelyn	Shani Wallace
Evan Lyons	Farley Granger
Minister	Victor Buono
Governor	John McGiver
Constable Hooks	Bernard Fox
Douglas Whitehead	Patric Knowles
Dybbi	Jamie Farr
Arnold	Norman Stuart
Jonesy	Ben Wright
Flo	Wanda Bailey
Dart Players	Steven Marlo, Leslie Thompson

Right: Stella Stevens, Roddy McDowall, Norman Stuart

Farley Granger, Stella Stevens Above: Stevens, Elsa Lanchester, Jamie Farr, Ben Wright, Bernard Fox

Norman Stuart, Elsa Lanchester Above: John McGiver, Wanda Bailey

THE DON IS DEAD

(UNIVERSAL) Producer, Hal B. Wallis; Director, Richard Fleischer; Screenplay, Marvin H. Albert; Based on his novel; Photography, Richard H. Kline; Editor, Edward A. Biery; Music, Jerry Goldsmith; Associate Producer, Paul Nathan; In color; Rated R; 115 minutes; November release.

CAST

Don Angelo	Anthony Quinn
Tony	Frederic Forrest
Frank	Robert Forster
Vince	Al Lettieri
Ruby	Angel Tompkins
Orlando	Charles Cioffi
Marie	Jo Anne Meredith
Don Bruno	J. Duke Russo
Mitch	Louis Zorich
Nella	Ina Balin
Vitto	George Skaff
Mike Spada	Robert Carricart
Johnny Tresca	Anthony Charnota

and Abe Vigoda, Frank de Kove, Joseph Santos

Right: Anthony Quinn

Angel Tompkins, Robert Forster
Above: Anthony Quinn, Robert Forster

Anthony Quinn, Angel Tompkins
Above: Robert Forster, Frederic Forrest

94

ROBIN HOOD

(BUENA VISTA) Producer-Director, Wolfgang Reitherman; Story, Larry Clemmons; Based on character and story conceptions by Ken Anderson; Directing Animators, Milt Kahl, Frank Thomas, Ollie Johnston, John Lounsbery; Music, George Bruns; Songs, Roger Miller, Floyd Huddleston, George Bruns, Johnny Mercer; Sung by Roger Miller, Nancy Adams, Phil Harris; Art Director, Don Griffith; Assistant Directors, Ed Hansen, Dan Alguire, Jeff Patch; Editors, Tom Acosta, Jim Melton; A Walt Disney production; In Technicolor; Rated G; 83 minutes; November release.

CAST

Voice of the Rooster	Roger Miller
Voice of Robin Hood	Brian Bedford
Voice of Maid Marian	Monica Evans
Voice of Little John	Phil Harris
Voice of Friar Tuck	Andy Devine
Voice of Lady Kluck	Carole Shelley
Voice of Prince John	Peter Ustinov
Voice of Sir Hiss	Terry-Thomas
Voice of Sheriff	Pat Buttram
Voice of Trigger	George Lindsey
Voice of Nutsy	Ken Curtis

CINDERELLA LIBERTY

(20th CENTURY-FOX) Producer-Director, Mark Rydell; Screenplay, Darryl Ponicsan; Based on his novel of the same title; Photography, Vilmos Zsigmond; Designer, Leon Ericksen; Editor, Donn Cambern; Music, John Williams; Lyrics and Vocals, Paul Williams; Assistant Director, Tim Zinneman; Costumes, Rita Riggs; A Sanford production; In Panavision and DeLuxe color; Rated R; 117 minutes; December release.

CAST

John Baggs, Jr	James Caan
Maggie Paul	Marsha Mason
Doug	Kirk Calloway
Forshay	Eli Wallach
Master at Arms	Burt Young
Alcott	Bruce Kirby, Jr.
Miss Watkins	Allyn Ann McLerie
Executive Officer	Dabney Coleman
Dr. Osgood	Fred Sadoff
Drunken Sailor	Allan Arbus
Dental Corpsman	Jon Korkes
Lewis	Don Calfa
Sam	Paul Jackson
Sailor #1	David Proval
Cook	Ted D'Arm's
Fleet Chick	Sally Kirkland
Nurse	Diane Schenker
Seaman #1	James Bigham
Seaman #2	Wayne Hudgins
Wave	Rita Joelson Chidester
Yeoman	Knight Landesman
Hot Dog Beggar	Spike Africa
Young Sailor	Chris F. Prebazac
Messboy	David Norfleet
Woman	Sara Jackson

and James De Closs (Sailor), Niles Brewster (Paymaster), Glen Freeman (Marine Guard), Jonathan Estrin (Officer), John Kauffman (Sailor), Christopher Rydell (Boy fishing), Joe Locke (Club Owner), Frank O'Neal (Sailor), Catherine M. Balzer (Examining Nurse), Frank H. Griffin, Jr. (Obstretrician), Nella Pugh (Delivery Nurse), Clayton Corzatte (Doctor), Joseph Candiotti (OOD)

James Caan, Marsha Mason

Top: Eli Wallach, James Caan

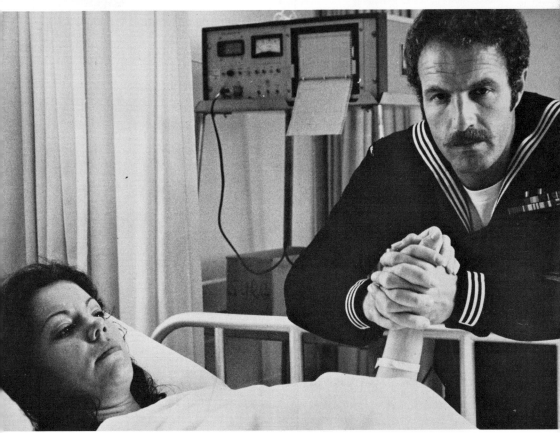

Marsha Mason, James Caan
Top: (L) Eli Wallach (R) James Caan, Marsha Mason

THE SEVEN UPS

(20th CENTURY-FOX) Producer-Director, Philip D'Antoni; Executive Producers, Kenneth Utt, Barry Weitz; Screenplay, Albert Ruben, Alexander Jacobs; Story, Sonny Grosso; Associate Producer and Editor, Gerald Greenberg; Photography, Urs Furrer; Designer Ed Wittstein; Assistant Directors, Ted Zachary, Irving Bigman, Walter Scotchdopole; Costumes, Joseph G. Aulisi; in DeLuxe color Rated PG; 103 minutes; December release.

CAST

Buddy Manucci	Roy Scheider
Vito	Tony Lo Bianco
Max Kalish	Larry Haines
Barilli	Victor Arnold
Mingo	Jerry Leon
Ansel	Ken Kercheva
Moon	Richard Lynch
Bo	Bill Hickman
Bruno	Ed Jordan
Bobby	David Wilson
Lt. Hanes	Robert Burr
Gilson	Rex Everhart
Festa	Matt Russo
Coltello	Lou Polan
Toredano	Joe Spinell
Henry Parten	William Shust
Mickey Parten	Roger Serbagi
Sara Kalish	Frances Chaney
Chef	Louis Yaccarino
Besta's son	Benedetto Marino
Fitz	Tom Signorelli
Fat Man	Thomas Rand
Nurse	Adeline Leonard
Barber	Frank Mascetta
Mrs. Pugliese	Mary Multari

Left: Roy Scheider

Tony Lo Bianco, Roy Scheider
Above: Larry Haines, Richard Lynch

Roy Scheider, Jerry Leon, Victor Arnold, Ken Kercheval Above: Larry Haines, Roy Scheider

THE LAUGHING POLICEMAN

(20th CENTURY-FOX) Producer-Director, Stuart Rosenberg; Screenplay, Thomas Rickman; Based on novel by Per Wahloo and Maj Sjowall; Photography, David Walsh; Music, Charles Fox; Editor, Robert Wyman; Assistant Directors, Mike Moder, Ron Wright, Charles Ziarko; In DeLuxe color; Rated Pg; 103 minutes; December release.

CAST

Jake Martin	Walter Matthau
Leo Larsen	Bruce Dern
Larrimore	Lou Gossett
Camerero	Albert Paulsen
Lt. Steiner	Anthony Zerbe
Pappas	Val Avery
Kay Butler	Cathy Lee Crosby
Bobby Mow	Mario Gallo
Monica	Joanna Cassidy
Grace Martin	Shirley Ballard
Schwermer	William Hansen
Collins	Jonas Wolfe
Haygood	Paul Koslo
Gus Niles	Lou Guss
Prostitute	Lee McCain
Pimp	David Moody
Rodney	Ivan Bookman
Maloney	Cliff James
Vickery	Gregg Sierra
Ripple	Warren Finnerty
Coroner	Matt Clark
Avakian's brother	Joe Bernard
Maydola	Melvina Smedley
Porno Cashier	Leigh French
Fowler	Jim Clawin
Dave Evans	Tony Costello

and John Francis (Russo), John Vick (Terry), Wayne Grace (Brennan), Cheryl Christiansen (Nurse), Jimmy Christy (Avakian), Dave Belrose (Ralph), Dawn Frame (Debbie), Ellen Nance, Lavelle Robey (Receptionists), Hobart Nelson (Jail Guard), Gus Bruneman (Squad Capt.), The San Francisco Strutters

Top: Walter Matthau, also right with Bruce Dern

Walter Matthau, Bruce Dern, Lou Gossett
Above: Matthau, Cathy Lee Crosby

SLEEPER

(UNITED ARTISTS) Executive Producer, Charles H. Joffe; Producer, Jack Grossberg; Direction and Screenplay, Woody Allen; Assistant Directors, Fred T. Gallo, Henry J. Lange, Jr.; Photography, David Walsh; Art Director, Dale Hennesy; Designer, Dianne Wager; Costumes, Joel Schumacher; Editor, Ralph Rosenblum; In color; Rated PG; 88 minutes; December release.

CAST

Miles Monroe	Woody Allen
Luna	Diane Keaton
Erno	John Beck
Dr. Nero	Marya Small
Dr. Orva	Bartlett Robinson
Dr. Melik	Mary Gregory
Rainer	Chris Forbes
Dr. Dean	Peter Hobbs
Jeb	Spencer Milligan
Sears	Stanley Ross
Janus	Whitney Rydbeck

Woody Allen, Diane Keaton
Top: Woody Allen

Woody Allen, also above (C), and top
with Diane Keaton

Woody Allen, also above with Diane Keaton,
and top with Mary Gregory, John McLiam

THE DAY OF THE DOLPHIN

(AVCO EMBASSY) Producer, Robert E. Relyea; Director, Mike Nichols; Screenplay, Buck Henry; Executive Producer, Joseph E. Levine; Associate Producer, Dick Birkmayer; Based on novel by Robert Merle; Music, Georges Delerue; Photography, William A. Fraker; Designer, Richard Sylbert; Editor, Sam O'Steen; Costumes, Anthea Sylbert; Assistant Director, Tom Schmidt; Art Director, Angelo Graham; Dolphins trained by Peter Moss; In Panavision and Technicolor; Rated PG; 104 minutes; December release.

CAST

Dr. Jake Terrell	George C. Scott
Maggie Terrell	Trish Van Devere
Mahoney	Paul Sorvino
Harold DeMilo	Fritz Weaver
David	Jon Korkes
Mike	Edward Herrmann
Maryanne	Leslie Charleson
Larry	John David Carson
Lana	Victoria Racimo
Wallingford	John Dehner
Schwinn	Severn Darden
Dunhill	William Roerick
Mrs. Rome	Elizabeth Wilson
Women at club	Julie Follansbee, Florence Stanley, Brooke Hayward, Pat Englund
Stone	Willie Meyers
Secretary	Phyllis Davis

Left: George C. Scott and Alpha

George C. Scott, Trish Van Devere, Alpha

**Fritz Weaver, George C. Scott
Above: George C. Scott and Alpha**

JONATHAN LIVINGSTON SEAGULL

(PARAMOUNT) Producer-Director, Hall Bartlett; Screenplay, Richard Bach, Hall Bartlett; From novel by Richard Bach; Photography, Jack Couffer; Editor, Frank Keller; Music, Neil Diamond, Lee Holdridge; Designer, Boris Leven; In DeLuxe color; Rated G; 114 minutes; December release.

CAST

Jonathan's voice	James Franciscus
Girl's voice	Juliet Mills
Elder's voice	Hal Holbrook
Chang's voice	Philip Ahn
Fletcher's voice	David Ladd
Kimmy's voice	Kelly Harmon
Mother's voice	Dorothy McGuire
Father's voice	Richard Crenna

Jason Miller, Max von Sydow, Linda Blair

THE EXORCIST

(WARNER BROTHERS) Executive Producer, Noel Marshall; Produced and Written by William Peter Blatty; Based on his novel; Director, William Friedkin; Photography, Owen Roizman, Billy Williams; Editors, Jordan Leondopoulos, Evan Lottman, Norman Gay, Bud Smith; Music, Jack Nitzsche; Designer, Bill Malley; Assistant Director, Terrence A. Donnelly; In Metrocolor; Rated R; 121 minutes; December release.

CAST

Mrs. MacNeil	Ellen Burstyn
Father Merrin	Max von Sydow
Lt. Kinderman	Lee J. Cobb
Sharon	Kitty Winn
Burke	Jack MacGowran
Father Karras	Jason Miller
Regan MacNeil	Linda Blair
Father Dyer	Rev. William O'Malley
Karras' Mother	Vasiliki Maliaros
Karras' Uncle	Titos Vandis
Bishop	Wallace Rooney
Assistant Director	Ron Faber
President of University	Rev. T. Bermingham

Top: Ellen Burstyn, Linda Blair
1973 Academy Award winner for Best Screenplay, and Best Sound

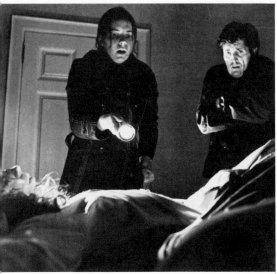

Linda Blair, Kitty Winn, Jason Miller
Top: Jason Miller, Max von Sydow

Linda Blair, Ellen Burstyn

PAPILLON

(ALLIED ARTISTS) Producers, Robert Dorfman, Franklin J. Schaffner; Executive Producer, Ted Richmond; Director, Franklin J. Schaffner; Screenplay, Dalton Trumbo, Lorenzo Semple, Jr.; Based on book by Henri Charriere; Photography, Fred Koenekamp; Editor, Robert Swink; Music, Jerry Goldsmith; Designer, Anthony Masters; Art Director, Jack Maxsted; Assistant Directors, Jose Lopez Rodero, Juan Lopez Rodero; A Corona/General production; In Technicolor; Rated PG; 150 minutes; December release.

CAST

Papillon	Steve McQueen
Dega	Dustin Hoffman
Indian Chief	Victor Jory
Julot	Don Gordon
Leper Colony Chief	Anthony Zerbe
Maturette	Robert Deman
Clusiot	Woodrow Parfrey
Lariot	Bill Mumy
Dr. Chatal	George Coulouris
Zoraima	Ratna Assan
Warden Barrot	William Smithers
Antonio	Gregory Sierra
Mother Superior	Barbara Morrison
Nun	Ellen Moss
Butterfly Trader	Don Hanmer
Commandant	Dalton Trumbo

Left: Steve McQueen, Dustin Hoffman

Don Gordon, Billy Mumy, Steve McQueen, Dustin Hoffman

Steve McQueen, Victor Jory
Top: Steve McQueen, Dustin Hoffman

Dustin Hoffman, Steve McQueen Above: McQueen,
Ratna Assan Top: Hoffman, Robert Deman

MAGNUM FORCE

(WARNER BROTHERS) Producer, Robert Daley; Director, Te
Post; Screenplay, John Milius, Michael Cimino; Based on Story b
John Milius; From original material by Harry Julian Fink, R. M
Fink; Photography, Frank Stanley; Editor, Ferris Webster; Musi
Lalo Schifrin; Art Director, Jack Collis; Assistant Director, We
McAfee; In Technicolor; Rated R: 124 minutes; December release

CAST

Harry Callahan	Clint Eastwoo
Lt. Briggs	Hal Holbroo
Early Smith	Felton Perr
Charlie McCoy	Mitchell Rya
Davis	David Sou
Sweet	Tim Matheso
Grimes	Robert Uric
Astrachan	Kip Nive
Carol McCoy	Christine Whit
Sunny	Adele Yoshiok

Top: Clint Eastwood

Clint Eastwood and policeman

Felton Perry, Clint Eastwood, Hal Holbrook Top Left: Clint Eastwood
Top Right: Clint Eastwood Below: Clint Eastwood, Hal Holbrook

THE STING

(UNIVERSAL) Producers, Tony Bill, Michael and Julia Phillips; Director, George Roy Hill; Screenplay, David S. Ward; Photography, Robert Surtees; Editor, William Reynolds; Music, Marvin Hamlisch; Art Director, Henry Bumstead; Assistant Director, Ray Gosnell; A Richard D. Zanuch-David Brown presentation; In Technicolor; Rated PG; 129 minutes; December release.

CAST

Henry Gondorff	Paul Newman
Johnny Hooker	Robert Redford
Doyle Lonnegan	Robert Shaw
Lt. Snyder	Charles Durning
Singleton	Ray Walston
Billie	Eileen Brennan
Kid Twist	Harold Gould
Niles	John Heffernan
FBI Agent	Dana Elcar
Erie Kid	Jack Kohoe
Loretta	Dimitra Arliss

Left: Robert Redford, Paul Newman

1973 Academy Award winner for Best Film, Best Director, Best Story and Screenplay, Best Editing, Best Scoring, Best Art and Set Direction, Best Costume Design

Paul Newman, Robert Redford Center: (L) Robert Redford, Robert Shaw, Charles Dierkop (R) Ray Walston, Eileen Brennan, Paul Newman

Robert Redford, Eileen Brennan Above: Harold Gould, Paul Newman, Ray Walston Top: Newman, Redford

Paul Newman, Robert Redford Above: Redford, Robertearl Jones, James Sloyan Top: Robert Shaw, Newman

111

SERPICO

(PARAMOUNT) Producer, Martin Bregman; Director, Sidney Lumet; Screenplay, Waldo Salt, Norman Wexler; Based on book by Peter Maas; Photography, Arthur J. Ornitz; Editors, Dede Allen, Richard Marks; Music, Mikis Theodorakis; Designer, Charles Bailey; Art Director, Douglas Higgins; Assistant Director, Burtt Harris; A Dino De Laurentiis-Artists Entertainment Complex presentation; In Technicolor; Rated R; 130 minutes; December release.

CAST

Frank Serpico	Al Pacino
Chief Green	John Randolph
Tom Keough	Jack Kehoe
Captain McClain	Biff McGuire
Laurie	Barbara eda-Young
Leslie	Cornelia Sharpe
Bob Blair	Tony Roberts
D. A.	Allan Rich
Rubello	Norman Ornellas
Lombardo	Ed Grover
Captain Tolkin	Gene Gross
Steiger	James Tolkin
Berman	Lewis J. Stadlen
Gilbert	John Lehne
Gallagher	M. Emmet Walsh
Daley	George Ede
Commissioner Delaney	Charles White
Pasquale	John Medici
Peluce	Al Henderson
Malone	Hank Garrett
Joey	Damien Leake
Potts	Joe Bova
Waterman	John Stewart
Larry	Woodie King
Barto	Ed Crowley
Smith	Nathan George
Palmer	Bernard Barrow
Mr. Serpico	Sal Carollo
Mrs. Serpico	Mildred Clinton
Dr. Metz	Gus Fleming
Corsaro	Richard Foronjy
Brown	Alan North
Kellogg	John McQuade
Sarno	Ted Beniades

Al Pacino, Franklin Scott Above: Sal Carollo, Mildred Clinton, Al Pacino

Top: Al Pacino Left: Al Pacino, Damien Leake

Al Pacino, Nathan George (R) Above: Pacino,
Ed Grover Top: Tony Roberts, Pacino

Al Pacino, Biff McGuire Above (C)
and Top: Al Pacino

THE LAST DETAIL

(COLUMBIA) Producer, Gerald Ayres; Director, Hal Ashby; Screenplay, Robert Towne; Based on novel by Darryl Ponicsan; Photography, Michael Chapman; Editor, Robert C. Jones; Music, Johnny Mandel; Songs, Jack Goga, K. Lawrence Dunham, Ron Nagel, Miles Goodman, Douglas Brayfield; Associate Producer, Charles Mulvehill; Costumes, Ted Parvin; Designer, Michael Haller; Assistant Directors, Wes McAfee, Gordon Robinson, Al Hopkins; An Acrobat Film in Metrocolor; Rated R; 105 minutes; December release.

CAST

Buddusky	Jack Nicholson
Mulhall	Otis Young
Meadows	Randy Quaid
M.A.A.	Clifton James
Young Whore	Carol Kane
Marine O.D.	Michael Moriarty
Donna	Luana Anders
Kathleen	Kathleen Miller
Nancy	Nancy Allen
Henry	Gerry Salsberg
Bartender	Don McGovern
Madame	Pat Hamilton
Taxi Driver	Michael Chapman
Sweek	Jim Henshaw
Nichiren Shoshu Members	Derek McGrath, Gilda Radner, Jim Horn, John Castellano

Otis Young, Randy Quaid, Jack Nicholson, also top left

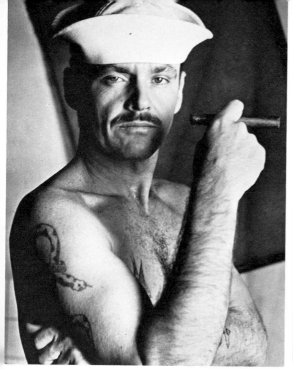

Otis Young, Jack Nicholson, Michael Moriarty
Above: Nicholson (also top), Nancy Allen

Randy Quaid, Jack Nicholson, also top with
Otis Young Above: Carol Kane, Nicholson

Zaldy Zshornack, Margaret Markov
in "Black Mama, White Mama"

Pam Grier, Margaret Markov, Laurie Burton,
Lynn Borden in "Black Mama, White Mama"

BLACK MAMA, WHITE MAMA (American International) Executive Producer, David J. Cohen; Producers, John Ashley, Eddie Romero; Director, Eddie Romero; Screenplay, H. R. Christian from story by Joseph Viola, Jonathan Demme; Photography, Justo Paulino; Music, Harry Betts; Editor, Asagni V. Pastor; Design, Roberto Formoso; A Four Star Associates presentation in Movielab Color; Rated R; 87 minutes; January release. CAST: Pam Grier (Lee), Margaret Markov (Karen), Sid Haig (Ruben), Lynn Borden (Densmore), Zaldy Zshornack (Ernesto), Laurie Burton (Logan), Eddie Garcia (Capt.), Alona Alegre (Juana), Dindo Fernando (Rocco), Vic Diaz (Vic), Wendy Green (Ronda), Lotis M. Key (Jeanette), Alfonso Carvajal (Galindo), Bruno Punzalah (Truck Driver), Ricardo Herrero (Luis), Jess Ramos (Alfredo)

SUGAR COOKIES (General Film) Executive Producer, Lloyd Kaufman; Producer, Ami Artzi; Director, Theodore Gershuny; Screenplay, Lloyd Kaufman, Theodore Gershuny; Associate Producers, Gerrard L. Glenn, Oliver W. Stone, Jeffrey Kappelman; Photography, Hasse Wellin; Editor, Dov Hoenig; Art Director, Thomas Sturges; Music, Gershon Kingsley; An Armor Films production in Eastmancolor; Rated X; January release. CAST: George Shannon (Max), Mary Woronov (Camilla), Lynn Lowry (Alta-Julie), Monique Van Vooren (Helene), Maureen Byrnes (Dola), Daniel Sadur (Gus), Ondine (Roderick), Jennifer Welles (Secretary), Anthony Pompei (Oliver), Reid Cruickshanks (Det. Schwartz), Thomas Mahony (Det. Joe), Ralph R. Ralph (Doctor), S. Lloyd Kaufman, Sr. (Lawyer), Shawn Randall (Girl), Allen Liffman (Man), Debbie Parness (Cindy), Beatrice Eisner (Boutique Girl), Beatrice Conrad, Uta Walters, Mary Schacheel, Nancy Ennis (Interview Girls)

LIFE STUDY (Nebbia) Produced, Directed, and Photographed by Michael Nebbia; Screenplay, Arthur Birnkrant; Based on story by Michael Nebbia; Editors, Ray Sandiford, Sidney Katz; In color; 99 minutes; January release. CAST: Bartholomew Miro, Jr. (Angelo), Erika Peterson (Myrna), Ziska (Angela), Gregory D'Alessio (Adrian), Tom Lee Jones (Gus), Rosetta Garuffi (Grandma), Anthony Forest (John), Yvonne Sherwell (Peggy)

IT HAPPENED IN HOLLYWOOD (Screw) Producer, Jim Buckley; Direction and Screenplay, Peter Locke; Photography, Steven Bower; Editor, Wes Craven; Music, Ron Frangipane, Al Steckler; Designer, Peter Bramley; In color; Rated X; 74 minutes; January release. CAST: Felicity Split, Mark Stevens, Al Levitsky, Alan Spitz, Al Goldstein, Richard Sternberger, Jim Buckley, Liz Torres

HIGH RISE (Maturpix) Produced, Directed, and Written by Danny Stone; Photography, Maurice Finkelstein; Editor, Robert Salvator; Music, Jacques Urbont; In color; Rated X; 66 minutes; January release. CAST: Tamie Trevor, Geri Miller, Richard Hunt, James Kleeman, Jutta David, Mireille Renaud, Samantha Whitney

THE AROUSERS (New World) Producer, Tamara Asseyev; Direction and Screenplay, Curtis Hanson; Music, Charles Bernstein; Photography, Daniel Lacombre, Edmund Anderson, Floyd Crosby; Editor, Gretel Erlich; Assistant Director, Ramzi Thomas; In Metrocolor; Rated R; 84 minutes; January release. CAST: Tab Hunter, Cherie Latimer, Linda Leider, Isabel Jewell, Nadyne Turney, Roberta Collins, Brandy Herred, Angel Fox, Katie McKeown, John Aprea, Josh Green, Rory Guy, Sandy Kenyon

MANSON (American International) Producer-Director, Laurence Merrick; Compiled and Written by Joan Huntington; Associate Producer, Leo Rivers; Editor, Clancy Syrko; Photography, Leo Rivers; Narrator, Jess Pearson; Assistant Director, Betty Adams; Art Director, Michael Roberts; Songs composed and performed by Paul Watkins and Brooks Poston; In Movielab color; Rated R; 83 minutes; January release. A documentary on Charles Manson with the following as themselves: Charles Manson, D. A. Vincent Bugliosi, Patricia Krenwinkle, Leslie Van Houten, Tex Watson, Robert Beausoliel, Steve Grogan, Bruce Davis, Mary Bruner.

PRISON GIRLS (American International) Producers, Nick Grippo, Burton Gershfeld; Director, Thomas DeBurton; Screenplay, Burton Gershfeld; In color and Optivision 3-D; Rated X; January release. CAST: Robin Whitting, Maria Arnold, Angie Monet, Ushi Diagart, Lisa Ashbury, Tracy Handfuss, Jamie McKenna, Ilona Lakes, Claire Bow, Lois Darst, Carol Peters

"Sugar Cookies"

"Sugar Cookies"

Tab Hunter, Cherie Ratimer
in "The Arousers"

Tab Hunter, Linda Leider
in "The Arousers"

RUNNING WITH THE DEVIL (Unisphere) An Allen Bazzini presentation; In Eastmancolor; No other credits available; Rated R; January release. CAST: Sean Kenny, Donna Stanley, Reagon Wilson, Jane Peters

THE SIN OF ADAM AND EVE (Dimension) In color; Rated R; No other credits available; January release. CAST: George Rivero, Candy Cave

LOVE ME DEADLY (Cinema National) In color; Rated R; No other credits available; January release. CAST: Mary Wilcox, Lyle Waggoner, Christopher Stone

IRISH WHISKEY REBELLION (GSF-Cinerama) Director, Chester Erskine; In Color; Rated PG; No other credits available; January release. CAST: William Devane, Anne Meara, Richard Mulligan, David Groh, Stephen Joyce

TEENAGE SEX REPORT (Cinemation) In color; Rated X; No other information available; January release.

SLAUGHTER HOTEL (Hallmark) In Eastmancolor; Rated R; No other information available; January release.

THE DIRTIEST GIRL I EVER MET (American International) Producer-Director, Pete Walker; In Eastmancolor; Rated R; January release. CAST: Janet Lynn (Carol), Robin Askwith (Joe), Peter Elliott (Philip), Jess Conrad (Jonathan), Stubby Kaye (Strangeways)

TWILIGHT PEOPLE (Dimension) Producers, John Ashley, Eddie Romero; In Metrocolor; Rated PG; January release. CAST: John Ashley, Pat Woodell, Pam Grier, Brooke Mills

SWEET SUGAR (Dimension) Producer, Charles S. Swartz; Director, Michel Levesque; Screenplay, Don Spencer; In Metrocolor; Rated R; January release. CAST: Phyllis Davis, Timothy Brown, Pam Collins, Angus Duncan, Ella Edwards, Jackie Giroux, Cliff Osmond, Albert Cole, Jim Houghton, Daryl Severns, James Whitworth

THE FEMALE RESPONSE (Trans-American) Producer, Richard Lipton; Director, Tim Kincaid; Screenplay, Tim Kincaid, David Newburge; Photography, Arthur D. Marks; Music, Bill Beynolds; Editors, Graham Place, Arthur Marks; In Eastmancolor; A Filmpeople presentation; Rated R; 88 minutes; January release. CAST: Raina Barrett (Leona), Jacque Lynn Colton (Rosalie), Michaela Hope (Sandy), Jennifer Welles (Andrea), Gene Wheeler (Victoria), Marjorie Hirsch (Marjorie), Roz Kelly (Gilda), Lawrie Driscoll (Karl), Edmund Donnelly (Mark), Todd Everett (Gary), Richard Wilkins (Tom), Phyllis MacBride (Rachel), Suzy Mann (Ramona), Curtis Carlson (Alex), Herb Streicher (Max), Anthony Scott Craig (Caller), Richard Lipton (Leland)

HOWZER (URI) Producer, Philip Clarke Kaufman; Direction-Screenplay, Ken Laurence; Photography, Bruce Logan; Music, Stephen Scull; In DeLuxe color; 82 minutes; January release. CAST: Royal Dano (Nick), Olive Deering (Mary), Virgil Frye (Joe), Peter Desiante (Howzer), Melissa Stocking (Debora), William Gray (Albert), and Edmund Gilbert, Allyn Ann McLerie, Elaine Partnow, Wonderful Smith, Steven Vaughan, David Dean, Ed Van Nordic

BIG FOOT (Ellman Enterprises) Producer, Tony Cardoza; Director, Robert F. Slatzer; Screenplay, James Gordon White, Robert F. Slatzer; In color; Rated GP; January release. CAST: Chris Mitchum, John Carradine, Joe Lansing, Lindsay Crosby, Ken Maynard

THE HITCHHIKERS (Entertainment Ventures) Producers, Directors, Screenplay, Ferd and Beverly Sebastian; Original Screenplay, Ann Cawthorne; Photography, Ferd Sebastian; Editor, Jeremy Hoenack; Music, Danny Cohen; In Movielab color; Rated R; 91 minutes; January release. CAST: Misty Rowe (Maggic), Norman Klar (Benson), Linda Avery (Diane), Tammy Gibbs (Karen), Kathy Stutsman (Jinx), Mary Thatcher (Brook), Denny Nichols (Truck Driver), Ted Ziegler (Deacon), Efrem Dockter (Store Manager), Lou Jofferd (Doctor), Blue McKenzie (Reb), Lee Morley (Car Salesman), Jim Sherwood (Nemo)

The Charles Manson family
in "Manson"

Richard Lipton, Roz Kelly
in "Female Response"

Art Lund, Fred Williamson
in "Black Caesar"

The Bar-Kays
in "Wattstax"

BLACK CAESAR (American International) Executive Producer, Peter Sabiston; Produced, Directed, and Screenplay by Larry Cohen; Photography, Fenton Hamilton; Associate Producer, James P. Dixon; Co-Producer, Janelle Cohen; Editor, George Folsey, Jr.; Music composed and performed by James Brown; Album by Polydor Records; A Larco Production in DeLuxe Color; Rated R; 92 minutes; February release. CAST: Fred Williamson (Tommy), D'Urville Martin (Rev. Rufus), Julius W. Harris (Gibbs), Don Pedro Colley (Crawdaddy), Gloria Hendry (Helen), Art Lund (McKinney), Val Avery (Cardoza), Minnie Gentry (Mama Gibbs), Phillip Roye (Joe), William Wellman, Jr. (Alfred), James Dixon (Bryant), Myrna Hansen (Virginia), Patrick McAllister (Grossfield), Cecil Alonzo (Motor), Allen Bailey (Sport), Omer Jeffrey (Tommy as boy), Michael Jeffrey (Joe as boy)

LOLLY-MADONNA XXX (MGM) Producer, Rodney Carr-Smith; Director, Richard C. Sarafin; Screenplay, Rodney Carr-Smith, Sue Grafton; Based on novel "Lolly-Madonna War" by Sue Grafton; Music, Fred Myrow; Photography, Philip Lathrop; Art Director, Herman Blumenthal; Editor, Tom Rolf; Assistant Directors, Mike Moder, Terry Carr; Song "Peaceful Country," Kim Carnes, David Ellingson; Sung by Kim Carnes; In Panavision and Metrocolor; Rated PG; 105 minutes; February release. CAST: Rod Steiger (Laban), Katherine Squire (Chickie), Scott Wilson (Thrush), Timothy Scott (Skylar), Ed Lauter (Hawk), Randy Quaid (Finch), Jeff Bridges (Zack), Robert Ryan (Pap), Tresa Hughes (Elspeth) Paul Koslo (Villum), Kiel Martin (Ludie), Gary Busey (Seb), Joan Goodfellow (Sister E), Season Hubley (Roonie)

ALABAMA'S GHOST (Ellman Enterprises) Produced, Directed, and Written by Fredric Hobbs; In DeLuxe color; Rated PG; February release. CAST: Christopher Brooks, E. Kerrigan Scott, Turk Murphy Jazz Band

BONNIE'S KIDS General Film Corp.) Producer, Chuck Stroud; Director, Arthur Marks; In color; Rated R; February release. CAST: Tiffany Bolling, Steve Sandor, Robin Mattson, Scott Brady, Alex Rocco, Tim Brown

WATTSTAX (Columbia) Producers, Larry Shaw, Mel Stuart; Director, Mel Stuart; Executive Producers, Al Bell, David L. Wolper; Associate Producer, Forest Hamilton; Photography, Roderick Young, Robert Marks, Jose Mignone, Larry Clark; Editors, Robert Lambert, David Newhouse, David Blewitt; Assistant Director, Charles Washburn; A Stax Films-Wolper Pictures production in color; Rated R; 102 minutes; February release. CAST: Richard Pryor, The Dramatics, Staple Singers, Kim Weston, Jimmy Jones, Rance Allen Group, William Bell, Louise McCord, Debra Manning, Eric Mercury, Freddy Robinson, Lee Sain, Ernie Hines, Little Sonny, Newcomers, Eddie Floyd, Temprees, Frederick Knight, The Emotions, Bar Kays, Albert King, Little Milton, Johnnie Taylor, Mel and Tim, Carla Thomas, Rufus Thomas, Luther Ingram, Isaac Hayes, Ted Lange, Elizabeth Cleveland, Raymond Allen, Andre Edwards, Patricia Henley, Eric Kilpatrick, Ernest King, Michael Gibson

TEENAGE COWGIRLS (Kairio) Producer, Hal Grunquist; Director, Ted Denver; In color; Rated X; 64 minutes; February release. CAST: Lon Johnny Wadd, Teresa Gillies, Felice Karr, Roberta Hine, Harold Banover

THE BACK ROW (Cedarlane) Director, Doug Richards; Music, William R. Cox; A Scorpio V production in color; Rated X; 85 minutes; February release. CAST: Casey Donovan (Unnamed Protagonist), George Payne (Kid from Montana), Robin Anderson (Hippy), David Knox (Sailor), Warren Carlton (Cashier), Robert Tristan (Roommate), Arthur Graham (Student), Chris Villette (Hard Hat)

TEN FROM YOUR SHOW OF SHOWS (Continental) Producer-Director, Max Liebman; Written by Mel Tolkin, Lucille Kallen, Mel Brooks, Tony Webster, Sid Caesar, Max Liebman; Designer, Frederick Fox; Costumes, Paul Dupont; Editor, Bob Bass; Rated G; 92 minutes; February release. CAST: Sid Caesar, Imogene Coca, Carl Reiner, Louis Nye, Howard Morris, Dorothy Patten, Jack Russell, Ray Drakely, Eleanor Williams, Swen Swenson, Ed Herlihy

Katherine Squire, Rod Steiger, Joan Goodfellow,
Robert Ryan in "Lolly-Madonna XXX"

Sid Caesar, Imogene Coca
in "Ten from Your Show of Shows"

John Savage, Donald Sutherland, Peter Boyle
in "Steelyard Blues"

Jane Fonda
in "Steelyard Blues"

STEELYARD BLUES (Warner Bros.) Executive Producer, Donald Sutherland; Producers, Tony Bill, Michael and Julia Phillips; Director, Alan Myerson; Screenplay, David S. Ward; Photography, Laszlo Kovacs, Stevan Larner; Art Director, Vincent Cresciman; Editors, Don Cambern, Robert Grovenor; Associate Producer, Harold Schneider; Music, Nick Gravenites, Paul Butterfield; Assistant Director, Sheldon Schrager; In Technicolor; Rated PG; 92 minutes; February release. CAST: Jane Fonda (Iris), Donald Sutherland (Veldini), Peter Boyle (Eagle), Garry Goodrow (Duval), Howard Hesseman (Frank), John Savage (The Kid), Richard Schaal (Zoo Official), Melvin Stewart (Black Man in Jail), Morgan Upton (Police Captain), Roger Bowen (Fire Commissioner), Howard Storm (Health Inspector), Jessica Myerson (Savage Rose), Dan Barrows (Rocky), Nancy Fish (Pool Hall Waitress), Lynn Bernay (Bar Waitress), Edward Greenberg (Rookie Cop)

CHILDHOOD II (Postape) Producer, Richard M. Gibson; Director, Martin J. Spinelli; Photography, Ken Basmajian; In Color; 85 minutes; February release. A documentary on group encounters.

BROTHER OF THE WIND (Sun International) Executive Producer, G. M. Ridges; Producers, Dick Robinson, John Mahon; Screenplay, John Mahon, John Champion; Narrator, Leon Ames; Director, Dick Robinson; Music, Gene Kauer, Douglas Lackey; In color; 87 minutes; February release. CAST: Dick Robinson

THE BIG BUST-OUT (New World) Producer-Director, Richard Jackson; Screenplay, Sergio Garrone; Photography, Robert Galeassi; Editor, Barbara Pokras; Music, Burt Rexon, Elsio Mancuso; In Technicolor; Rated R; 75 minutes; February release. CAST: Vonetta McGee, Monica Taylor, Linda Fox, Karen Carter, Gordon Mitchell, Christin Thorn, Tony Kendall, William Berger, Mara Krup, Giorgio Dolphin, Rebecca Mead, Miller Drake

SCREAM BLOODY MURDER (Indepix) Producer-Director, Marc B. Ray; Rated R; February release. CAST: Fred Holbert, Leigh Mitchell, Robert Knox, A. Maana Tanelah, Ron Bastone, Suzette Hamilton

THE BLIND DEAD (Hallmark) In color; Rated PG; No other information available; February release.

THE BLACK BUNCH (Entertainment Pyramid) Producer, Daniel Cady; Director, Henning Schellerup; In color; Rated X; February release. CAST: Gladys Bunker, Marshall Breedson, Evan Renshaw

TARZANA, THE WILD GIRL (Ellman Enterprises) Producer, Glen Hart; Director, James Reed; Screenplay, Philip Shaw; In Eastmancolor; Rated R; February release. CAST: Ken Clark, Beryl Cunningham, Franca Polesello, Frank Ressel, Andrew Ray, Alfred Thomas

THE EXPERIMENT (Jaguar) Producer, Barry Knight; Direction and Screenplay, Gorton Hall; Executive Producer, Mark Aaron; Photography and Editing, Barry Knight; In Eastmancolor; Rated X; 118 minutes; February release. CAST: Mike Stevens (Billy Joe), Joey Daniels (Gary Lee), Gorton Hall (Herm), Jimmy Hughes (Salesman), and Dave Craig, Tony Ross, Robert Weaver, Eva Faye, David Blair, Peter Thomas

LOLA (American International) Producer, Clive Sharp; Director, Richard Donner; In Technicolor; Rated PG; 88 minutes; February release. CAST: Charles Bronson (Scott), Susan George (Lola), Trevor Howard (Grandfather), Honor Blackman (Lola's Mom), Michael Craig (Lola's Dad), Orson Bean (Hal), Paul Ford (Scott's Dad), Jack Hawkins (Judge Draper), Robert Morley (Judge Roxburgh), Lionel Jeffries (Creighton)

KONGI'S HARVEST (Tam Communications) Director, Ossie Davis; Screenplay, Wole Soyinka; Based on his play; Photography, Ake Lindqvist; In color; 85 minutes; February release. CAST: Wole Soyinka (Kongi), Rashidi Onikoyi (Oba), Femi Johnson (Secretary), Dapo Adelugba (Daodu), Nina Baden-Semper (Segi), Orlando Martins (Dr. Gbenga)

Jeff Bridges, Season Hubley
in "Lolly-Madonna XXX"

"The Big Bust-out"

Robert Elfstrom
in "Gospel Road"

Barry Newman, Suzy Kendall
in "Fear Is the Key"

THE GOSPEL ROAD (20th Century-Fox) Producers, June Cash, Johnny Cash; Director, Robert Elfstrom; Screenplay, Johnny Cash, Larry Murray; Music, Larry Butler; Associate Producers, Reba Hancock, Saul Holiff, Barbara John, Lou Robin; Photography, Robert Elfstrom, Tom McDonough; Editor, John Craddock; Assistant Director, William Makley; Songs, John Denver, Larry Gatlin, Kris Kristofferson, Joe South, Harold and Don Reid, Christopher Wren, Johnny Cash; Sung by June Cash, Kris Kristofferson, Harold and Don Reid; In DeLuxe Color; Rated G; 93 minutes; March release. CAST: Robert Elfstrom (Jesus), June Carter Cash (Mary Magdalene), Larry Lee (John the Baptist), Paul Smith (Peter), Alan Dater (Nicodemus), Robert Elfstrom, Jr. (Child Jesus), Gelles LaBlanc (John), Terrance Winston Mannock (Matthew), Thomas Leventhal (Judas), John Paul Kay (James), Sean Armstrong (Thomas), Lyle Nicholson (Andrew), Steven Chernoff (Philip), Stuart Clark (Nathaniel), Ulf Pollack (Thaddeus), Jonathan Sanders (Simon)

PAINTERS PAINTING (New Yorker) Producer-Director, Emile de Antonio; Editor, Mary Lampson; Photography, Ed Emshwiller; In color and black and white; 116 minutes; March release. CAST: Willem de Kooning, Helen Frankenthaler, Hans Hoffman, Jasper Johns, Robert Motherwell, Barnett Newman, Kenneth Noland, Jules Olitski, Philip Pavia, Jackson Pollock, Larry Poons, Bob Rauschenberg, Frank Stella, Andy Warhol, Leo Castelli, Henry Geldzahler, Clement Greenberg, Tom Hess, Philip Johnson, Hilton Kramer, William Rubin, Robert Scull

BUMMER (Entertainment Ventures) Producers, David F. Friedman, William Allen Castleman; Director, William Allen Castleman; Screenplay, Alvin L. Fast; In color; Rated R; March release. CAST: Carol Speed, Connie Strickland, Dennis Burkley, Kipp Whitman, David Buchanan, David Ankrum

MIDNIGHT PLOWBOY (Boxoffice International) Executive Producer, Harry Novak; Producer-Director, Bethel Buckalew; In color; March release. CAST: John Tull, Nancee, Debbie Osborne, Christie Anna, Jack Richesim

THE BABY (Scotia International) Producers, Milton Polsky, Abe Polsky; Director, Ted Post; Screenplay, Abe Polsky; Executive Producers, Elliott Feinman, Ralph Hirsch; Music, Gerald Fried; In color; Rated PG; March release. CAST: Anjanette Comer, Ruth Roman, Mariana Hill, Suzan Zenor, David Manzy (Baby)

CAMPER JOHN (Cinemation) Producer, Peter Brown; Director, Sean McGregor; Rated R; March release. CAST: William Smith, Joe Flynn, Gene Evans, Barbara Luna

THE ROOM MATES (GFC) Producer, Charles Stroud; Director, Arthur Marks; In Eastmancolor; Rated R; March release. CAST: Pat Woodell, Marki Bey, Roberta Collins, Laurie Rose, Christina Hart

PLEASE DON'T EAT MY MOTHER (Boxoffice International) Alternate title "Please Release My Mother"; A Harry Novak presentation; In color; March release. CAST: Rene Bond, Buck Kartalian

GROUP MARRIAGE (Dimension) Producer, Charles S. Swartz; Director, Stephanie Rothman; In Metrocolor; Rated R; March release. CAST: Victoria Vetri, Aimee Eccles, Solomon Sturges, Claudia Jennings, Zack Taylor, Jeffrey Pomerantz, Milt Kamen

THE DEVIL IN MISS JONES (Marvin) Produced, Directed, Written, and Edited by Gerard Damiano; Photography, Harry Flecks; Music, Alden Shuman; In color; Rated X; 74 minutes; March release. CAST: Georgina Spelvin (Justine), John Clemens (Abaca), Harry Reams (Teacher), Albert Gork (Man in the cell), Marc Stevens, Rick Livermore, Sue Flaken

FEAR IS THE KEY (Paramount) Producers, Alan Ladd, Jr., Jay Kanter; Director, Michael Tuchner; Screenplay, Robert Carrington; Based on novel by Alistair MacLean; In Panavision and Technicolor; Rated PG; 103 minutes; March release. CAST: Barry Newman (John), Suzy Kendall (Sara), John Vernon (Vyland), Dolph Sweet (Jablonski), Ben Kingsley (Royale), Ray McAnally (Ruthven), Peter Marinker (Larry), Elliott Sullivan (Larry), Roland Brand (Deputy), Tony Anholt (FBI Man)

"Painters Painting"

Barry Newman
in "Fear Is the Key"

"Code Name Trixie"

Mel Stewart, Fuddle Bagley
in "Trick Baby"

CODE NAME TRIXIE (Cambist) formerly "The Crazies"; Producer, Al C. Croft; Director, George Romero; In color; 103 minutes; March release. CAST: Lane Carroll (Judy), W. G. McMillan (David), Harold Wayne Jones (Clank), Lloyd Hollar (Colonel), Richard Liberty (Artie), Lynn Lowry (Kathie), Richard France (Dr. Watts), Harry Spillman (Maj. Rider)

TRICK BABY (Universal) Producer, Marshal Backlar; Executive Producer, James Levitt; Director, Larry Yust; Screenplay, T. Raewyn, A. Neuberg, Larry Yust; Based on novel by Iceberg Slim; Photography, Isidore Mankofsky; Editor, Peter Parasheles; Music, James Bond; In color; Rated R; 89 minutes; March release. CAST: Jan Leighton (Carlson), Byron Sanders (Parkview Clerk), Dick Boccelli (Vincent), Jim Mapp (Doc), Bob Brooker (DuSable Clerk), Ronald Carter (Bartender), Celeste Creech, Deloris Brown-Harper (Hookers), Jacqueline Weiss (Aunt Rose), Father James Kelly (Priest), Charles Weldon (Tough), Charles Clarke (Cab Driver)

TWO PEOPLE (Universal) Producer-Director, Robert Wise; Screenplay, Richard DeRoy; Photography, Henri Decae; Art Director, Henry Michelson; Editor, William Reynolds; Music, David Shire; Assistant Director, Larbi Bennani; In Technicolor; 100 minutes; March release. CAST: Peter Fonda (Evan), Lindsay Wagner (Deirdre), Estelle Parsons (Barbara), Alan Fudge (Fitzgerald), Philippe March (Gilles), Frances Sternhagen (Mrs. McCluskey), Brian Lima (Marcus), Geoffrey Horne (Ron)

SCHLOCK (Jack H. Harris) Producer, James C. O'Rourke; Direction and Screenplay, John Landis; Photography, Bob Collins; Editor, George Folsey, Jr.; Assistant Director, Jonathan A. Flint; Music, David Gibson; Executive Producer, George Folsey, Jr.; A Gazotskie production in DeLuxe color; Rated PG; 77 minutes; March release. CAST: Saul Kahan, Joseph Piantadosi, Eliza Garrett, Eric Allison, Enrica Blankey, Charles Villiers, John Chambers

THE EROTIC FILMS OF PETER DE ROME (Hand-in-Hand) Produced, Directed, Photographed, and Edited by Peter De Rome; In color; Rated X; 95 minutes; March release.

THE YOUNG NURSES (New World) Producer, Julie Corman; Director, Clinton Kimbro; Screenplay, Howard R. Cohen; Photography, Sam Clement; Editor, Karen Johnson; Music, Greg Prestopino; Assistant Director, George Van Noy; Art Director, Barbara Peeters; Designer, Tim Kincaid; In Metrocolor; Rated R; 77 minutes; March release. CAST: Jean Manson (Kitty), Ashley Porter (Joanne), Angela Gibbs (Michelle), Zack Taylor (Donahue), Jack La Rue, Jr. (Ken), William Joyce (Fairbanks), Richard Miller (Policeman), Sally Kirkland (Patient), Allan Arbus (Krebs), Mary Doyle (Nurse), Don Keefer (Chemist), Nan Martin (Reporter), Jay Burton (Manager), Linda Towne (Chris), John Thompson (Chicken), Kimberly Hyde (Peppermint), James Anthony (Nurse), Jeff Young (Anesthetist), Tom Baker (Floyd), Caro Kenyatta (Lester), Man Tan Moreland, Sam Fuller

FREE (Indie-Pix) Producer, Director, Screenplay, Bert Tenzer; Photography, Tony Mitchel; Editor, Barbara Connell; In color; 80 minutes; March release. A documentary on "rock" fests featuring Mel Winkler, Louis Arroyo, Jimi Hendrix, Mountain, Van Morrison, Steppenwolf, Dr. John

THE FILTHIEST SHOW IN TOWN (William Mishkin) Produced, Directed, and Edited by Rick and Bob Endelson; Screenplay, Rick Endelson; Photography, Bob Endelson; Assistant Director, Victor Melt; In color; 80 minutes; March release. CAST: Dollya Sharp, Harry Reems, Tina Russel, Rudy Hornish, Alexander Sebastian, Judith Resnick, Arlana Blue, Joe Libido, Rudolph Rose, Bernard Erhard, Herbert Manguso, Richard Manchester, Mae Marmy, Rob Kendall, Alan Marlow, Sam Elias, Richard Tenbroke, Don Alter

FLY ME (New World) Producer-Director, Cirio Santiago; Screenplay, Miller Drake; Photography, Philip Sacdalan; Editor, Barbara Pokras; In Metrocolor; Rated R; 80 minutes; March release. CAST: Pat Anderson (Toby), Lenore Kasdorf (Andrea), Lyllah Torena (Sherry), Richard Young (Doctor), Naomi Stevens (Toby's mother), Richard Miller (Cab Driver), Vic Diaz (Police Chief)

Geoffrey Horne, Estelle Parsons, Lindsay
Wagner in "Two People"

Lenore Kasdorf
in "Fly Me"

Warren Oates, Ryan O'Neal, Jacqueline Bisset
in "The Thief Who Came to Dinner"

"Cannibal Girls"

THE THIEF WHO CAME TO DINNER (Warner Bros.) Producer-Director, Bud Yorkin; Screenplay, Walter Hill; Based on novel by Terrence L. Smith; Photography, Philip Lathrop; Designer, Polly Platt; Editor, John C. Horger; Music, Henry Mancini; Assistant Director, Associate Producer, D. Michael Moore; In color; Rated PG; 105 minutes; March release. CAST: Ryan O'Neal (Webster), Jacqueline Bisset (Laura), Warren Oates (Dave), Jill Clayburgh (Jackie), Charles Cioffi (Henderling), Neb Beatty (Deams), Austin Pendleton (Zukovsky), Gregory Sierra (Dynamite), Michael Murphy (Ted), John Hillerman (Laxker), Alan Oppenheimer (Insurance Man), Margaret Fairchild (Mrs. Donner), Jack Manning (Tom), Richard O'Brien (Sgt. Del Conte), George Morfogen (Rivera)

CANNIBAL GIRLS (American International) Executive Producer, Ivan Reitman; Producer, Daniel Goldberg; Director, Ivan Reitman; Screenplay, Robert Sandler; Photography, Robert Saad; Music, Doug Riley; Editor, Daniel Goldberg; Assistant Director, Dennis Matheson; In Movielab color; Rated R; 84 minutes; April release. CAST: Eugene Levy (Cliff), Andrea Martin (Gloria), Ronald Ulrich (Reverend), Randall Carpenter (Anthea), Bonnie Neilson (Clarissa), Mira Pawluk (Leona), Bob McHeady (Sheriff), Alan Gordon (1st Victim), Allan Price (2nd Victim), Earl Pomerantz (3rd Victim), May Jarvis (Mrs. Wainwright)

GANJA AND HESS (Kelly-Jordan) Executive Producers, Quentin Kelly, Jack Jordan; Producer, Chiz Schultz; Direction and Screenplay, Bill Gunn; Music, Sam Waymon; Photography, James E. Hinton; Designer, Tom John; Editor, Victor Kanefsky; Associate Producer, Joan Shigekawa; Assistant Director, Anthony Major; Costumes, Scott Barrie; Rated R; 110 minutes; April release. CAST: Duane Jones (Dr. Hess Green), Marlene Clark (Ganja), Bill Gunn (George), Sam Waymon (Rev. Williams), Leonard Jackson (Archie), Candece Tarpley (Girl in bar), Richard Harrow (Dinner Guest), John Hoffmeister (Jack), Betty Barney (Singer), Mabel King (Queen of Myrthia), Betsy Thurman (Poetess), Enrico Fales (Green's son), Tommy Lane (Pimp), Tara Fields (Woman with baby)

CIAO! MANHATTAN (Maron) Directed and Written by John Palmer, David Weisman; Editor, Robert Farren; Photography, John Palmer, Kiell Rostad; Music, John Phillips, Richie Havens, Kim Milford, Skip Battin, Kim Fowley; in color and black and white; Rated R; 90 minutes; April release. CAST: Edie Sedgwick (Susan), Wesley Hayes (Butch), Isabel Jewell (Mummy), Geoff Briggs (Geoffrey), Paul America (Paul), Jane Holzer (Charla), Roger Vadim (Dr. Braun), Jean Margouleff (Verdecchio)

DEVIL'S DUE (Norman Arno) Producer, Nino de Roma; Director, Ernest Danna; Screenplay, Gerry Pound; Editor, Nino de Roma; Music, Enneppitti; A Bacchus production in color; Rated X; 90 minutes; April release. CAST: Cindy West, Catherine Warren, Lisa Grant, Gus Thomas, Davy Jones, Angel Street, Mac Stevens

HUNGRY WIVES (Jack H. Harris) Producer, Nancy M. Romero; Directed, Written, Photographed, and Edited by George A. Romero; Music, Steve Gorn; A Latent Image production in color; Rated R; 89 minutes; April release. CAST: Jan White (Joan), Ray Laine (Gregg), Anne Muffly (Shirley), Joedda McClain (Nikki), Bill Thunhurst (Jack), Virginia Greenwald (Marion), Neil Fisher (Dr. Miller), Esther Lapidus (Sylvia), Jean Wechsler (Gloria), Shirley Strasser (Grace)

SCORPIO (United Artists) Producer, Walter Mirisch; Director, Michael Winner; Screenplay, David W. Rintels, Gerald Wilson; Story, David W. Rintels; Music, Jerry Fielding; Editor, Freddie Wilson; Photography, Robert Paynter; Art Director, Herbert Westbrook; Assistant Director, Michael Dryhurst; A Scimitar production; Presented by Mirisch Corp.; In color; Rated PG; 114 minutes; April release. CAST: Burt Lancaster (Cross), Alain Delon (Laurier), Paul Scofield (Zharkov), John Colicos (McLeod), Gayle Hunnicutt (Susan), J. D. Cannon (Filchock), Joanne Linville (Sarah), Melvin Stewart (Pick), Vladek Sheybal (Zemetkin), Mary Maude (Anne), Jack Colvin (Thief), James Sikking (Harris), Burke Byrnes (Morrison), William Smithers (Mitchell), Shmuel Rodensky (Lang), Howard Morton (Heck), Celeste Yarnall (Helen), Sandor Eles (Malkin), Frederick Jaeger (Novins), George Mikell (Dor), Robert Emhardt (Man in hotel)

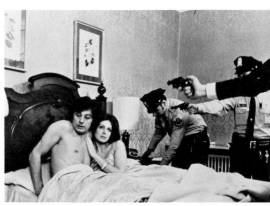

Bill Gunn, Duane Jones
in "Ganja & Hess"

Alain Delon, Gayle Hunnicutt
in "Scorpio"

**Anne Randall
in "Stacey!"**

**Randolph Roberts, Tiffany Bolling
in "Wicked, Wicked"**

THE MAD BOMBER (Cinemation) Produced, Directed, Written, and Photographed by Bert I. Gordon; Story, Marc Behm; Music, Michel Mention; Editor, Gene Ruggerio; Assistant Director, George Wagner; A Jerry Gross presentation; In color; Rated R; 91 minutes; April release. CAST: Vince Edwards (Geronimo), Chuck Connors (William), Neville Brand (Fromley), Hank Brandt (Blake), Christina Hart (Fromley's Victim), Faith Quabius (Martha), Ilona Wilson (Mrs. Fromley), Nancy Honnold (Anne)

STACEY! (New World) Producer, Leon Mirell; Director, Andy Sidaris; Screenplay, William Edgar; Story, Andy Sidaris, Leon Mirell; Executive Producer, Michael Trikilis; Associate Producer, Beverly McAfee; Photography, Mark Zavad; Editor, Craig Stewart; Music, Don Randi; Vocals, Pete Willcox; A Penn-Pacific Corp. presentation; In Metrocolor; Rated R; 82 minutes; April Release. CAST: Anne Randall, Marjorie Bennett, Anitra Ford, Alan Landers, James Westmoreland, Cristina Raines, Nicholas Georgiade, Richard LePore, John Alderman, Eddie Ryder, Madelaine Peterson, Michael Keep, Miki Garcia

FLESHPOT ON 42ND STREET (Mishkin) Producer, William Mishkin; Directed, Written, and Photographed by Andy Milligan; Editor, James Fox; In Eastmancolor; 80 minutes; April release. CAST: Diana Lewis (Dusty), Lynn Flanagan (Cherry), Bob Walters (Bob), Paul Matthews (Jimmy), Daniel Dietrich (Billy), and Dorin McGough, M. A. Whiteside, Joe Powers, Ron Keith, Earle Edgarson, Fred Lincoln, Fred Perisi

FAMILY HONOR (Cinerama) Produced and Written by Louis Pastore; Director, Clark Worswick; In color; A Rocinante Production; Rated R; April release. CAST: Antony Page, Vera Visconti, James Reyes

DIARY OF A TELEPHONE OPERATOR (GGP) In color; Rated PG; No other credits available; April release. CAST: Claudia Cardinale, Catherine Spaak, John Philip Law

WONDER WOMEN (General) Producer, Ross Hagen; Director, Robert O'Neil; Executive Producers, Donald Gottlieb, Ronald Remy; Screenplay, Lou Whitehill; Adaptation, Robert O'Neil; Photography, Ricardo M. David; Editor, Richard Greer; Art Director, Ben Otico; Music, Carson Whitsett; In Color; Rated PG; 82 minutes; April release. CAST: Nancy Kwan (Dr. Tsu), Ross Hagen (Mike), Maria De Aragon (Linda), Roberta Collins (Laura), Tony Lorea (Paulson/Lorenzo), Sid Haig (Gregorius), Vic Dias (Lapu), Claire Hagen (Vera), Shirley Washington (Maggie), Gail Hansen (Gail), Eleanor Siron (Mei-Ling), Bruno Punzalan (Nono), Joonee Gamboa (Won Ton Charlie), Rick Reveke (Attendant), Rudy De Jesus (Boy), Wendy Greene (Swimmer), Leila Benitez (Lillian), Ross Rival (Ramon)

WICKED, WICKED (MGM) Executive Producer, William T. Orr; Produced, Directed, and Written by Richard L. Bare; Music, Philip Springer; Photography, Frederick Gately; Art Director, Walter McKeegan; Editor, John F. Schreyer; Assistant Directors, Donald C. Klune, Ronald J. Martinez; A United National Pictures production in Duo-Vision, and color; Rated PG; 95 minutes; April release. CAST: David Bailey (Rick), Tiffany Bolling (Lisa), Randolph Roberts (Jason), Scott Brady (Sgt. Ramsey), Edd Byrnes (Hank), Diane McBain (Dolores), Roger Bowen (Manager), Madeleine Sherwood (Lenore), Indira Danks (Genny), Arthur O'Connell (Engineer), Jack Knight (Bill), Patsy Garrett (Housekeeper), Robert Nichols (Day Clerk), Kirk Bates (Owen), Maryesther Denver (Organist)

**Burt Lancaster
in "Scorpio"**

**Arthur O'Connell, David Bailey
in "Wicked, Wicked"**

Roger E. Mosley in
"Sweet Jesus, Preacher Man"

"Sweet Jesus, Preacher Man"

THE DEVIL'S WEDDING NIGHT (Dimension) Director, Paul Solday; Screenplay, Alan M. Harris, Ralph Zukor; In color; Rated R; April release. CAST: Mark Damon, Sarah Bay

TOGETHER FOR DAYS (Olas) Producer, Robert S. Buchanan; Director, Michael Shultz; Screenplay, William B. Branch; Story, Lindsay Smith; Photography, Donald H. Hudgins; Editor, Marshall M. Borden; Music, Coleridge-Taylor Perkinson; Art Director, Carlton Moulette; In DeLuxe color; Rated PG; 84 minutes; April release. CAST: Clifton Davis (Gus), Lois Chiles (Shelley), Northern Calloway (Calvin), Leonard Jackson (Phil), Gisela Caldwell (Karen), Woodie King (Jerry), Liz Wright (Miriam), Ben Jones (Doug), Andrea Frye (Sister Sonji), Gilbert Lewis (Big Bubba), Sam Jackson (Stan), Brooke Clift (Hanratty), Sherman Perkins (Murchinson), Scott Childress (1st Policeman), Michael Hatfield (2nd Policeman), Emmanuel Hall (Reporter), J. E. Nation (Guard), Dennis Henry (Sponsor), Robert Hills (Sponsor), Eileen Gordon (Hostess), Frank Hines (Shelley's Partner), Brad Blaisdell (Hippie), Georgia Allen (Gus' mother), Mimi Honce (Wig lady)

SOFT SHOULDERS, SHARP CURVES (Globe) A ContiFilm production in color; Rated X; No other information available; May release.

LITTLE LAURA AND BIG JOHN (Crown International) Producer, Lou Wiethe; Direction and Screenplay, Luke Moberly, Bob Woodburn; Based on story by Philip Weidling; Music, Bill Walker; In color; Rated R; May release. CAST: Fabian Forte (John), Karen Black (Laura), Ivy Thayer (Laura's mother), Kenny Miller, Paul Gleason

THREE DIMENSIONS OF GRETA (Dimension) Producer-Director, Pete Walker; In Eastmancolor and 3D; Rated R; May release. CAST: Leena Skoog, Tristan Rogers, Karen Boyes, Alan Curtis

LONELY WIVES (Hemisphere) In color; Rated X; No other credits available; May release. CAST: Ingred Van Bergen, Hilary Peters, Michael Butler, Marlene Reeves, Ralph Schumacher

FUN AND GAMES (Audubon) Producers, Marty Richards, Gill Champion; Director, Mervyn Nelson; In Eastmancolor; May release. CAST: Alice Spivak, David Drew, Bob Hodge, Calvin Culver

THE GATLING GUN (Ellman Enterprises) Producer, Oscar Nichols; Director, Robert Gordan; Screenplay, Mark Hanna, Joseph Van Winkle; A First Leisure production; In Technicolor; Rated PG; May release. CAST: Woody Strode, Guy Stockwell, Patrick Wayne, Robert Fuller, Barbara Luna, John Carradine

SWEET JESUS, PREACHER MAN (MGM) Executive Producer, Ronald Goldman; Producer, Daniel B. Cady; Director, Henning Schellerup; Screenplay, John Cerullo, M. Stuart Madden, Abbey Leitch; Music, Horace Tapscott; Photography, Paul E. Hipp; Editor, Warren Hamilton, Jr.; Assistant Director, Ernest Williams III; An Entertainment Pyramid-Capitol Cinema production in Metrocolor; Rated R; 103 minutes; May release. CAST: Roger E. Mosley (Holmes/Lee), William Smith (Martelli), Michael Pataki (Sills), Tom Johnigarn (Eddie), Joe Tornatore (Joey), Damu King (Sweetstick), Marla Gibbs (Beverly), Sam Laws (Deacon), Phil Hoover (George), Paul Silliman (Roy), Chuck Lyles (Detroit Charlie), Norman Fields (Police Captain), Della Thomas (Foxey), Amentha Dymally (Mrs. Greene), Patricia Edwards (Marion), Chuck Douglas, Jr. (Lenny), Vincent LaBauve (Bobby), Chuck Wells (Eli), Betty Coleman (Maxine), Lou Jackson (Randy), Lillian Tarry (Mother Gibbs), T. C. Ellis (Earl), Lee Frost (1st Policeman), JoAnn Bruno (Widow), Rev. K. D. Friend (Minister), Bill Quinn (Bodyguard), Bob Angelle, John Washington, Bruce Hall, Don Senette, Dan Black, Curtiss Price (Militants)

FIRST POSITION (Roninfilm) Conceived, Produced, and Directed by William Richert; Executive Producer, Jerry Seltzer; Photography, Gerald V. Cotts; Editor, David Hill; Associate Producers, Michael Zivian, Herb Michelson; Assistant Director, Robert Kenner; In color; 92 minutes; May release. CAST: Leon Danielian, Janis Roswick, Daniel Giagni, Valentina Pereyaslavec, David Prince, Yurek Lazowsky, Michael Maule, Andrei Kulik, Marlise Rockey, Valentina Vishnevsky, and students of the American Ballet Theatre School

"First Position"

Leon Danielian
in "First Position"

**Donna Jordan, Michael Sklar
in "L'Amour"**

**Don Johnson, Laurie Walters
in "The Harrad Experiment"**

THE P.O.W. (Dossick) Producers, David Mlotok, Jane Dossick; Direction and Screenplay, Phillip H. Dossick; Photography, Benjamin Gruberg; Editor, Phillip H. Dossick; Music, Martin Egan, Neal Goldstein; 82 minutes; May release. CAST: Howard Jahre (Howie), Rudy Hornish (Ruby), Wendy Messier (Wendy), Manuel Sicart (Manuel), Marcia Davis (Marcia), Shelley Kaplan (Shelley), Joanna Lee Dossick (Patty)

L'AMOUR (Altura) Executive Producer, Paul Morrissey; Direction and Screenplay, Andy Warhol, Paul Morrissey; Editors, Lana Jokel, Jed Johnson; Photography, Jed Johnson; Assistant Producer, Fred Hughes; Music, Ben Weisman; Song by Ben Weisman, Michael Sklar; Sung by Cass Elliot; In Eastmancolor; Rated R; 90 minutes; May release. CAST: Michael Sklar (Michael), Donna Jordan (Donna), Jane Forth (Jane), Max Delys (Max), Patti D'Arbanville (Patti), Karl Lagerfeld (Karl), Coral Labrie (Coral), Peter Greenlaw (Peter), Corey Tippin (Corey)

GIRLS ARE FOR LOVING (Continental) Producer, Ralph T. Desiderio; Direction and Screenplay, Don Schain; Photography, Howard Block; Music, Robert G. Orpin; Assistant Director, Dick Ashe; A Derio production in DeLuxe color; Rated R; 95 minutes; May release. CAST: Cheri Caffaro (Ginger), Timothy Brown (Clay), Jocelyn Peters (Ronnie), Scott Ellsworth (James), Fred Vincent (William), Robert C. Jefferson (Mateo), Rod Loomis (Mark), Larry Douglas (Mr. Secretary), Anthony C. Cannon (Neil), William Grannel (Jason), Yuki Shimoda (Ambassador)

STANLEY (Crown International) Producer-Director, William Grefe; Executive Producer, John Burrows; Screenplay, Gary Crutcher; In DeLuxe color; Rated PG; May release. CAST: Chris Robinson, Alex Rocco, Steve Alaimo, Susan Carroll, Mark Harris, Rey Baumel, Paul Avery, Marcie Knight

BOOTS TURNER (Rowland-Williams) Producers, Bill Rowland, Fred Williams; Direction and Screenplay, J. Edward, J. Lasko; May release. CAST: Terry Carter, Gwen Mitchell, Kyle Johnson, James Sikking, Art Lund

THE HARRAD EXPERIMENT (Cinerama) Executive Producer, Noel Marshall; Producer, Dennis F. Stevens; Director, Ted Post; Screenplay, Michael Werner, Ted Cassedy; Based on novel by Robert H. Rimmer; Music, Artie Butler; Photography, Richard H. Kline; Soundtrack Album by Capitol Records; Associate Producer, Mel Sokolow; Assistant Director, Jesse Corallo; Song by Charles Fox, Norman Gimbel; Sung by Lori Lieberman; Rated R; 96 minutes; May release. CAST: James Whitmore (Philip), Tippi Hedren (Margaret), Don Johnson (Stanley), B. Kirby, Jr. (Harry), Laurie Walters (Sheila), Victoria Thompson (Beth), Elliott Street (Wilson), Sharon Taggart (Barbara), Robert Middleton (Sidney), Billy Sands (Jack), Melody Patterson (Jeannie), Maggie Wellman (Cynthia), Michael Greene (Yoga instructor), Ron Kolman (Evan), Eric Server, Robert C. Ross (Workmen), and The Ace Trucking Company

EXTREME CLOSE-UP (National General) Producer, Paul N. Lazarus III; Director, Jeannot Szwarc; Screenplay, Michael Crichton; Associate Producers, Michael I. Rachmil, Kurt Villadsen; Music, Basil Poledouris; Photography, Paul N. Lohman; In color; Rated R; 80 minutes; May release. CAST: James McMullan (John), James A. Watson, Jr. (Tom), Kate Woodville (Sally), Bara Byrnes (Sylvia), Al Checco (Salesman)

LOVELAND (Illustrated) Producer, Lawrence Reynolds; Director, Richard Franklin; Screenplay, Harriet Rhodes; Photography, Eugene Moran; Editor, Lance Friedman; Music, Gardner Olson; Art Director, Gerald St. George; Associate Producer, Nelson Harvath; Assistant Director, J. S. Mansfield; In Technicolor; Rated X; 85 minutes; May release. CAST: Carla Montgomery, Burt Allen, Candy Miller, Leslie White, Bill Mantell, Randy Troy, Pamela Patton, Terry Larson, Genie Carson

SUNSEED (New Age) Producer, Ralph Harper Silver; Director, Frederick Cohn; Photography, Robert Frank, Baird Bryant; Editors, Frederick Cohn, Bill Yarhaus; Music, Sufi Choir; A Ram Film presentation in color; 92 minutes; May release. A documentary on yogis, gurus, and swamis.

**Cheri Caffaro in
"Girls Are for Loving"**

**Bara Byrnes, James McMullan
in "Extreme Close-Up"**

James Iglehart, Carol Speed
in "Savage"

Broderick Crawford, Ray Milland, Shani Wallis,
Louis Hayward in "Terror in the Wax Museum"

DEADLY FATHOMS (HMS) Producers, Mike Harris, Joe Almand; Screenplay, Dave O'Malley, Tom Chapman; Photography, Dick Winer; Music, Paul Lavalle; Commentary, Rod Serling; In color; Rated G; 93 minutes; May release. A documentary on the effects of "Operation Crossroads" atomic test at Bikini.

HOT CHANNELS (Distribpix) Produced, Directed, and Photographed by R. G. Benjamin; Screenplay, Alan Frybach, Paul Williams; Art Director, Peggy Magnet; Editors, Jerry Bone, Mick Beck; Music, Gilly; A Viaduck production; In Eastmancolor; Rated X; 70 minutes; May release. CAST: Davy Jones, Melanie Daniels, Catharine Warren, M. Tracis, Emmet Gregory, H. Quinlin.

SAVAGE! (New World) Producer-Director, Cirio H. Santiago; Screenplay, Ed Medard; Music, Don Julian; Photography, Philip Sacdalan; Editor, Richard Patterson; In Metrocolor; Rated R; 81 minutes; May release. CAST: James Iglehart, Carol Speed, Lada Edmund, Sally Jordan, Ken Metcalf, Rossana Ortiz, Vic Diaz, Eddie Gutierrez, Harley Paton, Marie Saunders, Aura Aurea.

TERROR IN THE WAX MUSEUM (Cinerama) Executive Producer, Charles A. Pratt; Producer, Andrew J. Fenady; Director, Georg Fenady; Screenplay, Jameson Brewer; Music, George Duning; Story, Andrew J. Fenady; Photography, William Jurgensen; Designer, Stan Jolley; Assistant Director, Floyd Joyer; Costumes, Oscar Rodriguez, Vou Lee Giokaris; A Fenady Associates production in association with Bing Crosby Productions; In DeLuxe color; Rated PG; 93 minutes; May release. CAST: Ray Milland (Flexner), Broderick Crawford (Burns), Elsa Lanchester (Julia), Maurice Evans (Inspector), Shani Wallis (Laurie), John Carradine (Dupree), Louis Hayward (Fowley), Patric Knowles (Southcott), Mark W. Edwards (Sgt. Hawks), Lisa Lu (Mme. Yang), Steven Marlo (Karkov), Ben Wright (Constable), Matilda Calnan (Charwoman), Peggy Stewart (Charwoman), Leslie Thompson (Constable), Nicole Shelby (Meg), and Don Herbert, Judy Wetmore, Jo Williamson, George Farina, Diane Wahrman, Rosa Huerta, Ben Brown, Rickie Weir, Paul Wilson, Ralph Cunningham, Don Williamson, Evelyn Reynolds.

POINT OF TERROR (Crown International) Producers, Chris Marconi, Peter Carpenter; Director, Alex Nichol; In DeLuxe color; Rated R; May release. CAST: Peter Carpenter (Tony), Dyanne Thorne (Andrea), Lory Hansen (Helayne), Paula Mitchell (Sally), Leslie Simms (Fran), Joel Marston (Martin), Roberta Robson (First Wife), Dana Diamond (Barmaid), Al Dunlap (Bartender), Ernest Charles (Detective), Tony Kent (Priest).

THE EROTIC ADVENTURES OF ZORRO (Entertainment Ventures) Producers, David F. Friedman, William Allen Castleman; Director, Robert Freeman; Screenplay, Mona Lott, Joy Boxe, David F. Friedman; Rated X; 101 minutes; June release. CAST: Douglas Frey, Robyn Whiting, Penny Boran, Jude Farese, John Alderman, Lynn Harris, Michelle Simon, Bruce Gibson, Sebastian Gregory, Mike Peratta, Ernie Dominy.

TRADER HORN (MGM) Producer, Lewis J. Rachmil; Director, Reza S. Badiyi; Screenplay, William Norton, Edward Harper; Story, Edward Harper; Music, Shelly Manne; Photography, Ronald W. Browne; Art Director, Jan Van Tamelen; Editor, George Folsey, Jr.; Assistant Directors, D. Jack Stubbs, Charles H. Norton; In Metrocolor; Rated PG; 105 minutes; June release. CAST: Rod Taylor (Trader Horn), Anne Heywood (Nicole), Jean Sorel (Emil), Don Knight (Sinclair), Ed Bernard (Apaque), Stack Pierce (Malugi), Eric Holland (Medford), Robert Miller Driscoll (Alfredo), King Solomon III (Red Sun), Willie Harris (Blue Star), Caro Kenyatta (Umbopa), Oliver Givens (Dancer), Curt Lowens (Schmidt), John Siegfried (German officer).

NIGHT OF THE COBRA WOMAN (New World) In Metrocolor; Rated R; No other information available; June release.

THE HAMMER OF GOD (No credits available) Rated R; In color; June release.

INVASION OF THE BEE GIRLS (Dimension) In color; Rated R; No other credits available; June release. CAST: William Smith, Anitra Ford, Victoria Vetri.

Broderick Crawford, wax figure, John Carradine
in "Terror in the Wax Museum"

126

Rod Taylor, Anne Heywood, Jean Sorel
in "Trader Horn"

Susan Anspach, Kris Kristofferson, George
Segal in "Blume in Love"

George Segal, Marsha Mason
in "Blume in Love"

HIGH PRIESTESS OF SEXUAL WITCHCRAFT (Triumvirate)
Producer, Mona Terry; Direction and Screenplay, Beau Buchanan;
No other credits; In color; Rated X; 90 minutes; June release. CAST:
Georgina Spelvin, Rick Livermore, Jean Palmer, Harding Harrison,
Marc Stevens

BLUME IN LOVE (Warner Bros.) Produced, Directed, and Written by Paul Mazursky; Photography, Bruce Surtees; Editor, Don
Cambern; Designer, Pato Guzman; Assistant Director, Irby Smith;
In Technicolor; Rated R; 115 minutes; June release. CAST: George
Segal (Blume), Susan Anspach (Nina), Kris Kristofferson (Elmo),
Marsha Mason (Arlene), Shelley Winters (Mrs. Cramer), Donald F.
Muhich (Analyst), Paul Mazursky (Blume's Partner), Erin O'Reilly
(Cindy), Annazette Chase (Gloria)

LITTLE CIGARS (American International) Producer, Albert
Band; Director, Chris Christenberry; Screenplay, Louis Garfinkle,
Frank Ray Perilli; Photography, John Stephens; Assistant Director,
Foster Phinney; Art Director, Alfeo Bocchicchio; Music, Harry
Betts; Editor, Eve Newman; A Samuel Z. Arkoff presentation; In
DeLuxe color; Rated PG; 92 minutes; June release. CAST: Angel
Tompkins (Cleo), Billy Curtis (Slick), Jerry Maren (Cadillac), Frank
Delfino (Monty), Emory Souza (Hugo), Felix Silla (Frankie), Joe De
Santis (Travers), Todd Susman (Buzz), Jon Cedar (Faust), Phil Kenneally (Ganz)

THE CHEERLEADERS (Cinemation) Producers, Paul Glickler,
Richard Lerner; Director, Paul Glickler; Screenplay, Mr. Glickler,
Tad Richards, Ace Baandige; Photography, Richard Lerner; Editors, Paul Glickler, Richard Lerner; Music, Dave Herman; Associate Producer, Robert Boggs; A Jerry Gross presentation; In color;
Rated X; 84 minutes; June release. CAST: Stephanie Fondue (Jeanie), Denise Dillaway (Claudia), Jovita Bush (Bonnie), Debbie Lowe
(Debbie), Sandy Evans (Susie), Kim Stanton (Patty), Richard Meatwhistle (Jon), John Jacobs (Norm), Raoul Hoffnung (Novi), Patrick
Wright (Coach), Terry Teague (Isabel), Jack Jonas (Daddy), Jay
Lindner (Mom), John Bracci (Vinnie), William Goldman (Sal), Bill
Lehrke (Waiter)

THIS IS A HIJACK (Fanfare) Producer, Paul Lewis; Executive
Producer, Joe Solomon; Director, Barry Pollack; Photography,
Bruce Logan; Editor, Peter Paeasheles; Music, Charles Alden; Art
Direction, Vincent Cresciman; In DeLuxe color; Rated PG; 90
minutes; June release. CAST: Adam Roarke (Christie), Neville
Brand (Dominic), Jay Robinson (Scott), Lynn Borden (Diane), Milt
Kamen (Phillips), John Alderman (Latimer), Sandy Balson (Mrs.
Phillips), Sam Chew (Pierce), Don Pedro Colley (Champ), Dub
Taylor (Sheriff), Carol Lawson (Mrs. Pierce), Jackie Giroux (Scott's
Girl), Barney Phillips (Banker), Patricia Winters (Latimer's Girl)

THE STEPMOTHER (Crown International) Produced, Directed,
and Written by Hikmet Avedis; Music and Song, Sammy Fain, Paul
Francis Webster; In DeLuxe color; Rated R: 94 minutes; June release. CAST: Alejandro Rey (Frank), John Anderson (Inspector),
Katherine Justice (Margo), Larry Linville (Dick), Marlene Schmidt
(Sonja), Claudia Jennings (Nude), Rudy Herrera, Jr. (Steve), John
D. Garfield (Goof), David Renard (Petro), Priscilla Garcia (His
Girl)

BAD CHARLESTON CHARLIE (International Cinema) Producer, Ross Hagen; Director, Ivan Nagy; Screenplay, Ross Hagen,
Ivan Nagy, Stan Kamber; Photography, Michael Neyman; Editors,
Walter, Thompson, Richard Garritt; Music, Luchi DeJesus; Art
Director, Raymond Markham; Assistant Director, Eric Lidberg; In
Eastmancolor; Rated PG; June release. CAST: Ross Hagen
(Charlie), Kelly Thordsen (Thad), Hoke Howell (Claude), Dal Jenkins (Ku Klux Klan Leader), Carmen Zapata (Lottie), Mel Berger
(Police Chief), John Carradine (Reporter), Ken Lynch (Sheriff),
John Dalk (Promoter), Tony Lorea (Criminal)

DUEL OF THE IRON FIST (Mahler) A United International film;
In color; Rated R; No other information available; June release.

THE CANDY SNATCHERS (GFC) Produced and Written by
Bryan Gindoff; Director, Guerdon Trueblood; A Marmot production; In color; Rated R; June release. CAST: Tiffany Bolling, Ben
Piazza, Susan Sennet, Brad David, Vincent Martorano

"Trader Horn"

"Little Cigars"

**Pam Grier, Robert Doqui
in "Coffy"**

**Clay O'Brien, James Garner
in "One Little Indian"**

COFFY (American International) Producer, Robert A. Papazian; Director, Jack Hill; Executive Producer, Salvatore Billitteri; Screenplay, Jack Hill; Assistant Director, Reuben Watt; Art Director, Perry Ferguson; Photography, Paul Lohmann; Editor, Charles McClelland; Music, Roy Ayers; In Movielab color; Rated R; 91 minutes; June release. CAST: Pam Grier (Coffy), Booker Bradshaw (Brunswick), Robert DoQui (King George), William Elliott (Carter), Allan Arbus (Vitroni), Sid Haig (Omar), Barry Cahill (McHenry), Morris Buchanan (Sugar-Man), Lee de Broux (Nick), Bob Minor (Studs), John Perak (Aleva), Ruben Moreno (Ramos), Carol Lawson (Priscilla), Linda Haynes (Meg), Lisa Farringer (Jeri)

ONE LITTLE INDIAN (Buena Vista) Producer, Winston Hibler; Director, Bernard McEveety; Screenplay, Harry Spalding; Photography, Charles F. Wheeler; Music, Jerry Goldsmith; Art Directors, John Mansbridge, LeRoy G. Deane; Editor, Robert Stafford; Associate Producer, Tom Leetch; Assistant Director, Ted Schilz; Costumes, Chuck Keehne, Emily Sundby; A Walt Disney production in Technicolor; Rated G; 90 minutes; June release. CAST: James Garner (Clint), Vera Miles (Doris), Clay O'Brien (Mark), Pat Hingle (Capt. Stewart), Andrew Prine (Chaplain), Morgan Woodward (Sgt. Raines), Jodie Foster (Martha), John Doucette, Robert Pine, Bruce Glover, Ken Swofford, Jay Silverheels, Walter Brooke, Rudy Diaz, John Flinn, Tom Simcox, Lois Red Elk, Hal Baylor, Terry Wilson, Paul Sorensen, Read Morgan, Jim Davis

DILLINGER (American International) Executive Producers, Samuel Z. Arkoff, Lawrence A. Gordon; Producer, Buzz Feitshans; Direction and Screenplay, John Milius; Associate Producer, Robert A. Papazian; Photography, Jules Breener; Music, Barry DeVorzon; Editor, Fred R. Feitshans, Jr.; Assistant Director, Donald C. Klune; In Movielab color; Rated R; 106 minutes; June release. CAST: Warren Oates (Dillinger), Ben Johnson (Melvin), Michelle Phillips (Billie), Cloris Leachman (Anna), Harry Dean Stanton (Homer), Geoffrey Lewis (Harry), John Ryan (Charles), Richard Dreyfuss (Baby Face), Steve Kanaly (Pretty Boy), John Martino (Eddie), Roy Jenson (Samuel), Read Morgan (Big Jim), Frank McRae (Reed)

FRASIER, THE SENSUOUS LION (LCS) Producer, Allan Sandler; Director, Pat Shields; Screenplay, Jerry Kobrin; Based on story by Sandy Dore; Photography, David L. Butler; Music, Robert Emenegger; Editor, Michael Brown; In DeLuxe color; Rated PG; 97 minutes; June release. CAST: Michael Callan (Marvin), Katherine Justice (Allison), Victor Jory (Voice of Frasier), Frank de Kova (The Man), Malachi Throne (Bill), Marc Lawrence (Chiarelli), Peter Lorre, Jr. (Boscov), Arthur Space (Dredge), Patrick O'Moore (Worcester), Lori Saunders (Minerva), Joe E. Ross (Kuback), Fritzi Burr (Marvin's Mother), A. E. Gould-Porter (Motel Manager), Ralph James (Reporter), Jerry Kobrin (Editor), John Qualen (Old Man), Florence Lake (Old Lady), Maryesther Denver (Nurse), Allison McKay (Wife in kitchen), Charles Woolf (Man in kitchen), John J. Fox (Fat Man), Paul Mousie Garner (Mah in bar), Frank Biro (Party Host)

THE WEDNESDAY CHILDREN (Venture) Producers, Homer Baldwin, Cal Clifford; Direction and Screenplay, Robert D. West; Photography, and Editing, Homer Baldwin; Music, Tom Baker, Dene Bays; In color; 88 minutes; June release. CAST: Marji Dodril (Mrs. Miller), Donald E. Murray (Miller), Tom Kelly (Scott), Carol Cary (Mrs. Berlow), Al Miskell (Fenton), Robert D. West (Minister)

TERMINAL ISLAND (Dimension) No credits available; In Metrocolor; Rated R; June release. CAST: Phyllis Davis, Don Marshall, Ena Hartman, Marta Kristen

SHOWDOWN (Universal) Producer-Director, George Seaton; Screenplay, Theodore Taylor; Story, Hank Fine; Associate Producer, Donald Roberts; Photography, Ernest Laszlo; Art Directors, Alexander Golitzen, Henry Bumstead; Costumes, Edith Head; Music, David Shire; Assistant Director, Jim Fargo; In Todd-Ao 35 and Technicolor; Rated PG; 99 minutes; July release. CAST: Rock Hudson (Chuck), Dean Martin (Billy), Susan Clark (Kate), Donald Moffat (Art), John McLiam (P. J.), Charles Baca (Martinez), Jackson Kane (Clem), Ben Zeller (Perry), John Richard Gill (Earl), Philip L. Mead (Jack), Rita Rogers (Girl), Vic Mohica (Big Eye), Raleigh Gardenhire (Joe), Ed Begley, Jr. (Pook), Dan Boydston (Rawls)

**Michelle Phillips, Warren Oates
in "Dillinger"**

**Susan Clark, Dean Martin, Rock Hudson
in "Showdown"**

"Hail to the Chief"

Tamara Dobson, Shelley Winters
in "Cleopatra Jones"

HAIL TO THE CHIEF (Cine-Globe) Producers, Roy Townshend, Paul Leaf; Executive Producer, Norman W. Cohen; Story and Screenplay, Larry Spiegel, Phil Dusenberry; Director, Fred Levinson; Photography, William Storz; Music, Trade Martin; Editor, Robert DeRise; In Metrocolor; Rated PG; 85 minutes; July release. CAST: Dan Resin (President), Richard B. Shull (Sec. of Health), Dick O'Neill (Attorney General), Joseph Sirola (Rev. Williams), Patricia Ripley (First Lady), Gary Sandy (Tom), Williard Waterman (Vice President), K. Callan (Burd), Constance Forslund (Sara), Phil Foster (Michael), Lee Meredith (Mrs. Moloney), Robert King (Reporter), Douglas Rutherford (Ellinson), Mary Louise Weller (Mrs. Ellinson), Peggy Pope (Sister Veronica), Ron Carrol (Professor), Brandon Maggert (Sgt. National Guard), Doyle Newberry (Speech Writer), Toni Reid (Doctor), Ted Gewant (Chief Justice), Jim Nurtaugh (Sgt. Johnson), Madison Arnold (Sgt. Mazzola)

SSSSSSSS (Universal) Executive Producers, Richard D. Zanuck, David Brown; Producer, Dan Striepeke; Director, Bernard L. Kowalski; Screenplay, Hal Dresner; Story, Dan Striepeke; Associate Producer, Robert Butner; Photography, Gerald Perry Finnerman; Art Director, John T. McCormack; Editor, Robert Watts; Music, Pat Williams; Assistant Directors, Gordon Webb, Charles Dismukes; In Technicolor; Rated PG; 99 minutes; July release. CAST: Strother Martin (Dr. Stoner), Dirk Benedict (David), Heather Menzies (Kristine), Richard B. Shull (Daniels), Tim O'Connor (Kogen), Jack Ging (Sheriff), Kathleen King (Kitty), Reb Brown (Steve), Ted Grossman (Deputy), Charles Seel (Old Man), Ray Ballard (Tourist), Brendan Burns (Jock 1), Rick Beckner (Jock 2), James Drum, Ed McCready, Frank Kowalski, Ralph Montgomery, Michael Masters (Hawkers), Charlie Fox (Arvin), Felix Silla (Seal Boy), Nobel Craig (Tim), Bobbi Kiger (Kootch dancer), J. R. Clark (Attendant), Chip Potter (Clerk)

BROTHER ON THE RUN (Southern Star) Producer, Fred Williams; Direction and Screenplay, Herbert Strock; Music, Johnny Pate; Title song sung by Adam Wade; In Eastmancolor; Rated R; July release. CAST: Terry Carter, Gwenn Mitchell, Kyle Johnson, James Sikking, Diana Eden

THE NEWCOMERS (Melody) Producers, Louis Su, R. E. Baringer; Director, Louis Su; Photography, Forrest Murray; Editor, Lois Fisher; Music, Milford Kulhagen; In Eastmancolor; Rated X; 75 minutes; July release. CAST: Georgina Spelvin, Harry Reams, Marc Stevens, Tina Russell, Derald Delancey, Cindy West, Davey Jones, Naomi Riis

SWEET SUZY (Signal 166) formerly "Blacksnake"; Producer-Director, Russ Meyer; Screenplay, Russ Meyer, Len Neubauer; Story, Russ Meyer, A. James Ryan; Photography, Arthur Ornitz; Editor, Fred Baratta; Music, Bill Loose, Al Teeter; Art Director, Rick Heatherly; In Movielab color; Rated R; 82 minutes; July release. CAST: Anouska Hempel (Susan), David Warbeck (Walker), Percy Herbert (Overseer), Milton McCollin (Joshua), Thomas Baptiste (Isaiah), Bernard Boston (Daladier), Vikki Richards (Slave), Dave Prowse (Walker's brother)

CLEOPATRA JONES (Warner Bros.) Producer, William Tennant; Co-Producer, Max Julien; Director, Jack Starrett; Screenplay, Max Julien, Sheldon Keller; Story, Max Julien; Photography, David Walsh; Editor, Allan Jacobs; Music, J. J. Johnson, Carl Brandt, Brad Shapiro; Title Theme, Joe Simon; Art Director, Peter Wooley; Assistant Director, Jack Roe; In Technicolor; Rated PG; 89 minutes; July release. CAST: Tamara Dobson (Cleopatra), Bernie Casey (Reuben), Shelley Winters (Mommy), Brenda Sykes (Tiffany), Antonio Fargas (Doodlebug), Bill McKinney (Purdy), Dan Frazer (Crawford), Stafford Morgan (Kert), Mike Warren (Andy), Albert Popwell, Caro Kenyatta (Johnson Boys), Esther Rolle (Mrs. Johnson), Paul Koslo, Joseph A. Tornatore (Mommy's Hoods), Hedley Mattingly (Chauffeur), George Reynolds, Theodore Wilson (Doodlebug's Hoods), Christopher Joy (Snake), Keith Hamilton (Maxwell), Angela Gibbs (Annie), John Garwood (Lt.), John Alderman (Mommy's Assistant)

THE DARING DOBERMANS (Dimension) Producer, David Chudnow; Director, Byron Ross Chudnow; In Metrocolor; Rated G; July release. CAST: Charles Knox Robinson, Tim Considine, David Moses, Claudio Martinez, Joan Caulfield

Heather Menzies, Strother Martin, Dirk Benedict
in "SSSSSSS"

Bernie Casey, Tamara Dobson
in "Cleopatra Jones"

Pam Grier, Don Mitchell, William Marshall,
in "Scream Blacula"

Hari Rhodes (R)
in "Detroit 9000"

SCREAM BLACULA SCREAM (American International) Producer, Joseph T. Naar; Director, Bob Kelljan; Screenplay, Joan Torres, Raymond Koenig, Maurice Jules; Story, Joan Torres, Raymond Koenig; Assistant Directors, Reuben Watt, John Poer; Photography, Isadore Mankofsky; Editor, Fabian Tordjman; Art Director, Al Brocchicchio; Music, Bill Marx; A Samuel Z. Arkoff presentation in Movielab color; Rated PG; 96 minutes; July release. CAST: William Marshall (Mamuwalde), Pam Grier (Lisa), Don Mitchell (Justin), Michael Conrad (Sheriff), Richard Lawson (Willis), Lynne Moody (Denny), Beverly Gill (Maggie), Bernie Hamilton (Ragman), Barbara Rhoades (Elaine), Janee Michelle (Gloria), Don Blackman (Doll Man), Van Kirksey (Prof. Walston), Arnold Williams (Louis)

I COULD NEVER HAVE SEX WITH ANY MAN WHO HAS SO LITTLE REGARD FOR MY HUSBAND (Cinema 5) Executive Producer, Norman I. Cohen; Producers, Gail and Martin Stayden; Director, Robert McCarty; Screenplay, Dan Greenburg; Based on his novel "Chewsday"; Associate Producers, Benni Korzen, Milton Felsen; Photography, Jeri Sopanen; Editor, John Carter; Music, Joe Liebman; Rated PG; 86 minutes; July release. CAST: Carmine Caridi (Marvin), Andrew Duncan (Stanley), Cynthia Harris (Laura), Lynne Lipton (Mandy), Gail and Martin Stayden (The DeVrooms), Dan Greenburg (Herb)

FOX STYLE (Presidial) In color; Rated R; No other credits available; July release. CAST: Chuck Daniel, Hank Rolike, Denise Denise, Juanita Moore

HOT SUMMER WEEK (Fanfare) Producer-Director, Thomas J. Schmidt; Screenplay, Larry Bischof, David Kaufman; Executive Producer, Joe Solomon; In color; Rated PG; July release. CAST: Kathleen Cody, Michael Ontkean, Diane Hull, Ralph Waite, John McMurty, Pamela Serpe, Riggs Kennedy

SWINGIN' WIVES (Hemisphere) In color; Rated X; No other credits available; July release. CAST: Gayle Mayberrie, Ron James, Linda Richards

DETROIT 9000 (General) Executive Producers, Donald Gottlieb, William Silberkleit; Producer-Director, Arthur Marks; Associate Producer, Charles Stroud; Screenplay, Orville Hampton; Based on story by Arthur Marks, Orville Hampton; Photography, Harry May; Music, Luchi DeJesus; In Panavision and CFI color; Rated R; 106 minutes; August release. CAST: Alex Rocco (Bassett), Hari Rhodes (Williams), Vonetta McGee (Roby), Ella Edwards (Helen), Scatman Crothers (Rev. Markham), Herbert Jefferson, Jr. (Ferdy), Robert Phillips (Capt. Chalmers), Rudy Challenger (Clayton), Ron McIlwain (Sam), Sally Baker (Ethel), George Skaff (Oscar), June Fairchild (Barbara), and Dilart Heyson, Davis Roberts, Jason Summers, John Nichols, Richard Bourin, Martha Jean Steinberg, Woody Willis, Bob Charlton, Ernie Winstanley, Council Cargle, Doris Ingraham, Ron Khoury, Jerry Dahlman, Whit Vernon, Don Hayes, Herb Weatherspoon, Michael Tylo

THE NAKED APE (Universal) Producer, Zev Bufman; Executive Producer, Hugh M. Hefner; Director, Donald Driver; Animation Director, Charles Swenson; Based on book by Desmond Morris; Photography, John Alonzo; Editor, Michael Economou, Robert L. Wolfe; Music, Jimmy Webb; Designer, Lawrence G. Paull; Assistant Director, Stuart Fleming; In Technicolor; Rated PG; 85 minutes; August release. CAST: Johnny Crawford (Lee), Victoria Principal (Cathy), Dennis Olivieri (Arnie)

SLAUGHTER'S BIG RIPOFF (American International) Producer, Monroe Sachson; Director, Gordon Douglas; Screenplay, Charles Johnson; Based on character created by Don Williams; Photography, Charles Wheeler; Editor, Christopher Holmes; Music, James Brown, Fred Wesley; In color; Rated R; 94 minutes; August release. CAST: Jim Brown (Slaughter), Ed McMahon (Duncan), Brock Peters (Reynolds), Don Stroud (Kirk), Gloria Hendry (Marcia), Richard Williams (Joe), Art Metrano (Burtoli), Judy Brown (Noria), Russ Marin (Crowder), Eddie Lo Russo (Arnie), Jackie Giroux (Mrs. Duncan), Tony Brubaker (Pratt). Gene LeBell (Leo), Fuji (Chin), Russ McGinn (Harvey)

"I Could Never Have Sex with Any Man Who
Has so Little Regard for My Husband"

Jim Brown, Gloria Hendry
in "Slaughter's Big Ripoff"

Ron Howard, Patricia Neal
in "Happy Mother's Day, Love George"

Cloris Leachman, Ron Howard
in "Happy Mother's Day, Love George"

THE VIRGIN WITCH (Joseph Brenner) Producer, Ralph Solomons; Director, Ray Austin; Screenplay, Klaus Vogel; A Univista production; In Eastmancolor; Rated R; 87 minutes; August release. CAST: Ann Michelle (Christine), Vicky Michelle (Betty), Keith Buckley (Johnny), Patricia Haines (Sybil), James Chase (Peter), Paula Wright (Mrs. Wendell), Neil Hallett (Gerald), Helen Downing (Abby)

HAPPY MOTHER'S DAY—LOVE, GEORGE (Cinema 5) Producer-Director, Darren McGavin; Screenplay, Robert Clouse; Photography, Walter Lassally; Editor, George Grenville; Music, Don Vincent; Assistant Director, Scott Maitland; Costumes, Robert Anton; In color; Rated PG; 90 minutes; August release. CAST: Patricia Neal (Cara), Cloris Leachman (Ronda), Bobby Darin (Eddie), Tessa Dahl (Celia), Ron Howard (Johnny), Kathie Browne (Crystal), Joe Mascolo (Piccolo), Simon Oakland (Ron), Thayer David (Minister), Gale Garnett (Yolanda), Roy Applegate (Porgie), Jan Chamberlain (Florence), Gerald E. Forbes (Bomber), Orest Ulan (Preacher), Clarence Greene Jeans (Mears)

LADY ICE (National General) Producer, Harrison Starr; Director, Tom Gries; Screenplay, Alan Trustman, Harold Clemens; Story, Alan Trustman; In color; Rated PG; 93 minutes; August release. CAST: Donald Sutherland (Andy), Jennifer O'Neill (Paula), Robert Duvall (Ford), Patrick Magee (Paul), Eric Braeden (Peter), Jon Cypher (Eddy)

VISIONS OF EIGHT (Cinema 5) Executive Producer, David L. Wolper; Producer, Stan Margulies; Directors, Milos Forman, Kon Ichikawa, Claude Lelouch, Juri Ozerov, Arthur Penn, Michael Pfleghar, John Schlesinger, Mai Zetterling; Music, Henry Mancini; Editors, Robert K. Lambert, Bea Dennis, Geoffrey Rowland; In Technicolor; 105 minutes; August release. Eight sequences filmed at the Olympiad in Munich.

THE POLICE CONNECTION (Cinemation) Original title "Detective Geronimo"; Producer-Director, Screenplay, Bert I. Gordon; Story, Marc Behm; Rated R; In color; August release. CAST: Vince Edwards, Chuck Connors, Neville Brand

THE CLONES (Filmmakers International) Producer, Paul Hunt; Directors, Paul Hunt, Lumar Card; Screenplay, Steve Fisher; Photography, Gary Graver; In Eastmancolor; Rated PG; August release. CAST: Michael Greene, Gregory Sierra, Otis Young, Susan Hunt, Stanley Adams, Barbara Burgdorph, John Barrymore, Jr.

THE BENGAL TIGER (Globe International) Producer-Director, Richard Martin; Associate Producer, Warren Gorney; Commentary, Trevor Black; Narrated by Edward Mulhare; Photography, Peter Jensen; Editor, Axel Hubert; Music, Gordon Zahler; In color; Rated G; 83 minutes; August release. A documentary.

FORBIDDEN UNDER THE CENSORSHIP OF THE KING (Lemming) Produced, Directed, and Written by Barry R. Kerr; Music, Michael Wright, Rupert Holmes, Pool-Pah; Animation, Betsy Stang; Producers, Steven B. Singer, Greg Pardes; In color; 84 minutes; August release. CAST: Herb Kaplow (Student), Marshall Anker (Exhibitionist), Bob Lavigne (Student), Lee Rey (Girl in theatre), Perry Gerwitz (Mortician), Alana Blue (Dead Body), Andrea Krangle (Ice Cream Girl), Leslie Gaye (Larisa), Jaime German (Ted), Billy Arrington (Voice)

MAURIE (National General) Producers, Frank Ross, Douglas Morrow; Director, Daniel Mann; Screenplay, Douglas Morrow; Photography, John Hora; Editor, Walter A. Hannemann; Art Director, Wally Berns; Assistant Director, Ridgeway Callow; An Ausable production; In Technicolor; Rated G; 113 minutes; August release. CAST: Bernie Casey (Maurice), Bo Swenson (Jack), Janet MacLachian (Dorothy), Stephanie Edwards (Carol), Paulene Myers (Rosie), Bill Walker (Stokes), Maidie Norman (Mrs. Stokes), Curt Conway (Dr. Stewart), Jitu Cumbuka (Oscar), Lori Busk (Lida), Tol Avery (Milton), Chris Schenkel

"Visions of Eight"

Chuck Connors in
"The Police Connection"

Scott Sealey, Kerwin Mathews
in "The Boy Who Cried Werewolf"

Kerwin Mathews, Elaine Devry
in "The Boy Who Cried Werewolf"

EROTIKUS (Hand-in-Hand) Producer, Tom DeSimone; Director, Nicholas Grippo; Narrated by Fred Halsted; In color and black and white; Rated X; 90 minutes; August release. A documentary on the homosexual movies.

THE BOY WHO CRIED WEREWOLF (Universal) Producer, Aaron Rosenberg; Director, Nathan H. Juran; Associate Producers, Russell Schoengarth, Vicki Rosenberg; Screenplay, Bob Homel; Photography, Michael P. Joyce; Editor, Barton Hayes; Music, Ted Stovall; Assistant Director, Larry Powell; An RKF production in Technicolor; Rated GP; 93 minutes; August release. CAST: Kerwin Mathews (Robert), Elaine Devry (Sandy), Scott Sealey (Richie), Robert J. Wilke (Sheriff), Susan Foster (Jenny), Jack Lucas (Harry), Bob Homel (Brother Christopher), George Gaynes (Dr. Marderosian), Loretta Temple (Monica), Dave Cass (Deputy), Herold Goodwin (Duncan), Tim Haldeman (1st Guard), John Logan (2nd Guard), Eric Gordon (Hippy Jesus Freak), Paul Baxley (First Werewolf)

STEEL ARENA (L-T) Producers, Mark L. Lester, Peter S. Traynor; Direction and Screenplay, Mark L. Lester; Photography, John A. Morrill; Editor, Dave Peoples; Music, Don Tweedy; Assistant Director, Rick Smith; In Technicolor; Rated PG; 98 minutes; September release. CAST: Dusty Russell, Gene Drew, Buddy Love, Dutch Schnitzer, Bruce Mackey (Crash Chambers), Laura Brooks (JoAnn)

WHATEVER HAPPENED TO MISS SEPTEMBER? (808 Pictures) Director, Jerry Denby; Photography, Joe Mangine; Screenplay, Adam Baum; Editor, Jonathan Richards; Music, Graff-Eshback; In Technicolor; Rated X; 80 minutes; September release. CAST: Tina Russell, Nick Harley, Jason Russell, Marc Stevens, Hardy Harrison, Marcello Bonino, Eric Edwards, Ultra Max, Kethy May, Mary Madigan, Janis King, Jean Jeffries

SUPERCHICK (Crown International) Producer, John Burrows; Director, Ed Forsyth; In color; Rated R; September release. CAST: Joyce Jillson, Louis Quinn, Tony Young, Thomas Reardon, Timothy Wayne Brown

CRYPT OF THE LIVING DEAD (Atlas) Producer, Lou Shaw; Director, Ray Danton; Story, Lois Gibson; Screenplay, Lou Shaw; In Metrocolor; Rated PG; September release. CAST: Andrew Prine, Mark Damon, Teresa Gimpera, Patty Sheppard, Francisco Brana

BEYOND ATLANTIS (Dimension) Producers, Eddie Romero, John Ashley; Director, Eddie Romero; Screenplay, Charles Johnson; In Metrocolor; Rated PG; September release. CAST: John Ashley, Patrick Wayne, Leigh Christian, George Nader

SLEEPY HEAD (No credits available) In color; Rated X; September release. Starring Georgina Spelvin

DON'T LOOK IN THE BASEMENT (Hallmark) Director, S. F. Brownrigg; Screenplay, Tim Pope; A Camera 2 production; In color; Rated R; 89 minutes; September release. CAST: Rosie Holotik (Charlotte), Ann McAdams (Dr. Masters), William Bill McGhee (Sam)

THE NEW YORK EXPERIENCE (Trans-Lux) Executive Producer, David M. Sacks; Producer, Paul Heller; Director, Writer, Designer, Rusty Russell; Photography, Ray Witlin, Werner Kuhn, Roy Inman, Rusty Russell, Edwin Forti, Michael Grumer; Editor, L. Deborah Klingman; A Trans-Lux/Bing Crosby presentation; In Technicolor; September release. CAST: Robin King, Maggi Thrall (Narrators), voices of Bill Alton, Ed Barth, Scott Beach, Bibi Besch, Rick Cimino, George Coe, Fay DeWitt, Dena Dietrich, Paul Dooley, Bob Kaliban, Deborah May, Jesse Osborn, Charlotte Rae, James Ray, Guy Sorel, and the wonderful people of New York City

I ESCAPED FROM DEVIL'S ISLAND (United Artists) Producers, Roger Corman, Gene Corman; Director, William Witney; Screenplay, Richard L. Adams; Photography, Rosalio Solano; Editors, Alan Collins, Tom Walls, Barbara Pokras; Music, Les Baxter; Art Director, Roberto Silva; Assistant Directors, Jaime Contreras, Cliff Bush; In DeLuxe color; Rated R; 87 minutes; September release. CAST: Jim Brown (Le Bras), Christopher George (Davert), Rick Ely (JoJo), Richard Rust (Zamorra)

Jim Brown (C), Christopher George
in "I Escaped from Devil's Island"

"I Escaped from Devil's Island"

Lawrence Cook, Martin Golar, J. A. Preston
in "The Spook Who Sat by the Door"

Paula Kelly in "The Spook
Who Sat by the Door"

THE SPOOK WHO SAT BY THE DOOR (United Artists) Producers, Ivan Dixon, Sam Greenlee; Director, Ivan Dixon; Screenplay, Sam Greenlee, Melvin Clay; Based on novel by Mr. Greenlee; Associate Producer, Thomas G. Neusom; Music, Herbie Hancock; Photography, Michel Hugo; Editor, Michael Kahn; Art Director, Leslie Thomas; Costumes, Henry Salley; In color; Presented by Bokari Ltd.; Rated PG; 102 minutes; September release. CAST: Lawrence Cook (Dan), Paula Kelly (Dahomey Queen), Janet League (Joy), J. A. Preston (Dawson), Paul Butler (Do-Daddy Dean), Don Blakely (Stud), David Lemieux (Pretty Willie), Byron Morrow (General), Jack Aaron (Carstairs), Joseph Mascolo (Senator), Beverly Gill (Willa), Bob Hill (Calhoun), Martin Golar (Perkins), Jeff Hamilton (Policeman), Margaret Kromgols (Old Woman), Tom Alderman (Security Officer), Stephen Ferry (Colonel), Kathy Berk (Doris), Stephen Ferry II (Boy Guardsman), Frank Lesley (Commentator), Harold Johnson (Jackson), Anthony Ray (Shorty), Audrey Stevenson (Mrs. Duncan), John Charles (Stew), Ponciano Olayta, Jr. (Soo), Sidney Eden (Inspector), Colostine Boatwright (Dancer), Johnny Williams (Waiter), Cora Williams, Bobbie Gene Williams, Ernie Robinson, Doug Johnson, Mark Williams, Robert Franklia, Jim Heard, Lenard Norris, Walter Lowe, Harold Harris, Kenneth Lee Orme, Don Greenlee, Johnnie Johnson, Maurice Wicks, Clinton Malcome, Larry Lawrence, Tyrone Livingston, James Mitchell, Frank E. Ford, Perry Thomas, Orlanders Thomas, Rodney McGrader, Ramon Livingston, Virgie Johnson

THE SLAMS (MGM) Producer, Gene Corman; Director, Jonathan Kaplan; Screenplay, Richard L. Adams; Photography, Andrew Davis; Editor, Morton Tubor; Music, Luther Henderson; Art Director, Jack Fisk; Assistant Directors, Thalmus Rasulala, Nate Long; a Penelope production; In Metrocolor; Rated R; 91 minutes; September release. CAST: Jim Brown (Curtis), Judy Pace (Iris), Roland Bob Harris (Stambell), Paul E. Harris (Jackson,) Frank de Kova (Capiello), Ted Cassidy (Glover), Frenchia Guizon (Macey), John Dennis (Flood), Jac Emel (Zack), Quinn Redeker (Warden), Betty Coles (Mother), Robert Phillips (Cohalt), Jan Merlin (Saddler)

THE LIGHT FROM THE SECOND STORY WINDOW (Jaquar) Produced, Directed, and Written by David L. Allen from his novel; Photography, Brad Kingston; Editor, David Wayne; In Eastmancolor; Rated X; 130 minutes; September release. CAST: David Allen (Lee), Ray Todd (Chuck), Joey Daniels (Big John), Jim Cassidy (Movie Star), Winston Kramer (Karl), Vicki Mills (Alma), and Richard Lindstrom, Eva Faye, Brad Preston, William Lasky, Felisha Fahr, Richard Lauette, Bob Weaver, Lou Claudio, Greg Phillips, Bob Ratcliffe, Steve Fox, John Mihu

THE EROTIC MEMOIRS OF A MALE CHAUVINIST PIG (Mature) Direction and Photography, John Butterworth; Screenplay, Ray Hoersch; In color; Rated X; 70 minutes; September release. CAST: Georgina Spelvin, Paul Taylor, Tiny Russell, Amy Matheau, Helen Madigan, Darby Lloyd Rains, Billy O'Shea

THE STUDENT TEACHERS (New World) Producer, Julie Corman; Director, Jonathan Kaplan; Screenplay, Danny Opatoshu; Photography, Steven Katz; Music, David Nichtern; Editor, George Van Noy; Art Director, Jim Newport; In Metrocolor; Rated R; 84 minutes; September release. CAST: Susan Damante, Brooke Mills, Brenda Sutton, Nora Heflin, Dick Miller, John Kramer, James Millhollin, Johnny Ray McGhee, Rich Duran, Douglas D. Anderson, Bob Harris, Charles Dierkop, Jac Emel, Tom Mohler, Rose Cypress, Gary Morgan, Ruth Warshawsky, Brad Jewett, Susan Madigan, Tracy Bogart, Gail Davies, Max Anderson, Amy Trachtenberg, Leslie Oliver, Paul Livadery, Chuck Norris, Vincent Barbi, Nick Dimitri, Jane Rosenfeld, Nancy Friedman

JIMI PLAYS BERKELEY (New Line Cinema) Produced by Electric Lady; Director, Peter Palafian; In color; 48 minutes; September release. CAST: Jimi Hendrix, Mitch Miller, Billy Cox

ARNOLD'S WRECKING CO. (Cine Globe) Producer, Otto G. Stoll III; Direction and Screenplay, Steve De Souza; Photography, Sam Virgoglini; Music, Laurel Brothers; Rated PG; 85 minutes; September release. CAST: Mike Ranshaw (Arnold), Steve De Souza (Kenny), Eddie Henderson (Rollo), Shirley Kauffman (Mae), Byron Schauer (Officer Ace)

Judy Pace
in "The Slams"

Brooke Mills, Brenda Sutton
in "The Student Teachers"

Karen Black
in "The Outfit"

Robert Duvall
in "The Outfit"

THE SECOND GUN (National General) Produced, Directed, Edited by Gerard Alcan; Based on the investigation of Theodore Charach; Music, Travis E. Pike; In color, black and white; 110 minutes; October release. A Documentary on the assassination of Robert F. Kennedy.

THE OUTFIT (MGM) Producer, Carter De Haven; Direction, Screenplay, John Flynn; Based on novel by Richard Stark; Music, Jerry Fielding; Photography, Bruce Surtees; Art Director, Tambi Larsen; Editor, Ralph E. Winters; Assistant Director, William McGarry; In color; Rated PG; 102 minutes; October release. CAST: Robert Duvall (Macklin), Karen Black (Bett), Joe Don Baker (Cody), Robert Ryan (Mailer), Timothy Carey (Menner), Richard Jaeckel (Chemey), Sheree North (Buck's Wife), Felice Orlandi (Frank), Marie Windsor (Madge), Jane Greer (Alma), Henry Jones (Doctor), Joanna Cassidy (Rita), Tom Reese (First Man), Elisha Cook (Carl), Bill McKinney (Buck), Ania O'Day (Herself), Archie Moore (Packard), Tony Young (Accountant), Roland LaStarza (Hit Man), Edward Ness (Ed), Roy Roberts (Bob), Toby Anderson (Parking Attendant), Emile Meyer (Amos), Roy Jenson (Al), Philip Kenneally (Bartender), Bern Hoffman (Sinclair), John Steadman (Gas Attendant), Paul Genge (Payoff Man), Francis De Sales (Jim), James Bacon (Bookie), Army Archerd (Butler), Tony Trabert (Himself)

HEX (20th Century-Fox) Executive Producer, Max L. Raab; Producer, Clark Paylow; Director, Leo Garen; Story, Doran William Cannon, Vernon Zimmerman; Screenplay, Leo Garen, Steve Katz; Associate Producer, William M. McCutcheon; Music, Pat Williams; Photography, Charles Rosher, Jr.; Art Directors, Gary Weist, Frank Sylos; Editors, Danford B. Greene, Stanford Allen; Assistant Director, Charles Myers; In DeLuxe color; 92 minutes; Rated PG; October release. CAST: Tina Herazo (Oriole), Hilarie Thompson (Acacia), John Carradine (Old Gunfighter), Keith Carradine (Whizzer), Mike Combs (Golly), Scott Glenn (Jimbang), Gary Busey (Giblets), Robert Walker (Chupo), Doria Cook (China), Iggie Wolfington (Cuzak), Patricia Ann Parker (Elma), Tom Jones (Elston), Dan Haggerty (Brother Billy)

I. F. STONE'S WEEKLY (Bruck) Produced, Directed, Photographed, and Edited by Jerry Bruck, Jr.; Narrated by Tom Wicker; In black and white; 62 minutes; October release. A documentary on Isadore Feinstein Stone.

YEAR OF THE WOMAN Producer, Porter Bibb; Directed and Written by Sandra Hochman; Photography, Claudia Weill, Juliana Wang; Editor, Patricia Powell; 80 minutes; October release. A documentary with Sandra Hochman, Liz Renay, Florynce Kennedy, Art Buchwald, Warren Beatty, Shirley MacLaine, Gloria Steinem, Shirley Chisholm, Norman Mailer, Bella Abzug, and others.

BEN-GURION REMEMBERS (Lawrence Fredricks Enterprises) Producers, Simon Hesera, Alan Kay; Director, Simon Hesera; Written by Mr. Hesera and Michael Bar-Zohar; 85 minutes; October release. A documentary in which Ben-Gurion discourses on his life and career.

THE NIGHT BEFORE (Hand-in-Hand) Producer, Jack Deveau; Direction and Photography, Arch Brown; Screenplay, Arch and Bruce Brown; Art Director, Bob Greco; Music, David Earnest; Editor, Robert Alvarez; In color; Rated X; 80 minutes; October release. CAST: Coke Hennessy (Hank), Michael Cade (Paul), Jamal Jones (Messenger), Nick Kastroff (Tim), Alexis Knight (Cyclist), Bob Plummer (Bill), Bill Yort (Pete), Tim Clark, Jeffrey Etting (Dancers)

LAST FOXTROT IN BURBANK (Federated Films) Producer-Director, Charles Band; Screenplay, Bill Haggard, Sam Vaughn; Photography, Tom Cecato; Editor, John T. Casino; Music, Gordon McGill; Assistant Director, Jory Valian; In color; Rated X; 65 minutes; October release. CAST: Michael Pataki (Paul), Sherry Denton (Jeanne), Simmy Bow (Marcel), Sally Marr (Mrs. Ketchenberg), William Quinn (Tom)

THE THUNDER KICK (Cannon) In color; Rated R; No other credits available; October release.

Scott Glenn, Keith Carradine, Mike Combs, Robert Walker, Tina Herazo, Hilarie Thompson in "Hex"

John Carradine, Keith Carradine
in "Hex"

Dean Stockwell
in "Werewolf in Washington"

Karl Malden
in "Summertime Killer"

RESURRECTION OF EVE (Mitchell Bros.) Producers, James L. and Artie Mitchell; Directors, Artie Mitchell, Jon Fontana; Screenplay, Artie Mitchell, Jon Fontana; Photography, Jon Fontana; Designer, Frank Gold; Music, Richard Wynkoop; Editors, Jon Fontana, Mark Bradford; In color; Rated X; October release. CAST: Nancy Weich (Eve), Mimi Morgan (Eve), Marilyn Chambers (Eve), Matthew Armon (Frank), Johnnie Keyes (Johnnie), Bentley Christmas (Mother), Dale Meador (Phil), Debbie Marinoff, Cozy Edmundson (Nurses), June Richards (Dallas), Pam Francis (Pam), Binky Bish (Manager)

WEREWOLF OF WASHINGTON (Diplomat) Producer, Nina Schulman; Direction and Screenplay, Milton Moses Ginsberg; Associate Producer, Stephen Miller; Photography, Bob Baldwin; Music, Arnold Freed; Editor, Mr. Ginsberg; A Millco production; 90 minutes; October release. CAST: Dean Stockwell (Jack), Biff McGuire (President), Clifton James (Attorney General), Beeson Carroll (Cmdr. Salmon), Jane House (Marion), Michael Dunn (Dr. Kiss), Barbara Siegel (Hippy), Stephen Cheng (Foreign Minister), Nancy Andrews (Mrs. Captree), Ben Yaffe (Judge), Jacqueline Brookes (Publisher), Thurman Scott (Hippy), Tom Scott (Reporter), Dennis McMullen (Astronaut), Jack Waltzer (Appointments Secretary), Randy Phillips (Federal Agent), Glenn Kezer (Admiral)

SANTEE (Crowin International) Producers, Deno Paoli, Edward Platt; Director, Gary Nelson; Screenplay, Tom Blackburn; Story, Brand Bell; Photography, Donald Morgan; Editor, George W. Brooks; Art Director, Mort Rabinowitz; Assistant Director, Michael Messinger; Music, Don Randi; A Vagabond production in color; Rated PG; 93 minutes; October release. CAST: Glenn Ford (Santee), Michael Burns (Jody), Dana Wynter (Valerie), Jay Silverheels (John Crow), and Harry Townes, John Larch, Robert Wilke, Bob Donner, Taylor Lacher, Lindsay Crosby, Charles Courtney, X Brand, John Hart, Ross McCubbin, Robert Mellard

THE DOBERMAN GANG (Dimension) Director, Byron Chudnow; In Metrocolor; Rated PG; October release. CAST: Byron Mabe, Hal Reed, Julie Parrish, Simmy Bow, Jojo D'Amoro

THE BROTHERS O'TOOLE (CVD) Producer, Charles E. Sellier; Director, Richard Erdman; In Eastmancolor; Rated G; October release. CAST: John Astin, Steve Carlson, Pat Carroll, Hans Conreid, Lee Merriwether, Allyn Joslyn, Richard Jury, Jesse White, Richard Erdman

TOM (Four Star International) Executive Producers, Mardi Rustam, Robert Brown; Producer, Alvin L. Fast; Director, Greydon Clark; Screenplay, Greydon Clark, Alvin L. Fast; Photography, Louis Horvath; Editor, Earl Watson, Jr.; Title song, Sheldon Lee; A Challenge production; In Eastmancolor; Rated R; 83 minutes; October release. CAST: Greydon Clark (Jim), Tom Johnigarn (Makinba), Aldo Ray (Lt. Stans), Jock Mahoney (Sgt. Berry), Jacqulin Cole (Nancy), Bambi Allen (Bobbie), Pamela Corbett (Tina), Fred Scott (Washington), Carl Craig (Willie)

SUMMERTIME KILLER (Avco Embassy) Producer-Director, Antonio Isasi; Screenplay, R. Buckley, B. Degas; Photography, Juan Gelpi; Rated PG; 100 minutes; October release. CAST: Karl Malden (Kiley), Christopher Mitchum (Ray), Olivia Hussey (Tonia), Raf Vallone (Lazaro), Claudine Auger (Michele)

JIMI HENDRIX (Warner Bros.) Producers, Joe Boyd, John Head, Gary Weis; Associate Producer, Leo Branton; Editor, Peter Colbert; In Technicolor; Rated R; 102 minutes; October release. A documentary about the rock star Jimi Hendrix.

LADY FRANKENSTEIN (New World) Producer, Harry Cushing; Director, Mel Welles; In Metrocolor; Rated R; October release. CAST: Sarah Bay (Tanya), Joseph Cotten (Baron), Paul Muller (Marsh), Mickey Hargitay (Captain)

GEORGE (Capital) Producer, Marshall Thompson; A Sol Fried-David Roth presentation; In Eastmancolor; Rated G; October release. Marshall Thompson, Jack Mullaney, Inge Schoner, George

APARTMENT ON THE 13th FLOOR (Hallmark) Director, Eloy De La Iglesia; An Atlas Film; In color; Rated R; November release. CAST: Vincent Parra, Emma Cohen

Olivia Hussey, Christopher Mitchum
in "Summertime Killer"

Jimi Hendrix
in "Jimi Hendrix"

Isaac Hayes
in "Black Moses"

Florence Marly, Barry Coe
in "Dr. Death"

THE BLACK MOSES OF SOUL (Aquarius) Producer-Director, Chuck Johnson; A Terry Levene presentation; In color; Rated G; November release. CAST: Isaac Hayes

A SCREAM IN THE STREETS (Boxoffice International) Producer, Harry Novak; Director, Carl Manson; Screenplay, Eric Norden; In color; November release. CAST: John Kirkpatric, Frank Bannon

I AM FRIGID . . . WHY? (Audubon) Director, Max Pecas; A Griffon Films production; In Eastmancolor; Rated R; November release. CAST: Sandra Julien, John Terrade

BLACKENSTEIN (Exclusive International) In DeLuxe color; Rated R; No other credits available; November release. CAST: John Hart, Ivory Stone, Andrea King, Liz Renay, Roosevelt Jackson, James Cougar, Cardella Di Milo, Joe De Sue, Nick Bolin, Andy C.

THE BIRDS AND THE BEADS (No credits available) In color; Rated X; November release. CAST: Georgina Spelvin, Tina Russell

LITTLE MISS INNOCENCE (Lima) Producer-Director, Chris Warfield; Photography, Ray Steckler; In Eastmancolor; November release. CAST: John Alderman, Sandy Dempsey, Judy Medford

ROSELAND (Boxoffice International) Directed, Written and Designed by C. Fredric Hobbs; A Harry Novak presentation; In DeLuxe color; Photographed and Edited by Gordon Mueller; 90 minutes; November release. CAST: E. Kerrigan Prescott (Adam), Christopher Brooks (Bosch), Peggy Browne (Princess Moon), Karen Ingenthron (Watkins), Victor Alter (Sistine Skate), Carla LiBrizzi (Gosamer Girl), Pierre Henri Delattre (Father Finney), Terry Wills (Nico), Andrea Schmidt (Miss Higgen), H. K. Bauer (Narrator)

GRACE'S PLACE (L.A.C.) Producer, Lou Campa; Director, Chuck Vincent; Photography, Steven Colwell; In color; Rated X; 78 minutes; November release. CAST: Rebecca Brooke, Jeffrey Hurst, John Westleigh, Jacqueline Penn, Sheila Shelley, Jon Catlin, Dian Chelsea, Nora Escuadero, Grace Tapery, Leon Curiel

BLUE SUMMER (Monarch) Produced, Directed, and Written by Chuck Vincent; Photography, Stephen Colwell; Music, Richard Billay; Performed by Sleepy Hollow; Editor, Marc Ubell; An Allan Shackleton presentation; In color; Rated X; 80 minutes; November release. CAST: Darcey Hollingsworth (Tracy), Bo White (Gene), Lilly Bo Peep (Bee), Joann Sterling (Sparky), Melissa Evers (Regina), Chris Jordan (No Name), Jacqueline Carol (Margaret), Any Mathieu (Deborah), Shana McGran (Liza), Eric Edwards (Fred), Larry Lima (Roger), Sylvia Bernstein (Gene's mother), Hardy Harrison (Gene's father), Jeff Allen (Motorcyclist), Joe Asaro (Heavy), Robert Joel (Preacher), Mike Ledis (Ed)

SOME CALL IT LOVING (CineGlobe) Producer-Director, James B. Harris; Associate Producer, Ramzi Thomas; Screenplay, James B. Harris; Photography, Mario Tosi; Editor, Paul Jasiukonis; Music, Richard Hazard; Costumes, Jax; A Two World Films presentation; In Technicolor; Rated R; 103 minutes; November release. CAST: Zalman King (Robert), Carol White (Scarlett), Tisa Farrow (Jennifer), Richard Pryor (Jeff), Veronica Anderson (Angelica), Logan Ramsey (Doctor), Brandy Herred (Cheerleader), Pat Priest (Nurse), Ed Rue (Mortician), Joseph DeMeo (Bartender)

DOCTOR DEATH: SEEKER OF SOULS (Cinerama) Producer-Director, Eddie Saeta; Screenplay, Sal Ponti; Music, Richard LaSalle; Photography, Kent Wakeford, Emil Oster; Editor, Tony DiMarco; Associate Producer, Sal Ponti; Art Director, Ed Graves; Costumes, Tom Dawson; Assistant Director, Irby Smith; A Freedom Arts Pictures production; In Movielab color; Rated R; 93 minutes; November release. CAST: John Considine (Dr. Death), Barry Coe (Fred), Cheryl Miller (Sandy), Stewart Moss (Greg), Leon Askin (Thor), Jo Morrow (Laura), Florence Marly (Tana), Sivi Aberg (Venus), Jim Boles (Franz), Athena Lorde (Spiritualist), Moe Howard (Volunteer), Robert E. Ball (Old Wizard), Patrick Dennis-Leigh (Old Man), Lin Henson (TV Watcher), Anna Bernard (Girl in phonebooth), Barbara Boles (Alice), Pierre Gonneau (Harry), Larry Rogers (Young man in park), Denise Denise (Girl with flat tire), Eric Boles (Man at seance), Jeffrey Herman (Man wanting new body), Leon Williams (Man to arrange seance), Larry "Seymour" Vincent (Strangler)

Richard Pryor
in "Some Call It Loving"

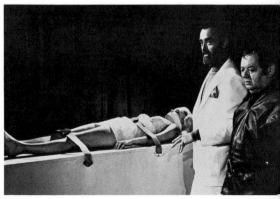

Sivi Aberg, John Considine, Leon Askin
in "Dr. Death"

Neile Adams McQueen
in "So Long, Blue Boy"

Pat Hingle in "Happy as the
Grass Was Green"

VALLEY OF BLOOD (Mica) Producer, John Daly; Director, Dean Turner; Screenplay, Wayne Forsythe; Music, Don Green, Crown Studios; Photography, Craig Faulkner, Ron Evans, John Evans; Editor, J. D. Turner; Assistant Directors, William Olive, James Wright; A Michael Hayes-C. L. Hayes-Woodrow Walker, Jr. presentation; In Capital Film color; In WideVision; Rating PG; 64 minutes; November release. CAST: Penny DeHaven, Ernie Ashworth, Zeke Clements, Wayne Forsythe, Rita Cristinziano, Joseph Turner, Herman Floyd

SO LONG, BLUE BOY (Maryon) Producer, Kenneth Sprague; Director, Gerald Gordon; Screenplay, David Long, Chris Long; Photography, James A. Larsen; Music, Bruce Buckingham; Editor, Al Street; Art Directors, Robinson Royce, Barren Rouche; Assistant Director, Sterling Franck; In CFI color; 100 minutes; November release. CAST: Arthur Franz (Ed), Rick Gates (Isaiah), Neile Adams McQueen (Julie), Richard Rowley (Dean), Pamela Collins (Cathy), Anne Seymour (Martha), Richard McMurray (Eli), Henry Brandon (Buck)

MADAME ZENOBIA (Screencom) Produced, Directed, and Photographed by Eduardo Cemano; In color; 80 minutes; November release. CAST: Tina Russell (Marcia), Derald Delancey (John), Elizabeth Donovan (Madame Zenobia), Rick Livermore (Eric), Inger Kissen (Lucy), Frank Martin (Rocky), David Jones (Clancy), J. C. Klitz (Old man), Claudia Miro (Heavenly Wench)

BLACK JACK (American International) Original title "Wild in the Sky"; Producers, William T. Naud, Dick Gautier; Director, William T. Naud; Story, William T. Naud, Dick Gautier, Peter Marshall; Screenplay, Dick Gautier, William T. Naud; Photography, Thomas E. Spalding; Editors, William T. Naud, Michael Kahn; Music, Jerry Styner; Presented by Ralph Andrews; A Bald Eagle production; In Movielab color; 87 minutes; Rated GP; December release. CAST: Georg Stanford Brown (Lynch), Brande de Wilde (Josh), Keenan Wynn (Gen. Gobohare), Tim O'Connor (Sen. Recker), Dick Gautier (Diver), James Daly (President), Robert Lansing (Maj. Reason), Larry Hovis (Capt. Breen), Bernie Kopell (Penrat), Joseph Turkel (Corazza), Dub Taylor (Roddenbery), Phil Vandervort (Woody)

DEEP SLEEP (Barferd) Producer, Andrew S. Cacksum; Director, Alfred Sole; Photography, Joe Friedman; Music, Butch Taylor; In color; Rated X; 72 mintutes; December release. CAST: Willard Butts, Mary Canary

THE LEGEND OF BOGGY CREEK (Halco) Producer-Director, Charles Pierce; Executive Producers, L. W. Ledwell, Charles Pierce; Screenplay, Earl E. Smith; Narrator, Vern Stearman; Photography, Charles Pierce; Editor, Thomas F. Boutress; Music, Jamie Mendoza-Nava; In Technicolor; Rated G; 90 minutes; December release.

HAPPY AS THE GRASS WAS GREEN (Martin) Producer, Burt Martin; Direction and Screenplay, Charles Davis; Based on novel by Merle Good; Photography, Stan Martin; Editor, Erwin Dumbrille; Music, Gordon Zahler; In CFI color; Rated PG; 105 minutes; December release. CAST: Geraldine Page (Anna), Pat Hingle (Eli), Graham Beckel (Eric), Rachel Thomas (Hazel), Steve Weaver (Jim), Elvin Byler (Rufus), Noreen Huber (Sarah), John Miller (Ben), Luke Sickles (Menno)

MY FAIR BABY (Arrow) Producer, Mortimer B. Goldberg; Photography, Al James; Art Director, Phyllis Stone; In color; Rated X; 82 minutes; December release. CAST: Noelle Karel, Bill Morgen, Michelle Magazine, Lou Steisel, Bruce Mortimer, Paul Munsinger

CHECKMATE (JER) Producer, John Amero; Director and Editor, Lem Amero; Screenplay, LaRue Watts; Photography, Roberta Findlay; In Movielab color; Rated R; 90 minutes; December release. CAST: Diana Wilson (Pepper), An Tsan Hu (Madame Chang), Don Draper (Mercer), J. J. Coyle (Snow), Caren Kaye (Alex), Kurt Mann (Jogger), Reg Roland (Andre), Ion De Hondol (Boris)

KEEP ON ROCKIN' (Pennebaker) Producer, D. A. Pennebaker; Photography, Barry Bergthorson, Jim Desmond, Randy Franklin, Richard Leacock, Richard Leiterman, Roger Murphy, Roger Neuwirth, D. A. Pennebaker; 95 minutes; December release. A documentary with rock artists Chuck Berry, Diddley Richard, Jerry Lee Lewis, Bo Diddley, Janis Joplin, Jimi Hendrix

Georg Stanford Brown, Brandon DeWilde, Phil
Vandervoort in "Black Jack"

Keenan Wynn
in "Black Jack"

Fred Williamson, Teresa Graves
in "That Man Bolt"

John Beal, Robin Strasser
in "The House that Cried Murder"

THAT MAN BOLT (Universal) Producer, Bernard Schwartz; Directors, Henry Levin, David Lowell Rich; Screenplay, Quentin Werty, Charles Johnson; Photography, Gerald Perry Finnerman; Editors, Carl Pingitore, Robert F. Shugrue; Music, Charles Bernstein; Art Director, Alexander Golitzen; Assistant Director, Phil Bowles; In Technicolor; Rated R; 103 minutes; December release. CAST: Fred Williamson (Bolt), Byron Webster (Griffiths), Miko Mayama (Dominique), Teresa Graves (Samantha), Satoshi Nakamura (Kumada), John Orchard (Carter), Jack Ging (Connie), Ken Kazama (Spider), Vassili Lambrinos (De Vargas)

BLADE (Joseph Green) Executive Producer, Ernest Pintoff; Producer-Director, George Manasse; Screenplay, Ernest Pintoff, Jeff Lieberman; Music, John Cacavas; Photography, David Hoffman; Editor, David Ray; Associate Producer, Drew Denbaum; Assistant Director, Gerald Gewirtz; In Eastman color; Rated R; 90 minutes; December release. CAST: John Marley (Blade), Jon Cypher (Petersen), Kathryn Walker (Maggie), William Prince (Powers), Michael McGuire (Quincy), Joe Santos (Spinelli), John Schuck (Reardon), Peter White (Freund), Keene Curtis (Steiner), Karen Machon (Connors), Raina Barrett (Novak), Ted Lange (Watson), Marshall Efron (Fat man), Arthur French (Sanchez), Steve Landesberg (Debaum), James Cook (Kaminsky), Jeanne Lange (Melinda), Michael Pendry (Bentley), Vince Cannon (Morgan), Frederick Rolf (Examiner), Hugh Hurd (Attorney), Eddie Lawrence (Producer), Jeri Miller (Caldwell)

THE DEADLY TRACKERS (Warner Bros.) Producer, Fouad Said; Executive Producer, Edward Rosen; Director, Barry Shear; Screenplay, Lukas Heller; Based on story "Riata" by Samuel Fuller; Photography, Gabriel Torres; Editors, Michael Economou, Carl Pingitore; Art Director, Javier T. Torija; Assistant Directors, John Quill, Jesus Marin; A Cine Film production; In Technicolor; Rated PG; 104 minutes; December release. CAST: Richard Harris (Kilpatrick), Rod Taylor (Brand), Al Lettieri (Guitierrez), Neville Brand (Choo Choo), William Smith (Schoolboy), Paul Benjamin (Jacob), Pedro Armendariz, Jr. (Blacksmith), Isela Varga (Maria), Kelly Jean Peters (Katharine)

THE HOUSE THAT CRIED MURDER (Unisphere) formerly "The Bride"; Producer, John Grissmer; Director, Jean-Marie Pelissie; Screenplay, John Grissmer, Jean-Marie Pelissie; Photography, Geoffrey Stephenson; Editor, Sam Moore; Music, Peter Bernstein; A Golden Gate production; In TVC color; Rated PG; 85 minutes; December release. CAST: Robin Strasser (Barbara), John Beal (Father), Arthur Roberts (David), Ivan Jean Saraceni (Ellen)

A TASTE OF HELL (Boxoffice International) Producer, John Garwood; Executive Producer, Ben Balatbat; Directors, Neil Yarema, Basil Bradbury; Screenplay, Neil Yarema; Photography, Fred Conde; Music, Nester Robles; In color by Movielab; Rated PG; 90 minutes; December release. CAST: John Garwood (Barry), Lisa Lorena (Maria), William Smith (Jack), Vic Diaz (Major), Lloyd Kino (Captain), Angel Buenaventura (Tomas), Ruben Rustia (Mario)

BLOOD OF THE DRAGON (Harnell) In color; Rated R; No other credits available; December release. Starring Wang Yu

FILM PORTRAIT (Anthology Film Archive) Produced and Edited by Jerome Hill; 90 minutes; December release. A documentary on Jerome Hill's career as a moviemaker.

DRACULA VS. FRANKENSTEIN (Independent International) Producers, Al Adamson, John Van Horn; Director, Al Adamson; Story and Screenplay, William Pugsley, Samuel M. Sherman; In DeLuxe color; Rated PG; 90 minutes; December release. CAST: J. Carrol Naish (Frankenstein), Lon Chaney (Groton), Zandor Vorkov (Dracula), Russ Tamblyn (Rico), Jim Davis (Martin)

HELL UP IN HARLEM (American International) Producer, Larry Cohen; Co-Producer, Janelle Cohen; Executive Producer, Peter Sabiston; Direction and Screenplay, Larry Cohen; Photography, Fenton Hamilton; Editors, Peter Holmes, Franco Guerri; Music, Freddie Perren, Fonce Mizell; Designer, Larry Lurin; In Movielab color; Rated R; 96 minutes; December release. CAST: Fred Williamson (Tommy), Julius W. Harris (Papa Gibbs), Gloria Hendry (Helen), Margaret Avery (Sister Jennifer), D'Urville Martin (Rev. Rufus), Tony King (Zach), Gerald Gordon (DiAngelo)

John Marley (L)
in "Blade"

Julius W. Harris, Fred Williamson, Margaret Avery,
D'Urville Martin "Hell up in Harlem"

ESTHER ANDERSON

TIMOTHY BOTTOMS

ROBERT DeNIRO

CANDY CLARK

MADELINE KAHN

JASON MILLER

MICHAEL MORIARTY

DIANE KEATON

MARSHA MASON

ROY SCHEIDER

BILLY DEE WILLIAMS

CINDY WILLIAMS

THE GODFATHER

(PARAMOUNT) Producer, Albert S. Ruddy; Director, Francis Ford Coppola; Associate Producer, Gray Frederickson; Screenplay, Mario Puzo, Francis Ford Coppola; Based on novel by Mr. Puzo; Photography, Gordon Willis; Designer, Dean Tavoularis; Music, Nino Rota; Costumes, Anna Hill Johnstone; Art Director, Warren Clymer; Assistant Directors, Fred Gallo, Samuel Verts, Steve Skloot; In Technicolor; Rating R; 175 minutes; March release.

CAST

Don Vito Corleone	Marlon Brando
Michael Corleone	Al Pacino
Sonny Corleone	James Caan
Clemenza	Richard Castellano
Tom Hagen	Robert Duvall
McCluskey	Sterling Hayden
Jack Woltz	John Marley
Barzini	Richard Conte
Kay Adams	Diane Keaton
Sollozzo	Al Lettieri
Tessio	Abe Vigoda
Connie Rizzi	Talia Shire
Carlo Rizzi	Gianni Russo
Fredo Corleone	John Cazale
Cuneo	Rudy Bond
Johnny Fontane	Al Martino
Mama Corleone	Morgana King
Luca Brasi	Lenny Montana
Paulie Gatto	John Martino
Bonasera	Salvatore Corsitto
Neri	Richard Bright
Moe Greene	Alex Rocco
Bruno Tattaglia	Tony Giorgio
Nazorine	Vito Scotti
Theresa Hagen	Tere Livrano
Phillip Tattaglia	Victor Rendina
Lucy Mancini	Jeannie Linero
Sandra Corleone	Julie Gregg
Mrs. Clemenza	Ardell Sheridan
Apollonia	Simonetta Stefanelli
Fabrizio	Angelo Infanti
Don Tommasino	Corrado Gaipa
Calo	Franco Citti
Vitelli	Saro Urzi

Left: Al Pacino, Marlon Brando, James Caan, John Cazale Top: Al Pacino, Marlon Brando

Robert Duvall, Tere Livrano, John Cazale, Gianni Russo, Talia Shire, Morgana King, Marlon Brando, James Caan, Julie Gregg, Jeannie Linero
BEST PICTURE OF 1972

MARLON BRANDO
in "The Godfather"
BEST PERFORMANCE BY AN ACTOR IN 1972

143

LIZA MINNELLI
in "Cabaret"
BEST PERFORMANCE BY AN ACTRESS IN 1972

JOEL GREY
in "Cabaret"
BEST SUPPORTING PERFORMANCE BY AN ACTOR IN 1972

EILEEN HECKART
in "Butterflies Are Free"
BEST SUPPORTING PERFORMANCE BY AN ACTRESS IN 1972

THE DISCREET CHARM OF THE BOURGEOISIE

(20TH CENTURY-FOX) Producer, Serge Silberman; Director, Luis Bunuel; Story and Screenplay, Luis Bunuel, Jean-Claude Carriere; Photography, Edmond Richard; Assistant Director, Pierre Lary; In DeLuxe Color; Rating PG; 100 minutes; October release.

CAST

Ambassador	Fernando Rey
Mrs. Thevenot	Delphine Seyrig
Mrs. Senechal	Stephane Audran
Florence	Bulle Ogier
Mr. Senechal	Jean-Pierre Cassel
Mr. Thevenot	Paul Frankeur
Bishop	Julien Bertheau
Colonel	Claude Pieplu
Home Secretary	Michel Piccoli
Peasant Girl	Muni

Right: Fernando Rey, Delphine Seyrig

Fernando Rey, Stephane Audran
Above: Rey, Jean-Pierre Cassel, Paul Frankeur

Jean-Pierre Cassel, Julien Bertheau

147

BEST FOREIGN LANGUAGE FILM OF 1972

Sandy Dennis

Karl Malden

Helen Hayes

Lee Marvin

Cloris Leachman

PREVIOUS ACADEMY AWARD WINNERS
(1) Best Picture, (2) Actor, (3) Actress, (4) Supporting Actor, (5) Supporting Actress, (6) Director, (7) Special Award, (8) Best Foreign Language Film

1927-28: (1) "Wings", (2) Emil Jannings in "The Way Of All Flesh", (3) Janet Gaynor in "Seventh Heaven", (6) Frank Borzage for "Seventh Heaven", (7) Charles Chaplin.

1928-29: (1) "Broadway Melody", (2) Warner Baxter in "Old Arizona", (3) Mary Pickford in "Coquette", (6) Frank Lloyd for "The Divine Lady".

1929-30: (1) "All Quiet On The Western Front", (2) George Arliss in "Disraeli", (3) Norma Shearer in "The Divorcee", (6) Lewis Milestone for "All Quiet On The Western Front".

1930-31: (1) "Cimarron", (2) Lionel Barrymore in "A Free Soul", (3) Marie Dressler in "Min and Bill", (6) Norman Taurog for "Skippy".

1931-32. (1) "Grand Hotel", (2) Fredric March in "Dr. Jekyll and Mr. Hyde", tied with Wallace Beery in "The Champ", (3) Helen Hayes in "The Sin of Madelon Claudet", (6) Frank Borzage for "Bad Girl".

1932-33: (1) "Cavalcade", (2) Charles Laughton in "The Private Life of Henry VIII", (3) Katharine Hepburn in "Morning Glory", (6) Frank Lloyd for "Cavalcade".

1934: (1) "It Happened One Night", (2) Clark Gable in "It Happened One Night", (3) Claudette Colbert in "It Happened One Night", (6) Frank Capra for "It Happened One Night", (7) Shirley Temple.

1935: (1) "Mutiny On The Bounty", (2) Victor McLaglen in "The Informer", (3) Bette Davis in "Dangerous", (6) John Ford for "The Informer", (7) D. W. Griffith.

1936: (1) "The Great Ziegfeld", (2) Paul Muni in "The Story of Louis Pasteur", (3) Luise Rainer in "The Great Ziegfeld", (4) Walter Brennan in "Come and Get It", (5) Gale Sondergaard in "Anthony Adverse", (6) Frank Capra for "Mr. Deeds Goes To Town".

1937: (1) "The Life of Emile Zola", (2) Spencer Tracy in "Captains Courageous", (3) Luise Rainer in "The Good Earth", (4) Joseph Schildkraut in "The Life of Emile Zola", (5) Alice Brady in "In Old Chicago", (6) Leo McCarey for "The Awful Truth", (7) Mack Sennett, Edgar Bergen.

1938: (1) "You Can't Take It With You", (2) Spencer Tracy in "Boys' Town", (3) Bette Davis in "Jezebel", (4) Walter Brennan in "Kentucky", (5) Fay Bainter in "Jezebel", (6) Frank Capra for "You Can't Take It With You", (7) Deanna Durbin, Mickey Rooney, Harry M. Warner, Walt Disney.

1939: (1) "Gone With The Wind", (2) Robert Donat in "Goodbye, Mr. Chips", (3) Vivien Leigh in "Gone With The Wind", (4) Thomas Mitchell in "Stagecoach", (5) Hattie McDaniel in "Gone With The Wind", (6) Victor Fleming for "Gone With The Wind", (7) Douglas Fairbanks, Judy Garland.

1940: (1) "Rebecca", (2) James Stewart in "The Philadelphia Story", (3) Ginger Rogers in "Kitty Foyle", (4) Walter Brennan in "The Westerner", (5) Jane Darwell in "The Grapes of Wrath", (6) John Ford for "The Grapes of Wrath", (7) Bob Hope.

1941: (1) "How Green Was My Valley", (2) Gary Cooper in "Sergeant York", (3) Joan Fontaine in "Suspicion", (4) Donald Crisp in "How Green Was My Valley", (5) Mary Astor in "The Great Lie", (6) John Ford for "How Green Was My Valley", (7) Leopold Stokowski, Walt Disney.

1942: (1) "Mrs. Miniver", (2) James Cagney in "Yankee Doodle Dandy", (3) Greer Garson in "Mrs. Miniver", (4) Van Heflin in "Johnny Eager", (5) Teresa Wright in "Mrs. Miniver", (6) William Wyler for "Mrs. Miniver", (7) Charles Boyer, Noel Coward.

1943: (1) "Casablanca", (2) Paul Lukas in "Watch On The Rhine", (3) Jennifer Jones in "The Song of Bernadette", (4) Charles Coburn in "The More The Merrier", (5) Katina Paxinou in "For Whom The Bell Tolls", (6) Michael Curtiz for "Casablanca".

1944: (1) "Going My Way", (2) Bing Crosby in "Going My Way", (3) Ingrid Bergman in "Gaslight", (4) Barry Fitzgerald in "Going My Way", (5) Ethel Barrymore in "None But The Lonely Heart", (6) Leo McCarey for "Going My Way", (7) Margaret O'Brien, Bob Hope.

1945: (1) "The Lost Weekend", (2) Ray Milland in "The Lost Weekend", (3) Joan Crawford in "Mildred Pierce", (4) James Dunn in "A Tree Grows in Brooklyn", (5) Anne Revere in "National Velvet", (6) Billy Wilder for "The Lost Weekend", (7) Walter Wanger, Peggy Ann Garner.

1946: (1) "The Best Years of Our Lives", (2) Fredric March in "The Best Years of Our Lives", (3) Olivia de Havilland in "To Each His Own", (4) Harold Russell in "The Best Years of Our Lives", (5) Anne Baxter in "The Best Years of Our Lives", (7) Laurence Olivier, Harold Russell, Ernst Lubitsch, Claude Jarman, Jr.

1947: (1) "Gentleman's Agreement", (2) Ronald Colman in "A Double Life", (3) Loretta Young in "The Farmer's Daughter", (4) Edmund Gwenn in "Miracle On 34th Street", (5) Celeste Holm in "Gentleman's Agreement", (6) Elia Kazan for "Gentleman's Agreement", (7) James Baskette, (8) "Shoe Shine."

1948: (1) "Hamlet", (2) Laurence Olivier in "Hamlet", (3) Jane Wyman in "Johnny Belinda", (4) Walter Huston in "The Treasure of The Sierra Madre", (5) Claire Trevor in "Key Largo", (6) John Huston for "The Treasure of The Sierra Madre", (7) Ivan Jandl, Sid Grauman, Adolph Zukor, Walter Wanger, (8) "Monsieur Vincent".

1949: (1) "All The King's Men", (2) Broderick Crawford in "All The King's Men", (3) Olivia de Havilland in "The Heiress", (4) Dean Jagger in "Twelve O'Clock High", (5) Mercedes McCambridge in "All The King's Men", (6) Joseph L. Mankiewicz for "A Letter To Three Wives", (7) Bobby Driscoll, Fred Astaire, Cecil B. DeMille, Jean Hersholt, (8) "The Bicycle Thief."

1950: (1) "All About Eve", (2) Jose Ferrer in "Cyrano de Bergerac", (3) Judy Holliday in "Born Yesterday", (4) George Sanders in "All About Eve", (5) Josephine Hull in "Harvey", (6) Joseph L. Mankiewicz for "All About Eve", (7) George Murphy, Louis B. Mayer, (8) "The Walls of Malapaga".

1951: (1) "An American in Paris", (2) Humphrey Bogart in "The African Queen", (3) Vivien Leigh in "A Streetcar Named Desire", (4) Karl Malden in "A Streetcar Named Desire", (5) Kim Hunter in "A Streetcar Named Desire", (6) George Stevens for "A Place In The Sun", (7) Gene Kelly, (8) "Rashomon."

1952: (1) "The Greatest Show On Earth", (2) Gary Cooper in "High Noon", (3) Shirley Booth in "Come Back, Little Sheba", (4) Anthony Quinn in "Viva Zapata", (5) Gloria Grahame in "The Bad and the Beautiful", (6) John Ford for "The Quiet Man", (7) Joseph M. Schenck, Merian C. Cooper, Harold Lloyd, Bob Hope, George Alfred Mitchell, (8) "Forbidden Games."

1953: (1) "From Here To Eternity", (2) William Holden in "Stalag 17", (3) Audrey Hepburn in "Roman Holiday", (4) Frank Sinatra in "From Here To Eternity", (5) Donna Reed in "From Here To Eternity", (6) Fred Zinnemann for "From Here To Eternity", (7) Pete Smith, Joseph Breen.

1954: (1) "On The Waterfront", (2) Marlon Brando in "On The Waterfront", (3) Grace Kelly in "The Country Girl", (4) Edmond

John Mills

Sophia Loren

Sidney Poitier

Anne Revere

Cliff Robertson

O'Brien in "The Barefoot Contessa", (5) Eva Marie Saint in "On The Waterfront", (6) Elia Kazan for "On The Waterfront", (7) Greta Garbo, Danny Kaye, Jon Whitely, Vincent Winter, (8) "Gate of Hell."

1955: (1) "Marty", (2) Ernest Borgnine in "Marty", (3) Anna Magnani in "The Rose Tattoo", (4) Jack Lemmon in "Mister Roberts", (5) Jo Van Fleet in "East of Eden", (6) Delbert Mann for "Marty", (8) "Samurai."

1956: (1) "Around The World in 80 Days", (2) Yul Brynner in "The King and I", (3) Ingrid Bergman in "Anastasia", (4) Anthony Quinn in "Lust For Life", (5) Dorothy Malone in "Written On The Wind", (6) George Stevens for "Giant", (7) Eddie Cantor, (8) "La Strada."

1957: (1) "The Bridge On The River Kwai", (2) Alec Guinness in "The Bridge On The River Kwai", (3) Joanne Woodward in "The Three Faces of Eve", (4) Red Buttons in "Sayonara", (5) Miyoshi Umeki in "Sayonara", (6) David Lean for "The Bridge On The River Kwai", (7) Charles Brackett, B. B. Kahane, Gilbert M. (Bronco Billy) Anderson, (8) "The Nights of Cabiria."

1958: (1) "Gigi", (2) David Niven in "Separate Tables", (3) Susan Hayward in "I Want to Live", (4) Burl Ives in "The Big Country", (5) Wendy Hiller in "Separate Tables", (6) Vincente Minnelli for "Gigi", (7) Maurice Chevalier, (8) "My Uncle."

1959: (1) "Ben-Hur", (2) Charlton Heston in "Ben-Hur", (3) Simone Signoret in "Room At The Top", (4) Hugh Griffith in "Ben-Hur", (5) Shelley Winters in "The Diary of Anne Frank", (6) William Wyler for "Ben-Hur", (7) Lee de Forest, Buster Keaton, (8) "Black Orpheus."

1960: (1) "The Apartment", (2) Burt Lancaster in "Elmer Gantry", (3) Elizabeth Taylor in "Butterfield 8", (4) Peter Ustinov in "Spartacus", (5) Shirley Jones in "Elmer Gantry", (6) Billy Wilder for "The Apartment", (7) Gary Cooper, Stan Laurel, Hayley Mills, (8) "The Virgin Spring."

1961: (1) "West Side Story", (2) Maximilian Schell in "Judgment At Nuremberg", (3) Sophia Loren in "Two Women", (4) George Chakiris in "West Side Story", (6) Robert Wise for "West Side Story", (7) Jerome Robbins, Fred L. Metzler, (8) "Through A Glass Darkly."

1962: (1) "Lawrence of Arabia", (2) Gregory Peck in "To Kill A Mockingbird", (3) Anne Bancroft in "The Miracle Worker", (4) Ed Begley in "Sweet Bird of Youth", (5) Patty Duke in "The Miracle Worker", (6) David Lean for "Lawrence of Arabia", (8) "Sundays and Cybele."

1963: (1) "Tom Jones", (2) Sidney Poitier in "Lilies of The Field", (3) Patricia Neal in "Hud", (4) Melvyn Douglas in "Hud", (5) Margaret Rutherford in "The V.I.P.'s", (6) Tony Richardson for "Tom Jones", (8) "8½".

1964: (1) "My Fair Lady", (2) Rex Harrison in "My Fair Lady", (3) Julie Andrews in "Mary Poppins", (4) Peter Ustinov in "Topkapi", (5) Lila Kedrova in "Zorba The Greek", (6) George Cukor for "My Fair Lady", (7) William Tuttle, (8) "Yesterday, Today and Tomorrow."

1965: (1) "The Sound Of Music", (2) Lee Marvin in "Cat Ballou", (3) Julie Christie in "Darling", (4) Martin Balsam in "A Thousand Clowns", (5) Shelley Winters in "A Patch Of Blue", (6) Robert Wise for "The Sound of Music", (7) Bob Hope, (8) "The Shop On Main Street".

1966: (1) "A Man For All Seasons", (2) Paul Scofield in "A Man For All Seasons", (3) Elizabeth Taylor in "Who's Afraid Of Virginia Woolf?", (4) Walter Matthau in "The Fortune Cookie", (5) Sandy Dennis in "Who's Afraid of Virginia Woolf?", (6) Fred Zinnemann for "A Man For All Seasons", (8) "A Man and A Woman."

1967: (1) "In The Heat Of The Night", (2) Rod Steiger in "In The Heat Of The Night", (3) Katharine Hepburn in "Guess Who's Coming To Dinner", (4) George Kennedy in "Cool Hand Luke", (5) Estelle Parsons in "Bonnie and Clyde", (6) Mike Nichols for "The Graduate", (8) "Closely Watched Trains."

1968: (1) "Oliver!", (2) Cliff Robertson in "Charly", (3) Katharine Hepburn in "The Lion in Winter" and Barbra Streisand in "Funny Girl", (4) Jack Albertson in "The Subject Was Roses", (5) Ruth Gordon in "Rosemary's Baby", (6) Carol Reed for "Oliver!", (7) Onna White for "Oliver!" choreography, John Chambers for "Planet of the Apes" make-up, (8) "War and Peace."

1969: (1) "Midnight Cowboy", (2) John Wayne in "True Grit", (3) Maggie Smith in "The Prime of Miss Jean Brodie", (4) Gig Young in "They Shoot Horses, Don't They?", (5) Goldie Hawn in "Cactus Flower", (6) John Schlesinger for "Midnight Cowboy", (7) Cary Grant, (8) "Z."

1970: (1) "Patton", (2) George C. Scott in "Patton", (3) Glenda Jackson in "Women in Love," (4) John Mills in "Ryan's Daughter," (5) Helen Hayes in "Airport," (6) Franklin J. Schaffner for "Patton," (7) Lillian Gish, Orson Welles, (8) "Investigation of a Citizen above Suspicion."

1971: (1) "The French Connection," (2) Gene Hackman in "The French Connection," (3) Jane Fonda in "Klute," (4) Ben Johnson in "The Last Picture Show," (5) Cloris Leachman in "The Last Picture Show," (6) William Friedkin for "The French Connection," (7) Charles Chaplin, (8) "The Garden of the Finzi-Continis."

1972: (1) "The Godfather," (2) Marlon Brando in "The Godfather," (3) Liza Minelli in "Cabaret," (4) Joel Grey in "Cabaret," (5) Eileen Heckart in "Butterflies Are Free," (6) Bob Fosse for "Cabaret," (7) Edward G. Robinson, (8) "The Discreet Charm of the Bourgeoisie."

Maggie Smith

Paul Scofield

Barbra Streisand

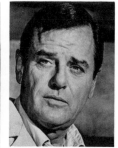

Gig Young

Elizabeth Taylor

FOREIGN FILMS OF 1973

LAST TANGO IN PARIS

(UNITED ARTISTS) Producer, Alberto Grimaldi; Direction and Story, Bernardo Bertolucci; Screenplay, Bernardo Bertolucci, Vranco Arcalli; Editor, Vranco Arcalli; Photography, Vittorio Storaro; Music, Gato Barbieri; Designer, Maria Paola Maino; Costumes, Gitt Magrini; Assistant Directors, Fernand Moszkowicz, Jean David Lefebvre; In color; Rated X; 125 minutes; February release.

CAST

Paul	Marlon Brando
Jeanne	Maria Schneider
Concierge	Darling Legitimus
Tom	Jean-Pierre Leaud
TV Script Girl	Catherine Sola
TV Cameraman	Mauro Marchetti
TV Sound Engineer	Dan Diament
TV Assistant Cameraman	Peter Schommer
Catherine	Catherine Allegret
Monique	Marie-Helene Breillat
Mouchette	Catherine Breillat
Small Mover	Stephane Kosiak
Tall Mover	Gerard Lepennec
Rosa's Mother	Maria Michi
Rosa	Veronica Lazare
Olympia	Luce Marquand
Bible Salesman	Michel Delahaye
Miss Blandish	Laura Betti
Marcel	Massimo Girotti
Prostitute	Giovanna Galletti
Her Customer	Armand Ablanalp
Jeanne's Mother	Gitt Magrini
Barge Captain	Jean Luc Bideau
Christine	Rachel Kesterber
President of Tango Jury	Mimi Pinson
Tango Orchestra Leader	Ramon Mendizabal

Right: Marlon Brando

Jean-Pierre Leaud, Maria Schneider

Maria Schneider, also top with
Marlon Brando

Marlon Brando, Maria Schneider
Above: Catherine Allegret, Marlon Brando

LADY CAROLINE LAMB

(UNITED ARTISTS) Producer, Fernando Ghia; Direction and Screenplay, Robert Bolt; Executive Producer, Franco Cristaldi; Associate Producer, Bernard Williams; Editor, Norman Savage; Photography, Oswald Morris; Art Director, Carmen Dillon; Costumes, David Walker; Assistant Directors, David Tringham, Michael Stevenson; Music, Richard Rodney Bennett; Dance Movement, Eleanor Fazan; In Color; Rated PG; 123 minutes; February release.

CAST

Lady Caroline Lamb	Sarah Miles
William Lamb	Jon Finch
Lord Byron	Richard Chamberlain
Canning	John Mills
Lady Melbourne	Margaret Leighton
Lady Bessborough	Pamela Brown
Miss Milbanke	Silvia Monti
The King	Ralph Richardson
Duke of Wellington	Laurence Olivier
Government Minister	Peter Bull
Mr. Potter	Charles Carson
Lady Pont	Sonia Dresdel
St. John	Nicholas Field
Girl in blue	Felicity Gibson
Apothecary	Robert Harris
Radical Member	Richard Hurndall
Irish Housekeeper	Paddy Joyce
Benson	Bernard Kay
Miss Fairfax	Janet Key
Coachman	Mario Maranzana
ADC to Wellington	Robert Mill
Restaurant Functionary	Norman Mitchell
Murray	John Moffatt
Agent	Trevor Peacock
Mrs. Butler	Maureen Pryor
Lady Holland	Fanny Rowe
Buckham	Stephen Sheppard
Black Pug	Roy Stewart
Admiral	Ralph Truman
Lord Holland	Michael Wilding

Left: Jon Finch, Sarah Miles, John Mills
Top: Sarah Miles, Richard Chamberlain

Richard Chamberlain, Margaret Leighton

Laurence Olivier, Sarah Miles

BAXTER

(NATIONAL GENERAL) Producer, Arthur Lewis; Director, Lionel Jeffries; Executive Producers, Howard G. Barnes, John L. Hargreaves; Screenplay, Reginald Rose; Music, Michael J. Lewis; Photography, Geoffrey Unsworth; Editor, Teddy Darvas; Art Director, Anthony Pratt; Assistant Director, Kip Gowans; An Anglo-Emi/Group W presentation in color; Rated PG; 105 minutes; February release.

CAST

Dr. Clemm	Patricia Neal
Roger Tunnell	Jean-Pierre Cassel
Chris Bentley	Britt Ekland
Mrs. Baxter	Lynn Carlin
Rober Baxter	Scott Jacoby
Nemo	Sally Thomsett
Mr. Rawling	Paul Eddington
Mr. Baxter	Paul Maxwell
Mr. Walsh	Ian Thomson
Mr. Fishie	Ronald Leigh-Hunt
Mrs. Newman	Frances Bennett
George	George Tovey

Top: Lynn Carlin, Patricia Neal
Below: Britt Ekland, Scott Jacoby,
Jean-Pierre Cassell Top Right:
Jean-Pierre Cassell, Britt Ekland

Patricia Neal, Scott Jacoby, also
above with Lynn Carlin

THE VAULT OF HORROR

(CINERAMA) Producers, Max J. Rosenberg, Milton Subotsky; Executive Producer, Charles W. Fries; Production Executive, Paul Thompson; Screen play, Milton Subotsky; Director, Roy Ward Baker; Assistant Director, Anthony Waye; Photography, Denys Coop; Art Director, Tony Curtis; Editor, Oswald Hafenrichter; A Metromedia/Amicus production in color; Rating R; 93 minutes; March release.

CAST

"Midnight Mess"
Rogers	Daniel Massey
Donna	Anna Massey
Clive	Mike Pratt
Old Waiter	Erik Chitty
Waiter	Jerold Wells

"Bargain in Death"
Maitland	Michael Craig
Alex	Edward Judd
Tom	Robin Nedwell
Jerry	Geoffrey Davies
Gravedigger	Arthur Mullard

"This Trick'll Kill You"
Sebastian	Curt Jurgens
Inez	Dawn Addams
Indian Girl	Jasmina Hilton
Fakir	Ishaq Bux

"The Neat Job"
Critchit	Terry Thomas
Eleanor	Glynis Johns
Jane	Marianne Stone
Wilson	John Forbes-Robertson

"Drawn and Quartered"
Moore	Tom Baker
Diltant	Denholm Elliott
Breedley	Terence Alexander
Gaskill	John Witty

Top Right: Tom Baker, Denholm Elliott

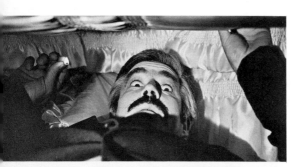

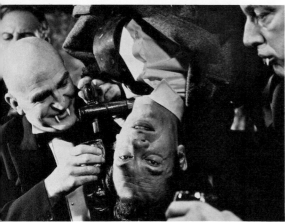

Daniel Massey
Above: Michael Craig

Terry-Thomas, Glynis Johns
Above: Curt Jurgens

WHITE SISTER

(COLUMBIA) Producer, Carlo Ponti; Director, Alberto Lattuada; Executive Producer, Gianni Cecchin; Screenplay, Iaia Fiastri, Alberto Lattuada, Tonino Guerra, Ruggero Maccari; Story, Tonino Guerra, Ruggero Maccari; Photography, Iafio Contini; Music, Fred Bongusto; Art Director, Vincenzo Del Prato; Costumes, Mario Ambrosino; Editor, Sergio Montanari; Assistant Director, Mino Giarda; Color; Rated PG; 96 minutes; March release.

CAST

Sister Germana	Sophia Loren
Annibale Pezzi	Adriano Celentano
Chief Physician	Fernando Rey
Guido	Juan Luis Galiardo
Libyan Brigadiere	Luis Marin
Dr. Arrighi	Giuseppe Maffioli
Dr. Filippini	Sergio Fasanelli
Sister Teresa	Pilar Gomez Ferrer
Sister Caterina	Patrizia de Clara
Rosa	Teresa Rabal
Martina	Valentine
Mrs. Ricci	Tina Aumont
Stolenghi	Bruno Biasibetti
Igino	Antonio Alfonso
Valenzani	Aldo Farina
Sister Germana as a child	Alessandra Mussolini
Attilio	Ezio Curti
Nin	Franio Curti
Chiacchiera	Bruno Sciponi
Giacomino	Massimiliano Filoni
Giacomino's mother	Maria Marchi
Licia	Francesca Modigliani
Ina	Carla Galletti
Spigni	Angelo Bellia
Quinto	Enzo Cannalvale
Policemen	Ettore Bussoli, Enzo Turchini
Milcare	Guido Spadea
Militario	Mario Comaschi
Cook	Dori Dorika
Arab Girl Mother	Merriana Henrique
Bandits	Gianni Magni, Attilio Meanti, Carlo Gaddi

Top: Maria Laura de Franceschi,
Sophia Loren

Sophia Loren, also top
with Adriano Celentano

155

Nicole Courcel, Lino Ventura

MONEY, MONEY, MONEY

(CINERAMA) Executive Producer, Alexandre Mnouchkine; Direction and Screenplay, Claude Le Louch; Dialogue, Claude Le Louch, Pierre Uytterhoeven; Assistant Director, Claude Pinoteau; Photography, Jean Collomb; Editor, Janine Boublil; Music, Francis Lai; A GSF presentation in color; Rated R; 115 minutes; March release.

CAST

Lino	Lino Ventura
Jacques	Jacques Brel
Simon	Charles Denner
Johnny Hallyday	Johnny Hallyday
Charlot	Charles Gerard
Aldo	Aldo Maccione
Nicole	Nicole Courcel
Femme de L'Ambassadeur	Prudence Harrington
L'Ambassadeur	Andre Falcon
L'Avocat General	Gerard Sire
Avocat de la Defense	Yves Robert
Fils de Lino	Xavier Gelin
Ernesto Juarez	Jean-Louis Bunuel

And Michele Alet, Madly Bamy, Sophie Boudet, Annie Ho, Annie Kerani

Top: Lino Ventura, Aldo Maccione, Charles Gerard, Charles Denner, Jacques Brel Center: (L)Lino Ventura, Jacques Brel (R) Jean-Louis Bunuel

THEATRE OF BLOOD

(UNITED ARTISTS) Producers, John Kohn, Stanley Mann; Executive Producers, Gustave Berne, Sam Jaffe; Director, Douglas Hickox; Screenplay, Anthony Greville-Bell; Music, Michael J. Lewis; Photography, Wolfgang Suschitzky; Assistant Director, Dominic Fulford; Designer, Michael Seymour; Costumes, Michael Baldwin; Editor, Malcolm Cooke; Choreography, Tutte Lemkow; In color; Rated R; 104 minutes; April release.

CAST

Edward Lionheart	Vincent Price
Edwina Lionheart	Diana Rigg
Peregrine Devlin	Ian Hendry
Trevor Dickman	Harry Andrews
Miss Chloe Moon	Coral Browne
Oliver Larding	Robert Coote
Solomon Psaltery	Jack Hawkins
George Maxwell	Michael Hordern
Horace Sprout	Arthur Lowe
Meredith Merridew	Robert Morley
Hector Snipe	Dennis Price
Mrs. Psaltery	Diana Dors
Mrs. Sprout	Joan Hickson
Mrs. Maxwell	Renee Asherson
Rosemary	Madeline Smith
Inspector Boot	Milo O'Shea
Sgt. Dogge	Eric Sykes
Agnes	Brigid Eric Bates
Police Photographer	Tony Calvin
Policemen	Bunny Reed, Peter Thornton
Meths Drinkers	Tutte Lemkow, Jack Maguire,

Joyce Graham, John Gilpin, Eric Francis, Sally Gilmore, Stanley Bates, Declan Mulholland

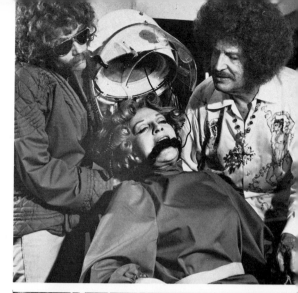

Right: Harry Andrews, Vincent Price, Diana Rigg
Top: Diana Rigg, Coral Browne, Vincent Price

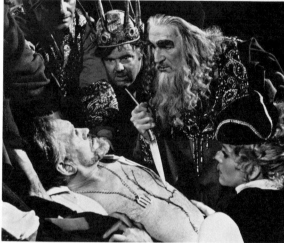

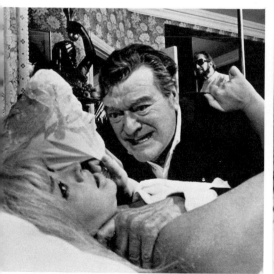

Diana Dors, Jack Hawkins, Vincent Price

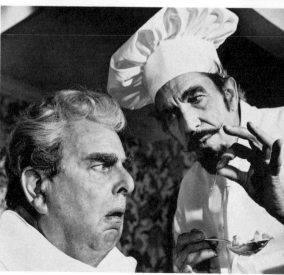

Robert Morley, Vincent Price

THE NELSON AFFAIR

(UNIVERSAL) Producer, Hal B. Wallis; Director, James Cellan Jones; Screenplay, Terence Rattigan; Based on his play "A Bequest to the Nation"; Photography, Gerry Fisher; Editor, Anne V. Coates; Music, Michel Legrand; In Panavision and Technicolor; Rated PG; 118 minutes; April release.

CAST

Lady Hamilton	Glenda Jackson
Lord Nelson	Peter Finch
Captain Hardy	Michael Jayston
Lord Minto	Anthony Quayle
Lady Nelson	Margaret Leighton
George Matcham, Jr.	Dominic Guard
George Matcham, Sr.	Nigel Stock
Catherine Matcham	Barbara Leigh-Hunt
Lord Barham	Roland Culver
Admiral Villeneuve	Andre Maranne
Rev. William Nelson	Richard Mathews
Sarah Nelson	Liz Ashley
Capt. Blackwood	John Nolan

Right: Peter Finch, Glenda Jackson

Peter Finch, Glenda Jackson Above: Clelia Matania, Anthony Quayle, Glenda Jackson

John Nolan, Peter Finch, Glenda Jackson Above: Peter Finch (L), Glenda Jackson, Dominic Guard

LOVE AND PAIN
and the whole damn thing

(COLUMBIA) Producer-Director, Alan J. Pakula; Screenplay, Alvin Sargent; Associate Producer, Thomas Pevsner; Art Director, Enrique Alarcon; Editor, Russell Lloyd; Photography, Geoffrey Unsworth; Assistant Director, Miquel Gil; Music, Michael Small; Rated R; 110 minutes; April release.

CAST

Lila Fisher	Maggie Smith
Walter Elbertson	Timothy Bottoms
The Duke	Don Jaime de Mora y Aragon
Spanish Gentleman	Emiliano Redondo
Dr. Elbertson	Charles Baxter
Mrs. Elbertson	Margaret Modlin
Melanie Elbertson	May Heatherley
Carl	Lloyd Brimhall
Dr. Edelheidt	Elmer Modlin
Tourist Guide	Andres Monreal

Right: Maggie Smith, Timothy Bottoms

Timothy Bottoms, Maggie Smith
Above: Maggie Smith, Emiliano Redondo

Jaime de Mora y Aragon, Maggie Smith
Above: Timothy Bottoms, Maggie Smith

STATE OF SIEGE

(CINEMA5) Producer, Jacques Perrin; Director, Constantin Costa-Gavras; Screenplay, Franco Solinas, Constantine Costa-Gavras; Music, Mikis Theodorakis; Photography, Pierre William Glenn; Designer, Jacques D'Ovidio; Editor, Francoise Bonnot; Assistant Director, Christian De Chalonge; A Cinema 10 and Reggane Films production; 120 minutes; April release.

CAST

Philip Michael Santore	Yves Montand
Captain Lopez	Renato Salvatori
Carlos Ducas	O. E. Hasse
Hugo	Jacques Weber
Este	Jean-Luc Bideau
Mrs. Philip Santore	Evangeline Peterson
Minister of Internal Security	Maurice Teynac
Woman Senator	Yvette Etievant
Minister of Foreign Affairs	Harald Wolff
President of the Republic	Nemesio Antunes
Deupty Fabbri	Andre Falcon
Fontana	Mario Montilles
Lee	Jerry Brouer
Journalist	Jean-Francois Gobbi
Spokesman for Internal Security	Eugenio Guzman
Dean of Law Faculty	Maurice Jacquemont
Romero	Roberto Navarette
Student	Gloria Lass
Manuel	Alejandro Cohen
Alicia	Martha Contreras

Top: Maurice Teynac
Below: Yvette Etievant

Yves Montand, also top
Above: O. E. Hasse (R)

160

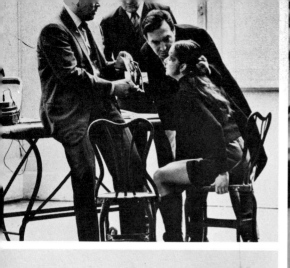

Yves Montand, Jacques Weber
Above: Jean-Luc Bideau

Yves Montand
Top: Jacques Weber

BROTHER SUN, SISTER MOON

(PARAMOUNT) Producer, Luciano Perugia; Director, Franco Zeffirelli; Screenplay, Suso Cecchi d'Amico, Kenneth Ross, Lina Wertmuller, Franco Zefferelli; Photography, Ennio Guarniere; Editors, Reginald Hills, John Rushton; Music, Donovan; Designer, Lorenzo Mongiardino; Art Director, Gianni Quaranta; Assistant Director, Carlo Cotti; A Euro International production; In Technicolor; Rated PG; 121 minutes; April release.

CAST

Francesco	Graham Faulkner
Clare	Judi Bowker
Pope Innocent III	Alec Guinness
Bernardo	Leigh Lawson
Paolo	Kenneth Cranham
Silvestro	Michael Feast
Giocondo	Nicholas Willatt
Pica	Valentina Cortese
Pietro di Bernardone	Lee Montague
Bishop Guido	John Sharp
Consul	Adolfo Celi
Deodato	Francesco Guerrieri

Left: Graham Faulkner

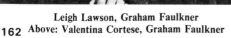

Leigh Lawson, Graham Faulkner
162 Above: Valentina Cortese, Graham Faulkner

Judi Bowker, Graham Faulkner
Above: Graham Faulkner, Alec Guinness

THE DAY OF THE JACKAL

(UNIVERSAL) Producer, John Woolf, Director, Fred Zinnemann; Co-Producers, David Deutsch, Julien Derode; Screenplay, Kenneth Ross; From book by Frederick Forsyth; Photography, Jean Tournier; Editor, Ralph Kemplen; Music, Georges Delerus; Designers, Willy Holt, Ernest Archer; Assistant Directors, Louis Pitzele, Peter Price; Costumes, Elizabeth Haffenden, Joan Bridge, Rosine Delamare; An Anglo-French Co-Production by Warwich Film Productions Ltd. and Universal Productions France; In Technicolor; Rated PG; 142 minutes; May release.

CAST

"The Jackal"	Edward Fox
Lloyd	Terence Alexander
Colonel Rolland	Michel Auclair
The Minister	Alan Badel
Inspector Thomas	Tony Britton
Casson	Denis Carey
The President	Adrien Cayla-Legrand
Gunsmith	Cyril Cusack
General Colbert	Maurice Denham
Interrogator	Vernon Dobtcheff
Pascal	Jacques Francois
Denise	Olga Georges-Picot
Flavigny	Raymond Gerome
St. Clair	Barrie Ingham
Caron	Derek Jacobi
Lebel	Michel Lonsdale
Wolenski	Jean Martin
Forger	Ronald Pickup
Colonel Rodin	Eric Porter
Bernard	Anton Rodgers
Colette	Delphine Seyrig
Mallinson	Donald Sinden
Bastien-Thiry	Jean Sorel
Montclair	David Swift
Berthier	Timothy West

Top: Olga Georges-Picot, Derek Jacobi, Michel Lonsdale Below: Edward Fox, Delphine Seyrig Top Right: Edward Fox, Eric Porter, Donald Swift, Dennis Carey

Edward Fox
Above: Jean Martin

A DOLL'S HOUSE

(PARAMOUNT) Producer, Hillard Elkins; Director, Patrick Garland; Screenplay, Christopher Hampton; Based on play by Henrik Ibsen; Photography, Arthur Ibbetson; Editor, John Glen; Music, John Barry; Art Director, Elliott Scott; Costumes, Beatrice Dawson; Assistant Director, Peter Price; In color; Rated G; 95 minutes; May release.

CAST

Nora Helmer	Claire Bloom
Torvald Helmer	Anthony Hopkins
Dr. Rank	Ralph Richardson
Krogstad	Denholm Elliott
Kristine Linde	Anna Massey
Anne-Marie	Edith Evans
Helen	Helen Blatch
Emmy	Stafanie Summerfield
Ivar	Mark Summerfield
Bob	Kimberley Hampton
Old Woman	Daphne Rigg

Right: Edith Evans, Claire Bloom

Claire Bloom, Denholm Elliott
Above: Ralph Richardson, Anthony Hopkins,
Claire Bloom

Claire Bloom, also above
with Anna Massey

164

FISTS OF FURY

(**NATIONAL GENERAL**) Producer, Raymond Chow; Direction and Screenplay, Lo Wei; Art Director, Chien Hsin; Photography, Chen Ching Chu; Assistant Producers, Liu Liang Hua, Lei Chen; Assistant Directors, Chin Yao Chang, Chen Cho; In color; Rated R; 103 minutes; May release.

CAST

Cheng	Bruce Lee
Mei	Maria Yi
Mi	Hang Ying Chieh
Mi's son	Tony Liu
Prostitute	Malalene
Chen	Paul Tien

and Miao Ke Hsiu, Li Quin, Chin Shan, Li Hua Sze

Right: Bruce Lee

Bruce Lee

Bruce Lee

165

A WARM DECEMBER

(NATIONAL GENERAL) Producer, Melville Tucker; Director, Sidney Poitier; Screenplay, Lawrence Roman; Photography, Paul Beeson; Editors, Pembroke Herring, Peter Pitt; Art Director, Elliot Scott; Assistant Directors, David Tomblin, Brian Cook; Music, Coleridge-Taylor Perkinson; A Verdon production; First Artists presentation; In color; Rated PG; 103 minutes; May release.

CAST

Matt Younger	Sidney Poitier
Catherine	Esther Anderson
Stefanie	Yvette Curtis
Henry Barlow	George Baker
Myomo	Johnny Sekka
George Oswandu	Earl Cameron
Marsha Barlow	Hilary Crane
Burberry	John Beardmore
General Kuznovski	Milos Kirek
Carol and Janie	Ann and Stephanie Smith
Singer in club	Letta Mbulu

Left: Sidney Poitier, Johnny Sekka, Earl Cameron
Top: Esther Anderson, Yvette Curtis, Sidney Poitier

Esther Anderson, Sidney Poitier

Sidney Poitier

LIVE AND LET DIE

(UNITED ARTISTS) Producers, Albert R. Broccoli, Harry Saltzman; Director, Guy Hamilton; Screenplay, Tom Mankiewicz; Music, George Martin; Title Song, Paul and Linda McCartney; Performed by "Wings" and Mr. McCartney; Photography, Ted Moore; Assistant Director, Derek Cracknell; Art Director, Syd Cain; Editors, Bert Bates, Raymond Poulton, John Shirley; Choreographer, Geoffrey Holder; Costumes, Julie Harris; In color; Rated PG; 121 minutes; June release.

CAST

James Bond	Roger Moore
Kananga/Mr. Big	Yaphet Kotto
Solitaire	Jane Seymour
Sheriff Pepper	Clifton James
Tee Hee	Julius W. Harris
Baron Samedi	Geoffrey Holder
Leiter	David Hedison
Rosie	Gloria Hendry
"M"	Bernard Lee
Moneypenny	Lois Maxwell
Adam	Tommy Lane
Whisper	Earl Jolly Brown
Quarrel	Roy Stewart
Strutter	Lon Satton
Cab Driver	Arnold Williams
Mrs. Bell	Ruth Kempf
Charlie	Joie Chitwood
Beautiful Girl	Madeline Smith
Dambala	Michael Ebbin
Sales Girl	Kubi Chaza
Singer	B. J. Arnau

Top: Roger Moore, also right
with Jane Seymour

Roger Moore, Gloria Hendry

O LUCKY MAN!

(WARNER BROTHERS) Producers, Michael Medwin, Lindsay
Anderson; Director, Lindsay Anderson; Screenplay, David Sherwin;
Based on idea by Malcolm McDowell; Photography, Miroslav Ond-
ricek; Designer, Jocelyn Herbert; Art Director, Alan Withy; Edi-
tors, Tom Priestley, David Gladwell; Associate Producer, Basil
Keys; Music and Songs, Alan Price; Assistant Director, Derek
Cracknell; A Memorial Enterprises/Sam Film production; In Tech-
nicolor; Rated R; 186 minutes; June release.

CAST

Mick	Malcolm McDowell
Sir James/Monty	Ralph Richardson
Duff/Johnson/Munda	Arthur Lowe
Gloria/Mme. Paillard/Mrs. Richards	Rachel Roberts
Patricia	Helen Mirren
Tea Lady/Neighbor	Dandy Nichols
Neighbor/Usher/Sister Hallet	Mona Washbourne
Factory Chairman/Prison Governor	Peter Jeffrey
Stewart/Millar/Meths Drinker	Graham Crowden
Jenkins/Interrogator/Salvation Army Major	Philip Stone
Himself	Alan Price
Stone/Steiger/Executive/Warder	Wallas Eaton
M.C./Warner/Male Nurse	Warren Clarke
Barlow/Superintendent	Bill Owen
Oswald	Edward Judd
Mrs. Naidu	Pearl Nunez
Mary Ball/Vicar's Wife	Mary Macleod
William/Interrogator/Released Prisoner	Michael Bangerter
Duke of Belminster/Captain/Power	
Station Technician	Michael Medwin

Top: Helen Mirren, Malcolm McDowell

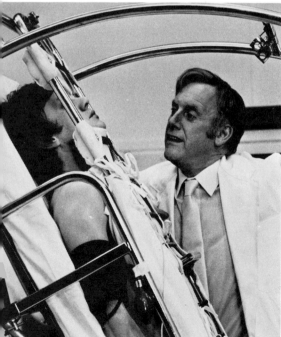

Malcolm McDowell, Graham Crowden

Alan Price Top: Pearl Nunez, Malcolm
McDowell, Arthur Lowe, Frank Cousins, Ralph
Richardson

Malcolm McDowell

169

PLAYTIME

(CONTINENTAL) Producer-Director, Jacques Tati; Screenplay, Jacques Tati, J. Lagrange; Photography, Jean Badal, Andreas Winding; Designer, Eugene Roman; Editor, Gerrard Pollicand; A Specta Films production; In Eastmancolor; 108 minutes; June release.

CAST

Mr. Hulot	Jacques Tati
Young Stranger	Barbara Dennek
Young Stranger's Friend	Jacqueline Lecomte
Secretary	Valerie Camille
Eyeglasses Saleswoman	France Rumilly
Customer Strand	France Delahalle
Ladies at Lampost	Laure Paillette, Colette Proust
Mrs. Giffard	Erika Dentzler
Girl at cloakroom	Yvette Ducreux
Mrs. Schultz' Companion	Rita Maiden
Singer	Nicole Ray

Right: Jacques Tati

Barbara Dennek, Jacques Tati

THE HIRELING

(COLUMBIA) Producer, Ben Arbeid; Executive Producer, Terence Baker; Director, Alan Bridges; Screenplay, Wolf Mankowitz; Based on novel by L. P. Hartley; Music, Marc Wilkinson; Photography, Michael Reed; Designer, Natasha Kroll; Editor, Peter Weatherley; Costumes, Phyllis Dalton; Assistant Director, Simon Relph; A World Film Services/Champion production in color; Rated PG; 95 minutes; June release.

CAST

Leadbetter	Robert Shaw
Lady Franklin	Sarah Miles
Cantrip	Peter Egan
Mother	Elizabeth Sellars
Connie	Carolin Mortimer
Mrs. Hansen	Patricia Lawrence
Edith	Petra Markham
Davis	Ian Hogg
Doreen	Christine Hargreaves

and Lyndon Brook, Alison Leggatt

Right: Robert Shaw, Sarah Miles

Robert Shaw, Sarah Miles

A TOUCH OF CLASS

(AVCO EMBASSY) Producer-Director, Melvin Frank; Screenplay, Melvin Frank, Jack Rose; Photography, Austin Dempster; Editor, Bill Butler; Music, John Cameron; Songs, George Barrie, Sammy Cahn; Designer, Terry Marsh; Art Director, Alan Tompkins; Assistant Director, Simon Relph; A Brut Productions presentation with Joseph E. Levine; In Technicolor; Rated PG; 106 minutes; June release.

CAST

Steve Blackburn	George Segal
Vicki Allessio	Glenda Jackson
Walter Menkes	Paul Sorvino
Gloria Blackburn	Hildegard Neil
Wendell Thompson	Cec Linder
Patty Menkes	K. Callan
Marsha Thompson	Mary Barclay
Cecil	Michael Elwyn
Night Hotel Manager	Nadim Sawalha
Derek	Ian Thompson
Miss Ramos	Eve Karpf
Dr. Alvarez	David De Keyser
Dora French	Gaye Brown

Top: George Segal, Glenda Jackson
1973 Academy Award for Best Actress
was won by Glenda Jackson

George Segal, Glenda Jackson

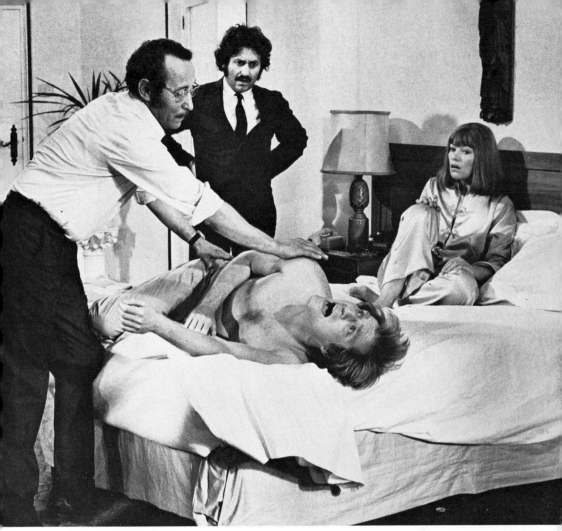

**George Segal, Glenda Jackson Top: David
DeKeyser, Nadim Sawalha, Segal, Jackson**

George Segal, Glenda Jackson

THE MACKINTOSH MAN

(WARNER BROTHERS) Producer, John Foreman; Director, John Huston; Screenplay, Walter Hill; Based on novel "The Freedom Trap" by Desmond Bagley; Photography, Oswald Morris; Designer, Terry Marsh; Editor, Russell Lloyd; Art Director, Alan Tomkins; Associate Producer, William Hill; Music, Maurice Jarre; Assistant Director, Colin Brewer; In Technicolor; Rated PG; 100 minutes; July release

CAST

Rearden	Paul Newman
Mrs. Smith	Dominique Sanda
Sir George Wheeler	James Mason
Mackintosh	Harry Andrews
Slade	Ian Bannen
Brown	Michael Hordern
Soames—Trevelyan	Nigel Patrick
Brunskill	Peter Vaughan
Judge	Roland Culver
Taafe	Percy Herbert
Jack Summers	Robert Lang
Gerda	Jenny Runacre
Buster	John Bindon
Prosecutor	Hugh Manning
Malta Police Commissioner	Wolfe Morris
O'Donovan	Noel Purcell
Jervis	Donald Webster
Palmer	Keith Bell
Warder	Niall MacGinnis

Left: Dominique Sanda, Paul Newman

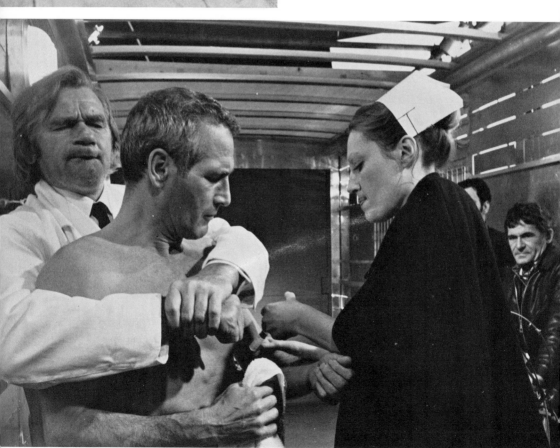

Percy Herbert, Paul Newman, Jenny Runacre

Paul Newman, Eric Mason Above: James Mason,
Dominique Sanda Top: Newman, Sanda

Paul Newman Above: James
Mason, Harry Andrews

175

DEAF SMITH AND JOHNNY EARS

(MGM) Producers, Joseph Janni, Luciano Perugia; Director, Paolo Cavara; Screenplay, Harry Essex, Oscar Saul; Music, Daniele Patucchi; Songs sung by Ann Collin; Photography, Tonino Delli Colli; Designer, Francesco Calabrese; Editor, Mario Morra; Costumes, Pasquale Nigro; Assistant Director, Fabrizio Sergenti; In Technicolor; Rated PG; 91 minutes; July release.

CAST

Erasmus "Deaf" Smith	Anthony Quinn
Johnny Ears	Franco Nero
Susie	Pamela Tiffin
General Morton	Franco Graziosi
Hester	Ira Furstenberg
Hoffman	Renato Romano

and Adolfo Lastretti, Antonio Faa Di Bruno, Francesca Benedetti, Cristina Airoldi, Romano Puppo, Franca Sciutto, Enrico Casadei, Lorenzo Fineschi, Mario Carra, Georgio Dolfin, Luciano Rossi, Margherita Trentini, Tom Felleghy, Fulvio Grimaldi, Paolo Pierani

Top: Anthony Quinn Below: Franco Nero,
Pamela Tiffin Top Left: Anthony Quinn

Franco Nero, Pamela Tiffin
Above: Anthony Quinn, Franco Nero

THE TALL BLOND MAN WITH ONE BLACK SHOE

(**Cinema 5**) Producers, Alain Poire, Yves Robert; Director, Yves Robert; Screenplay, Yves Robert, Francis Veber; Photography, Rene Mathelin; Editor, Ghislaine Desjonqueres; Music, Vladimir Kosma; Rated PG; 90 minutes; August release.

CAST

Francois	Pierre Richard
Milan	Bernard Blier
Toulouse	Jean Rochefort
Christine	Mireille Darc
Maurice	Jean Carmet
Paulette	Colette Castel
Perrache	Paul Le Person
Botrel	Jean Obe
Georghiu	Robert Castel
M. Boudart	Robert Caccia
Faux Livreur	Robert Dalban
Poucet	Jean Saudray
Mme. Boudart	Arlette Balkis
Chef d'orchestre	Yves Robert

Right: Pierre Richard

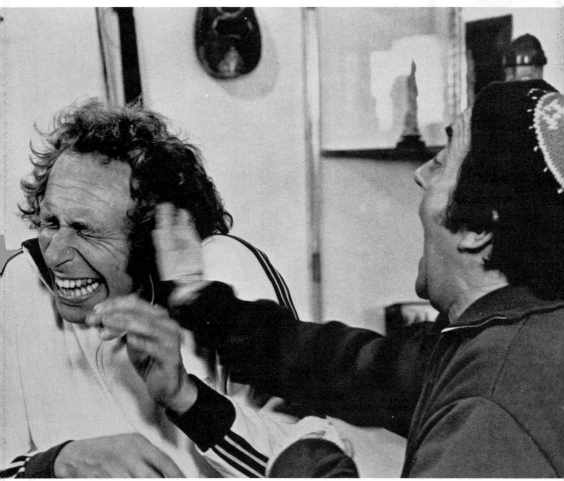

Pierre Richard (L)

NIGHT WATCH

(AVCO EMBASSY) Producers, Martin Poll, George W. George, Barnard Straus; Director, Brian G. Hutton; Screenplay, Tony Williamson; Additional dialogue, Evan Jones; Based on play by Lucille Fletcher; Photography, Billie Williams; Art Director, Peter Murton; Associate Producer, David White; Editor, John Jympson; Music, John Cameron; Costumes, Valentino; Presented by Joseph E. Levine and Brut Productions; In Panavision and Technicolor; Rated PG; 105 minutes; August release.

CAST

Ellen Wheeler	Elizabeth Taylor
John Wheeler	Laurence Harvey
Sarah Cooke	Billie Whitelaw
Appleby	Robert Lang
Tony	Tony Britton
Inspector Walker	Bill Dean
Sergeant Norris	Michael Danvers-Walker
Dolores	Rosario Serrano
Secretary	Pauline Jameson
Girl in car	Linda Hayden
Carl	Kevin Colson
Florist	Laon Maybanke

Left: Elizabeth Taylor

Laurence Harvey, Elizabeth Taylor, Billie Whitelaw

Elizabeth Taylor, Laurence Harvey, also top
Above: Elizabeth Taylor, Billie Whitelaw

Elizabeth Taylor, also above
with Robert Lang

DAY FOR NIGHT

(WARNER BROTHERS) Director, Francois Truffaut; Screenplay, Mr. Truffaut, Jean-Louis Richard, Suzanne Schiffman; Executive Producer, Marcel Berbert; Photography, Pierre-William Glenn; Editors, Yann Dedet, Martine Barraque; Music, Georges Delerue; In color; 116 minutes; Rated PG; September release.

CAST

Ferrand	Francois Truffaut
Julie	Jacqueline Bisset
Alphonse	Jean-Pierre Leaud
Severine	Valentina Cortese
Alexandre	Jean-Pierre Aumont
Lilianna	Dani
Stacey	Alexandra Stewart
Bertrand	Jean Champion

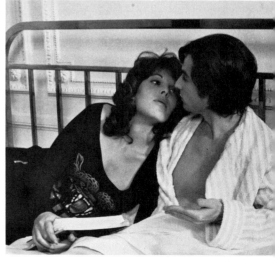

Dani, Jean-Pierre Leaud

Top: Jean Champion, Francois Truffaut (R)

*1973 Academy Award for Best Foreign
Language Film*

Jean-Pierre Leaud, Jean-Pierre Aumont, Jacqueline Bisset, Valentina Cortese
Top: (L) Jacqueline Bisset, Jean-Pierre Aumont, (R) Leaud , Dani
Center: (L) Aumont, Leaud (R) Jacqueline Bisset

181

LE RETOUR D'AFRIQUE

(NEW YORKER) Produced, Directed, and Written by Alain Tanner; Photography, Renato Berta, Carlo Varini; Music, J. S. Bach; A Group 5—Filman Thrope, NEF Paris production; In black and white; 108 minutes; September release.

CAST

Francoise	Josee Destoop
Vincent	Francois Marthouret
Emilio	Juliet Berto
Girl	Anne Wiazemsky

Left: Josee Destoop, Francois Marthouret

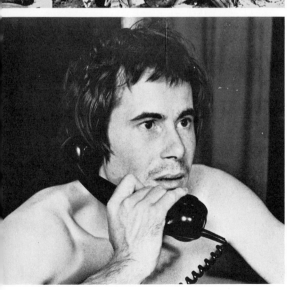

Francois Marthouret, also above left

Francois Marthouret, Josee Destoop

A KING IN NEW YORK

(CLASSIC ENTERTAINMENT) Produced, Directed, and Written by Charles Chaplin; Rated G; 105 minutes; December release. First released in England in September 1957.

CAST

King Shadhov	Charles Chaplin
Ann Kay	Dawn Addams
The Ambassador	Oliver Johnston
Queen Irene	Maxine Audley
Lawyer Green	Harry Green
Headmaster	Phil Brown
Macabee Senior	John McLaren
School Superintendent	Allan Gifford
Night Club Vocalist	Shani Wallace
Night Club Vocalist	Jay Nichols
Rupert Macabee	Michael Chaplin
Mr. Cromwell	John Ingram
Mr. Johnson	Sidney James
Prime Minister	Jerry Desmonde
Lift Boy	Robert Arden
Comedy Act	Lauri Lupina-Lane, George Truzzi

Top: Charles Chaplin (C), also below,
and top right

Charles Chaplin, also above
with Dawn Addams

HENRY VIII AND HIS SIX WIVES

(ANGLO EMI) Producer, Roy Baird; Executive Producer, Mark Shivas; Director, Waris Hussein; Screenplay, Ian Thorne; Photography, Peter Suschitzky; Music, David Munrow; Editor, John Bloom; Designer, Roy Stannard; Costumes, John Bloomfield; Assistant Director, Derek Cracknell; Choreographer, Terry Gilbert; Presented by Nat Cohen; In Technicolor; Rated PG; 125 minutes; September release.

CAST

King Henry VIII	Keith Michell
Thomas Cromwell	Donald Pleasence
Anne Boleyn	Charlotte Rampling
Jane Seymour	Jane Asher
Katherine of Aragon	Frances Cuka
Catherine Howard	Lynne Frederick
Anne of Cleves	Jenny Bos
Catherine Parr	Barbara Leigh-Hunt
Norfolk	Michael Gough
Suffolk	Brian Blessed
Thomas More	Michael Goodliffe
Cranmer	Bernard Hepton
Gardiner	Garfield Morgan
Wolsey	John Bryans
Wriothesley	John Bennett
Fisher	Peter Madden
Mary	Sarah Long
Warham	Richard Warner
Sir Ralph Ellerker	Michael Godfrey
Edward Seymour	Michael Byrne
Thomas Seymour	Peter Clay
Thomas Culpepper	Robin Sachs
Chapuys	Nicholas Amer

and Basil Clarke (Abbot), Alan Rowe (French Ambassador), Clive Merrison (Weston), David Baillie (Norris), Mark York (Brereton), Margaret Ward (Lady Rochford), Colin Rix (Bowes), Damien Thomas (Smeaton), Imogen Claire (Maria de Salinas)

Lynne Frederick

Frances Cuka

Charlotte Rampling

Jenny Bos

Barbara Leigh-Hunt

Jane Asher

Top: Donald Pleasence, Keith Michell
Left Center: Keith Michell, Michael Gough

184

LATE AUTUMN

(NEW YORKER) Director, Yasujiro Ozu; Screenplay, Kogo Noda, Yasujiro Ozu; Photography, Ushun Atsuta; Art Direction, Tatsuo Hamada; Music, Takanobu Saito; In Agfacolor; 127 minutes; October release.

CAST
The Mother .... Setsuko Hara
The Daughter .... Yoko Tsukasa
The Uncle .... Chishu Ryu
The Daughter's friend .... Mariko Okada
The Young Man .... Keiji Sada

Right: Yoko Tsukasa, Setsuko Hara

Setsuko Hara, Yoko Tsukasa, Nobuo Nakamara, Chishu Ryu

A DOLL'S HOUSE

(TOMORROW ENTERTAINMENT) Producer-Director, Joseph Losey; Screenplay, David Mercer from Michael Meyer's English translation of Henrik Ibsen's play; Photography, Gerry Fisher; Editor, Reggie Beck; Art Director, Eileen Diss; Costumes, John Furniss, Edith Head; Music, Michel Legrand; Presented by World Film, Services; In color; Rated G; 106 minutes; October release.

CAST

Nora	Jane Fonda
Torvald	David Warner
Dr. Rank	Trevor Howard
Kristine Linde	Delphine Seyrig
Krogstad	Edward Fox
Anne-Marie	Anna Wing
Olssen	Pierre Oudrey
Ivar	Frode Lien
Emmy	Tone Floor
Bob	Morten Floor
Dr. Rank's Maid	Ingrid Natrud
Helmer's Maid	Freda Krigh
Krogstad's Daughter	Ellen Holm
Krogstad's Son	Dagfinn Hertzberg

Right: Jane Fonda, Edward Fox

**Jane Fonda, David Warner,
also above**

**Jane Fonda, also above
with Delphine Seyrig**

THE OPTIMISTS

(**PARAMOUNT**) Producers, Adrian Gaye, Victor Lyndon; Direction and Screenplay, Anthony Simmons, Tudor Gates; Based on novel "The Optimists of Nine Elms" by Mr. Simmons; Photography, Larry Pizer; Editor, John Jympson; Music, Lionel Bart; Executive Producer, Ronald S. Kass; Art Director, Robert Cartwright; Assistant Directors, Tony Hopkins, Richard Merrick; A Cheetah production for Sagittarius; In Eastmancolor; Rated G; 110 minutes; October release.

CAST

Sam	Peter Sellers
Liz	Donna Mullane
Mark	John Chaffey
Bob Ellis	David Daker
Chrissie Ellis	Marjorie Yates
Ellis Baby	Katyana Kass
Dog's Home Secretary	Patricia Brake
Park Keeper	Michael Graham Cox
Park Policeman	Bruce Purchase
Dustmen	Bernie Searl, Tommy Wright
Mrs. Bonini	Pat Ashton
Laundry Ladies	Pat Becket, Daphne Lawson, Candyce Jane Brandl, Hilary Pritchard

Right: Peter Sellers

Donna Mullane, John Chaffey
Above: Peter Sellers

Peter Sellers
Above: John Chaffey, Donna Mullane

187

THE NEW LAND

(WARNER BROS.) Producer, Bengt Forslund; Directed, Photographed, and Edited by Jan Troell; Screenplay, Bengt Forslund, Jan Troell; From novel by Vilhelm Moberg; Art Director, P. A. Lundgren; Music, Bengt Ernryd, George Oddner; Costumes, Ulla-Britt Söderlund; A Svensk Filmindustri production; In Technicolor; Rated PG; 161 minutes; October release.

CAST

Karl Oskar	Max von Sydow
Kristina	Liv Ullmann
Robert	Eddie Axberg
Jonas Petter	Hans Alfredson
Anders Mansson	Halvar Bjork
Danjel	Allan Edwall
Samuel Nojd	Peter Lindgren
Arvid	Pierre Lindstedt
Petrus Olausson	Oscar Ljung
Judit	Karin Nordstrom
Pastor Torner	Per Oscarsson
Fina-Kajas	Agneta Prytz
Ulrika	Monica Zetterlund
Mario Vallejos	Georg Anaya
The Doctor	Ed Carpenter
Mr. Abbott	Larry Clementson
Pastor Jackson	Tom C. Fouts

Left: Max von Sydow, Liv Ullmann

Eddie Axberg, Liv Ullmann, Max von Sydow

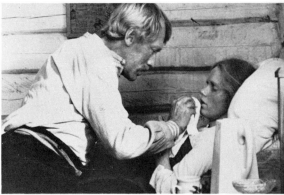

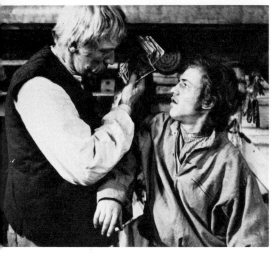

**Max von Sydow, Eddie Axberg Above: Liv
Ullmann, von Sydow Top: Monica Zetterlund,
Max von Sydow**

**Max von Sydow, Monica Zetterlund Above:
Max von Sydow, Liv Ullmann**

TRIPLE ECHO

(ALTURA) Producer, Graham Cottle; Director, Michael Apted; Screenplay, Robin Chapman; From novel by H. E. Bates; Photography, John Coquillon; Music, Marc Wilkinson; Editor, Barrie Vince; A Senat production; In Eastmancolor; Rated R; 90 minutes; October release.

CAST

Alice	Glenda Jackson
Barton	Brian Deacon
Sergeant	Oliver Reed
Subaltern	Anthony May
Stan	Gavin Richards
Christine	Jenny Lee Wright
Shopkeeper	Daphne Heard

Left: Brian Deacon, Glenda Jackson
Top: Oliver Reed, Brian Deacon

Glenda Jackson, Oliver Reed

THE OUTSIDE MAN

(UNITED ARTISTS) Producer, Jacques Bar; Director, Jacques Deray; Screenplay, Jean-Claude Carriere, Jacques Deray, Ian McLellan Hunter; Story, Jean-Claude Carriere, Jacques Deray; Photography, Terry K. Meade, Silvano Ippoliti; Music, Michel Legrand; Lyrics, Charles Burr; Title Song sung by Joe Morton; Assistant Directors, R. Robert Rosenbaum, Georges Pellegrin, Robert Enretto; Designer, Harold Michelson; Art Director, Kenneth A. Reid; Editors, Henri Lanoe, William K. Chulack; In color; Rated PG; 104 minutes; October release.

CAST

Lucien	Jean-Louis Trintignant
Nancy	Ann-Margret
Lenny	Roy Scheider
Jackie	Angie Dickinson
Jane	Georgia Engel
Anderson	Felice Orlandi
Carl	Carlo De Mejo
Antoine	Michel Constantin
Alex	Umberto Orsini
Second Hawk	Carmine Argenziano
Butler	Rice Cattani
Victor	Ted Corsia
Hitchhiker	Edward Greenberg
Salesgirl	Philippa Harris
Eric	Jackie Haley
Department Store Manager	John Hillerman
First Hawk	Jon Korkes
Rosie	Connie Kreski
Desk Clerk	Ben Piazza
Miller	Alex Rocco
Make-up Girl	Talia Shire
Paul	Lionel Vitrant

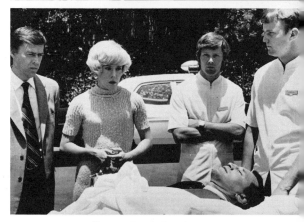

Top: Roy Scheider, Ann-Margret (R) Jean-Louis
Trintignant, Roy Scheider Below: Umberto
Orsini, Angie Dickinson (L) Trintignant,
Carlo de Mejo, Ann-Margret

Georgia Engel, Roy Scheider
Above: Ted de Corsia, Jean-Louis Trintignant

ENGLAND MADE ME

(CINE GLOBE) Producer, Jack Levin; Associate Producers, Jerome Z. Cline, David C. Anderson; Executive Producer, C. Robert Allen; Director, Peter Duffell; Screenplay, Desmond Cory, Peter Duffell; Based on novel by Graham Greene; Photography, Ray Parslow; Music, John Scott; Designer, Tony Woollard; Costumes, John Furniss; Editor, Malcolm Cooke; Assistant Director, Bata Maricic; An Atlantic Productions film; A Two World Films presentation; In Eastman Color; Rated PG; 100 minutes; November release.

CAST

Erik Krogh	Peter Finch
Anthony Farrant	Michael York
Kate Farrant	Hildegard Neil
F. Minty	Michael Hordern
Haller	Joss Ackland
Liz Davidge	Tessa Wyatt
Fromm	Michael Sheard
Stein	Bill Baskiville
Reichminster	Demeter Bitenc
Nikki	Mira Nikolic
Hartmann	Vladimir Bacic
Night Club Singer	Maja Papandopulo
Heinrich	Vladan Zivkovic
Maria	Cvetka Cupar

Top: Michael York, Hildegard Neil

Peter Finch

THE FRENCH CONSPIRACY

(CINE GLOBE) Producer, Yvon Guedel; Director, Yves Boisset; Screenplay, Ben Barzman, Basilio Franchina; Adaptation and Dialogue, Jorge Semprun; Music, Ennio Morricone; Photography, Ricardo Aronovich; Assistant Directors, Claude Othnin Girard, Thierry Chabert; Costumes, Pierre Nourry; A Two World Films presentation; In color; Rated PG; 125 minutes; November release.

CAST

Darien	Jean-Louis Trintignant
Kassar	Michel Piccoli
Sadiel	Gian Maria Volonte
Edith	Jean Seberg
Rouannet	Francois Perier
Garcin	Philippe Noiret
Lempereur	Michel Bouquet
Vigneau	Bruno Cremer
Acconeti	Daniel Ivernel
Howard	Roy Scheider

Right and Top: Jean-Louis Trintignant, Jean Seberg

Roy Scheider, Jean Seberg

THE SERPENT

(AVCO EMBASSY) Producer-Director, Henri Verneuil; Screenplay, Henri Verneuil, Gilles Perrault; Based on novel by Pierre Nord; Photography, Claude Renoir; Assistant Director, Marc Grunebaum; Designer, Jacques Saulnier; Editor, Pierre Gillette; Music, Ennio Morricone; Presented by Joseph E. Levine; In Panavision and DeLuxe color; Rated PG; 113 minutes; November release.

CAST

Vlassov	Yul Brynner
Allan Davies	Henry Fonda
Philip Boyle	Dirk Bogarde
Berthon	Philippe Noiret
Tavel	Michael Bouquet
Lepke	Martin Held
Computer Programming Chief	Farley Granger
Annabel Lee	Virna Lisi
Deval	Guy Trejan
Suzanne	Marie Dubois
Interrogator	Robert Alda

Right: Henry Fonda, Yul Brynner

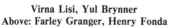

Virna Lisi, Yul Brynner
Above: Farley Granger, Henry Fonda

Henry Fonda, Dirk Bogarde Above: Yul
Brynner, Philippe Noiret, Henry Fonda

ASH WEDNESDAY

(PARAMOUNT) Producer, Dominick Dunne; Director, Larry Peerce; Screenplay, Jean-Claude Tramont; Photography, Ennio Guarnieri; Editor, Marion Rothman; Music, Maurice Jarre; Art Director, Philip Abramson; Assistant Director, Steven Barnett; A Saggitarius production; In Technicolor; Rated R; 99 minutes; November release.

CAST

Barbara Sawyer	Elizabeth Taylor
Mark Sawyer	Henry Fonda
Erich	Helmut Berger
David	Keith Baxter
Dr. Lambert	Maurice Teynac
Kate Sawyer	Margaret Blye
German Woman	Monique Van Vooren
Bridge Player	Henning Schlueter
Mario	Dino Mele
Mandy	Kathy Van Lypps
Nurse Ilse	Dina Sassoli
Paolo	Carlo Puri
Comte D'Arnoud	Andrea Esterhazy
Simone	Jill Pratt
Silvana Del Campo	Irina Wassilchikoff
Viet Hartung	Muki Windisch-Graetz
Helga	Nadia Stancioff
Prince Von Essen	Rodolfo Lodi
Gregory De Rive	Raymond Vignale
Tony Gutierrez	Jose De Vega
Samantha	Samantha Starr

Top: Keith Baxter, Elizabeth Taylor Below:
Henry Fonda, Taylor, Margaret Blye Top
Right: Henry Fonda, Elizabeth Taylor

Elizabeth Taylor, also above
with Helmut Berger

195

Rudolf Nureyev, Lucette Aldous

Lucette Aldous, Rudolf Nureyev

DON QUIXOTE

(CONTINENTAL) Producer, John Hargreaves; Directors, Rudolf Nureyev, Robert Helpmann; Photography, Geoffrey Unsworth; Designer and Costumes, Barry Kay; Music, Ludwig Minkus; Choreography, Rudolf Nureyev after Petipa; Associate Producer, Pat Condon; Art Director, William Hutchinson; Editor, Anthony Buckley; Assistant Directors, Bryan Ashbridge, Wallace Potts; In color; Rated G; 107 minutes; November release.

CAST

Don Quixote	Robert Helpmann
Sancho Panza	Ray Powell
Basilio	Rudolf Nureyev
Lorenzo	Francis Croese
Kitri	Lucette Aldous
Gamache	Colin Peasley
Street Dancer	Marilyn Rowe
Espada	Kelvin Coe
Kitri's Friends	Gailene Stock, Carolyn Rappel
Gypsy Dancers	Alan Alder, Paul Saliba
Gypsy Queen	Susan Dains
Gypsy King	Ronald Bekker
Gypsy Girls	Julie da Costa, Leigh Rowles
Dulcinea	Lucette Aldous
Queen of the Dryads	Marilyn Rowe
Cupid	Patricia Cox
Fandango Couple	Janet Vernon, Gary Norman
Matadors	Ronald Bekker, John Meehan, Tex McNeill, Rodney Smith, Joseph Janusaitis, Frederick Wener

Dancers of the Australian Ballet

ALFREDO, ALFREDO

(PARAMOUNT) Director, Pietro Germi; Story and Screenplay, Leo Benvenuti, Piero de Bernardi, Tullio Pinelli, Pietro Germi; Photography, Aiace Parolin; Editor, Sergio Montanari; Designer, Carlo Egidi; Music, Carlo Rustichelli; Assistant Directors, Silla Bettini, Gianni Cozzo; An RPA-Rizzoli-Francoriz production; In Techcolor; Rated R; 100 minutes; December release.

CAST

Alfredo	Dustin Hoffman
Mariarosa	Stefania Sandrelli
Carolina	Carla Gravina
Carolina's Mother	Clara Colosimo
Carolina's Father	Daniele Patella
Mariarosa's Mother	Danika La Loggia
Mariarosa's Father	Saro Urzi
Alfredo's Father	Luigi Baghetti
Oreste	Duilio Del Prete

Right: Saro Urzi, Dustin Hoffman, Stefania Sandrelli, Danika La Loggia

**Dustin Hoffman, Carla Gravina
Above: Hoffman, Stefania Sandrelli**

Dustin Hoffman

HAPPY NEW YEAR

(AVCO EMBASSY) Produced, Directed, and Written by Claude Lelouch; Photography, Jean Collomb; Music, Francis Lai; Presented by Joseph E. Levine; In color; Rated PG; 112 minutes; December release.

CAST

Simon	Lino Ventura
Francoise	Francoise Fabian
Charles	Charles Gerard
Jeweler	Andre Falcon
Italian Lover	Silvano Tranquilli
First Intellectual	Claude Mann
Parisian Lover	Frederic De Pasquale
Salesgirl	Bettina Rheims
Madame Felix	Lilo De La Passardiere
Prison Warden	Gerard Sire
Guest Appearance by	Mireille Mathieu

Right: Lino Ventura, Charles Gerard

Lino Ventura, Francoise Fabian

Lino Ventura

Francoise Fabian
Top: Lino Ventura, Andre Falcon

DON'T LOOK NOW

(PARAMOUNT) Executive Producer, Anthony B. Unger; Producer, Peter Katz; Director, Nicolas Roeg; Screenplay, Alan Scott, Chris Bryant; Story, Daphne du Maurier; Photography, Anthony Richmond; Art Director, Giovanni Soccol; Editor, Graeme Clifford; Music, Pino Donnagio; Associate Producer, Federico Mueller; Assistant Director, Francesco Cinieri; An Anglo-Italian Co-Production by Casey Productions, and Eldorado Films; A British Lion presentation; In Panavision and Technicolor; Rated R; 110 minutes; December release.

CAST

Laura Baxter	Julie Christie
John Baxter	Donald Sutherland
Heather	Hilary Mason
Wendy	Clelia Mantana
Bishop Barbarrigo	Massimo Serato
Inspector Longhi	Renato Scarpa
Workman	Giorgio Trestini
Hotel Manager	Leopoldo Trieste
Anthony Babbage	David Tree
Mandy Babbage	Ann Rye
Johnny Baxter	Nicholas Salter
Christine Baxter	Sharon Williams
Detective Sabbione	Bruno Cattaneo
Dwarf	Adelina Poerio

**Left: Julie Christie, Hilary Mason,
Clelia Matania**

Donald Sutherland, Julie Christie

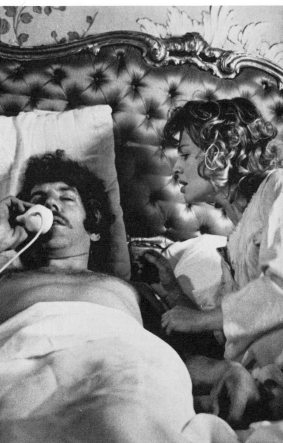

Donald Sutherland, Julie Christie Top: Julie
Christie, Hilary Mason, Clelia Matania

Donald Sutherland, Julie Christie

Giulio Brogi, Alida Valli
in "The Spider's Stratagem"

"The Flavor of Green Tea over Rice"

IF I HAD A GUN (A jay) Director, Stefan Uher; Screenplay, Milan Ferko, Stefan Uher; Based on novel by Milan Ferko; Photography, Vincent Rosinec; Music, Ilja Zeljenka; Art Director, Anton Krajcovic; Black and white; 90 minutes; January release. CAST: Marian Bernat (Boy), Josef Graf (Friend), Ludevit Kroner (Father), Emilia Dosekova (Mother), Hana Grissova (Girl), and B. Hausnerova, M. Furinova, D. Lapunik.

THE SPIDER'S STRATAGEM (New Yorker) Producer, Giovanni Bertolucci; Director, Bernardo Bertolucci; Screenplay, Bernardo Bertolucci, Edoardo De Gregoria, Marilu Pavolini, after the Jorge Louis Borges story; Photography, Vitorrio Storaro; Editor, Roberto Perpignani; Art Director, Maria Paola Maino; Music, Schoenberg, Verdi; Assistant Director, Giuseppe Bertolucci; In Technicolor; Rated GP; 97 minutes; January release. CAST: Giulio Brogi (Athos Sr. and Jr.), Alida Valli (Draifa), Tino Scotti (Costa), Pippo Campanini (Gaibazzi), Franco Giovanelli (Rasori), Allen Midgett (Sailor)

THE FLAVOR OF GREEN TEA OVER RICE (New Yorker) Producer, Shockiku/Ofuna; Director, Yasujiro Ozu; Screenplay, Ozu, and Kogo Noda; Photography, Yuharu Atsuta; In black and white; 115 minutes; January release. CAST: Shin Saburi, Michiyo Kogura, Koji Tsuruta, Keiko Tsushima, Kuniko Miyake, Chikaga Awashima, Chishu Ryu, Yuko Mochizuki.

TRINITY IS STILL MY NAME (Avco Embassy) Producer, Italo Zingarelli; Direction and Screenplay, E. B. Clucher; Photographer, Aldo Giordani; Designer, Enzo Bulgarelli; Music, Guido and Maurizio De Angelis; A West Film production in color; Presented by Joseph E. Levine; 121 minutes; January release. CAST: Terence Hill (Trinity), Bud Spencer (Bambino), Harry Carey, Jr. (Father), Jessica Dublin (Pioneer), Yanti Somer (Pioneer), Enzo Tarascio (Sheriff), Pupo De Luca (Padre)

THE NAKED COUNTESS (Crown International) Producer, Carl Spiehs; Direction and Screenplay, Curt Nachman; In color; Rated R; January release. CAST: Ursula Blauth, W. G. Lukschy, Elke Hart, Michael Cromer

THE FIRST CIRCLE (Paramount) Executive Producer, Zvi Kolitz; Direction and Screenplay, Aleksander Ford; From novel by Aleksander I. Solzhenitsyn; Photography, Wladyslaw Forbert; Editor, Carl Lerner; Music, Roman Palester; In Eastmancolor; Rated R; 95 minutes; January release. CAST: Gunthier Malzacher (Gleb), Elzbieta Czyzewska (Simonchka), Peter Steen (Volodin), Vera Chekova (Clara), Ole Ernest (Doronin), Ingolf David (Rubin), Prebrn Neegaard (Bobyin), Preben Lerdorff Rye (Cheinov), Per Bentzon Goldschmidt (Bulatov), Ole Ishoy (Siromakha)

INNOCENT BYSTANDERS (Paramount) Producer, George H. Brown; Director, Peter Collinson; Screenplay, James Mitchell; Based on novel by James Munro; Photography, Brian Probyn; Art Director, Maurice Carter, Editor, Alan Pattillo; Music, John Keating; Assistant Director; Clive Reed; A Sagittarius production; In Eastmancolor; Rated PG; 111 minutes; January release. CAST: Stanley Baker (John), Geraldine Chaplin (Miriam), Donald Pleasence (Loomis), Dana Andrews (Blake), Sue Lloyd (Joanna), Derrin Nesbitt (Andrew), Vladek Sheybal (Aaron), Warren Mitchell (Omar), Cec Linder (Mankowitz), Howard Goorney (Zimmer), J. C. Devlin (Waiter), Ferdy Mayne (Marcus), Clifton Jones (Hetherton), John Collin (Azimov), Aharon Impale (Gabril), Yuri Borienko (Guard), Frank Maher (Daniel), Michael Poole (Zhelkov), Tom Bowman (Guard)

EAGLE OVER LONDON (Cine Globe) Producer, Edmondo Amati; Director, Enzo G. Castellari; Photography, Alejandro Ulloa; Music, Francesco De Masi; In Technicolor; 100 minutes; January release. CAST: Frederick Stafford, Van Johnson, Francisco Rabal, Evelyn Stewart, Luigi Pistilli, Renzo Palmer, Edy Biagetti, Luis Davila, Christian Hay, Jacques Berthier, Teresa Gimpera

ISLAND OF THE BURNING DAMNED (Maron) Producer, Tom Blakely; Director, Terence Fisher; In color; Rated GP; January release. CAST: Christopher Lee (Hanson), Patrick Allen (Jeff), Jane Merrow (Angela), Sarah Lawson (Mrs. Callan), Peter Cushing (Dr. Stone), William Lucas (Stanley), Kenneth Cope (Mason), Jack Bligh (Siddle)

Bud Spencer, Terence Hill
in "Trinity Is Still My Name"

Stanley Baker, Geraldine Chaplin
in "Innocent Bystanders"

Christiane Kruger
in "Little Mother"

Stanley Baker
in "Innocent Bystanders"

LITTLE MOTHER (Audubon) Producer-Director, Radley Metzger; Associate Producer, Ava Leighton; Screenplay, Brian Phelan; Photography, Hans Jura; Editor, Amedeo Salfa; Music, George Craig; In Eastmancolor; Rated R; 90 minutes; January release. CAST: Christiane Kruger (Marina), Siegfried Rauch (Pinares), Ivan Desny (Umberia), Mark Damon (Riano), Anton Diffring (Cardinal), Elga Sorbas (Annette)

UNDER MILK WOOD (Altura) Executive Producers, Jules Buck, Hugh French; Direction and Screenplay, Andrew Sinclair; Based on play by Dylan Thomas; Photography, Bob Huke; Music, Brian Cascoigne; Editor, Willy Kempien; A Timon Films production in color; Rated PG; 90 minutes; January release. CAST: Richard Burton (Voice), Elizabeth Taylor (Rosie), Peter O'Toole (Capt. Cat), Glynis Johns (Myfanwy), Vivien Merchant (Mrs. Pugh), Sian Phillips (Mrs Ogmore), Victor Spinetti (Mog), Ryan Davies (Voice), Angharad Rees (Gossamer), Ray Smith (Waldo), Ann Beach (Polly), Talfryn Thomas (Pugh), Meg Wynn Owen (Lily)

EXQUISITE CADAVER (Wheeler) Producer-Director, Vicente Aranda; Screenplay, Mr. Aranda, A. Radinad; Photography, Juan Amoros, Fernando Arribas; Music, Marco Rossi; In Eastmancolor; 108 minutes; January release. CAST: Capucine (Parker), Judy Matheson (Esther), Teresa Gimpera (Teresa), Carlos Estrada (Husband)

THE LEGEND OF FRENCHY KING (SNC) Director, Christian-Jacque; Screenplay, Marie-Ange Anies, Jean Nemours, Guy Casaril, Clement Bywood, Daniel Boulanger; Photography, Henri Persin; Editor, Nicole Guadauchon; Music, Francis Lai; In Eastmancolor; Rated R; January release. CAST: Brigitte Bardot (Frenchy), Claudia Cardinale (Maria), Michael J. Pollard (Marshal), Emma Cohen (Sister), Micheline Presle (Aunt), and France Dougnac, Patty Shepard

THREE CORNERED BED (Jerand) In color; Rated R; No other credits available; January release. Starring Marie Liljedahl

ALL THE RIGHT NOISES (20th Century-Fox) Producers, Max L. Raab, Si Litvinoff; Associate Producer, Anthony Hope; Direction and Screenplay, Gerry O'Hara; From his novel; Photography, Gerry Fisher; Art Director, Terry Pritchard; Editor, Antony Gibbs; Music, Melanie; In color; Rated GP; 92 minutes; January release. CAST: Tom Bell (Len), Olivia Hussey (Val), Judy Carne (Joy), John Standing (Bernie), Roy Herrick (Camera Operator), Edward Higgens (Ted), Chloe Franks (Jenny), Gareth Wright (Ian), Gordon Griffith (Terry), Robert Keegan (Len's Father), Lesley Down (Laura), Peter Burton (Stage Manager), Chrissie Shrimpton (Waitress), Stacy Davies (Stage hand), Otto Diamont (Conductor), Roderick Jones (First Musician), Larry Burns (Second Musician)

TWITCH OF THE DEATH NERVE (Hallmark) Direction and Screenplay, Mario Bava; Music, Stelvio Copriani; In color; Rated R; January release. CAST: Claudine Auger, Claudio Volonto, Ana Maria Rosati, Laura Betti, Luigi Pistilli, Brigitte Skay

THE NIGHT EVELYN CAME OUT OF THE GRAVE (Phase One) Director, Emilio P. Miraglia; Screenplay, Fabio Pittoru, Massimo Felisatti, Emilio Miraglia; Photography, Gastone DiGiovanni; Music, Bruno Nicolai; A Phoenix Cinematografica production; In Technicolor; Rated R; 99 minutes; January release. CAST: Anthony Steffen, Marina Malfatti, Rod Murdock, Giacoma Rossi Stuart, Umberto Raho, Roberto Maidera, Joan C. Davies, Erica Blanc

DEATH OF A JEW (Cine Globe) Director, Denys de la Patelliere; Screenplay, Vahe Katcha, Denys de la Patelliere; Photography, Alain Levant; A Films Copernic production; Rated PG; 98 minutes; January release; CAST: Assaf Dayan (Shimon), Akim Tamiroff (Mehdaloun), Jean Claudio (Kassik)

THE FAMILY (International Coproduction) Director, Sergio Sollima; In Technicolor; Rated R; February release. CAST: Charles Bronson, Telly Savalas, Jill Ireland, Umberto Orsini, Michel Constantin

"Eagles over London"

Charles Bronson
in "The Family"

"Jory"

"Emitai"

JORY (Avco Embassy) Executive Producer, Leopoldo Silva; Producer, Howard G. Minsky; Associate Producers, Barry Minsky, Gerald Herman; Director, Jorge Fons; Screenplay, Gerald Herman, Robert Irving; Based on novel by Milton R. Bass; Music, Al DeLory; Photography, George Stahl; Designer, Earl Hedrick; Editors, Fred Chulack, Sergio Ortega; Presented by Joseph E. Levine; In color; February release. CAST: John Marley (Roy), B. J. Thomas (Jocko), Robby Benson (Jory), Brad Dexter (Jack), Claudio Brook (Ethan), Patricia Aspillaga (Carmelita), Todd Martin (Barron), Ben Baker (Jordan), Carlos Cortes (Logan), Linda Purl (Amy), Anne Lockhart (Dora), Betty Sheridan (Mrs. Jordan), Ted Marlkand (Evans), Quintin Bulnes (Walker), John Kelly (Thatcher), Eduardo Lopez Rojas (Cookie)

BARON BLOOD (American International) Producer, Alfred Leone; Director, Mario Bava; Screenplay, Vincent G. Fotre; Music, Les Baxter; Rated PG; 90 Minutes; February release. CAST: Joseph Cotten (Alfred), Elke Sommer (Eva), Massimo Girotti (Karl), Antonio Cantafora (Peter), Alan Collins (Fritz), Humi Raho (Police Inspector), Rada Rassimov (Christine), Dieter Tressler (Dortmundt)

TOUT VA BIEN (New Yorker) Producer, Jean-Pierre Rassam; Direction and Screenplay, Jean-Luc Godard, Jean-Pierre Gorin; Photography, Armand Marco; Editor, Kernout Peiter; 95 minutes; February release. CAST: Yves Montand (He), Jane Fonda (She), Vittorio Caprioli (Factory Manager), Jean Pignol (Delegate), Pierre Ondry (Frederic), Illizabeth Chauvin (Genevieve), Eric Chartier (Lucien), Yves Gabrielli (Leon)

I LOVE YOU ROSA (Leisure Media) Executive Producer, Yoram Globus; Producer, Menahem Golan; Direction and Screenplay, Moshe Mizrahi; Photography, Adam Greenberg; Editor, Dov Hoenig; Music, Dov Seltzer; Presented by Peter Gettinger, Oliver A. Unger; In color; 84 minutes; February release. CAST: Michal Bat-Adam (Rosa), Gabi Otterman (Nessim), Yosef Shiloah (Eli), Avner Chezkiyahu (Rabbi), Levana Finkelstein (Jemila), Moshe Tal (Nessim grown up), Elisheva Michaeli (Mother)

EMITAI (New Yorker) "Lord of the Sky"; Producer, Paulin Soumanou Vieya; Director, Ousmane Sembene; Photography, Michel Remaudeau; Editor, Gilbert Kikoine; A Films Domirev production in color; 103 minutes; February release. CAST: Robert Fontaine (Commandant), Michel Renaudeau (Lt.), Pierre Blanchard (Colonel), and Ibou Camara, Ousmane Camara, Joseph Diatta, Dji Niassebanor, Sibesalang, Kalifa (Villagers)

THE HARDER THEY COME (New World) Producer-Director, Perry Henzell; Screenplay, Perry Henzell, Trevor D. Rhone; Music, Jimmy Cliff, Desmond Dekker, The Slickers; Photography, Peter Jassop, David McDonald; Editor, John Victor Smith; Presented by Roger Corman; In Metrocolor; Rated R; 100 minutes; February release. CAST: Jimmy Cliff, Carl Bradshaw, Janet Bartley, Winston Stona, Ras Daniel Hartman, Basil Keane, Bobby Charlton, The Maytals

LUDWIG (MGM) Director, Luchino Visconti; Story and Screenplay, Luchino Visconti, Enrico Medioli, Suso Cecchi D'Amico; Executive Producer, Robert Gordon Edwards; Music, Schumann, Wagner, Offenbach; Photography, Armando Nannuzzi; Art Directors, Mario Chiari, Mario Scisci; Editor, Ruggero Mastroianni; Costumes, Piero Tosi; Assistant Director, Albino Cocco; Presented by Ugo Santalucia; In Panavision and Technicolor; Rated R; 186 minutes; February Release. CAST: Helmut Berger (Ludwig), Romy Schneider (Elizabeth), Trevor Howard (Wagner), Silvana Mangano (Cosima Von Bulow), Gert Frobe (Hoffman), Helmut Griem (Durcheim), Isabella Telezynska (Queen Mother), Umberto Orsini (Count von Holstein), John Moulder Brown (Prince Otto), Sonia Petrova (Sophie), Folker Bohnet (Joseph Kainz), Adriana Asti (Lila), Marc Porel (Richard Hornig), Nora Ricci (Countess Ida), Mark Burns (Han Von Bulow), Maurizio Bonuglia (Mayor), and Alexander Allerson, Bert Bloch, Manfred Furst, Kurt Grosskurt, Anna Maria Hanschke, Gerhard Herter, Jan Linhart, Carla Mancini, Gernot Mohner, Clara Moustawcesky, Alain Naya, Allesandro Perrella, Karl Heinz Peters, Wolfram Schaerf, Henning Schluter, Helmut Stern, Eva Tavazzi, Louise Vincent, Gunnar Warner, Karl Heinz Windhorst, Rayka Yurit

Michal Bat-Adam, Moshe Tal in "I Love You, Rosa"

Helmut Berger, Silvano Mangano, Trevor Howard in "Ludwig"

"The Creeping Flesh"

Samit Bhanja, Kaberi Bose
in "Days and Nights in the Forest"

THE CREEPING FLESH (Columbia) Producer, Michael Redbourn; Director, Freddie Francis; Screenplay, Peter Spenceley, Jonathan Rumbold; Photography, Norman Warwick; Music, Paul Ferris; Editor, Oswald Hafenrichter; Executive Producer, Norman Priggen; A World Film Services production in color; Rated PG; 89 minutes; February release. CAST: Christopher Lee (James), Peter Cushing (Emmanuel), Lorna Heilbron (Penelope), George Benson (Waterlow), Kenneth J. Warren (Lenny)

A REFLECTION OF FEAR (Columbia) Producer, Howard B. Jaffe; Director, William A. Fraker; Screenplay, Edward Hume; Based on novel "Go to Thy Deathbed" by Stanton Forbes; Music, Fred Myrow; Photography, Laszlo Kovacs; Editor, Richard Brockway; Art Director, Joel Schiller; Assistant Director, John Chulay; Costumes, Patti Norris; In color; Rated PG; 89 minutes; February release. CAST: Robert Shaw (Michael), Sally Kellerman (Anne), Mary Ure (Katherine), Sondra Locke (Marguerite), Mitchell Ryan (McKenna), Gordon DeVol (Hector), Gordon Anderson (Voice of Aaron), Victoria Risk (Peggy), Leonard John Crofoot (Aaron), Michael St. Clair (Kevin), Liam Dunn (Coroner), Michelle Marvin (Nurse), Michele Montau (Mme. Caraquet)

THE ASPHYX (Paragon) Producer, John Brittany; Director, Peter Newbrook; Screenplay, Brian Comfort; Photography, Freddie Young; In color; Rated PG; 93 minutes; February release. CAST: Robert Stephens (Hugo), Robert Powell (Giles), Jane Lapotaire (Christina), Alex Scott (President), Ralph Arliss (Clive), Fiona Walker (Anna), Terry Scully (Pauper), John Lawrence (Mason), David Gray (Vicar), Tony Caunter (Warden), Paul Bacon (First Member)

THE PRIEST AND THE GIRL (New Yorker) Producer, Luis Carlos Barreto; Directed and Written by Joaquim Pedro de Andrade; Photography, Marlo Carneiro; Music, Carlos Lira; 87 minutes; In black and white; February release. CAST: Paulo Jose (Priest), Helena Ignez (Girl), Mario Lago (Old Man), Fauzi Arap (Druggist)

DAYS AND NIGHTS IN THE FOREST (Pathe Contemporary) Direction, Screenplay, Music, Satyajit Ray; From novel by Sunil Ganguly; Photography, Soumendu Roy; Art Director, Bansi Chandragupta; Editor, Dulal Dutta; A Prya Films production in black and white; 115 minutes; March release. CAST: Soumitra Chatterjee (Ashim), Subhendu Chatterjee (Sanjoy), Samit Bhanja (Harinath), Robi Ghose (Sekhar), Sharmila Tagore (Aparna), Kaberi Bose (Jaya), Simi (Duli), Pahari Sanyal (Sadashiv), Aperna Sen (Atasi)

I AM A DANCER (Anglo-Emi) Producer, Evdoros Demetriou; Director, Pierre Jourdan; Associate Producer, Denise Tual; Narration written by John Percival; Spoken by Bryan Forbes; Musical Director, Evdoros Demetriou; Editors, Catherine Henry, Timothy Gee; Designer, Sydney Beytex; In color; 93 minutes; March release. CAST: Rudolf Nureyev, Margot Fonteyn, Carla Fracci, Lynn Seymour, Deanne Bergsma

THE HERO (Avco Embassy) formerly "Bloomfield"; Producers, John Heyman, Wolf Mankowitz; Director, Richard Harris; Screenplay, Wolf Mankowitz; Story, Joseph Gross; Editor, Kevin Connor; Music, Johnny Harris; Rated PG; 97 minutes; March release. CAST: Richard Harris (Eitan), Romy Schneider (Nira), Kim Burfield (Nimrod), Maurice Kaufman (Yasha), Yossi Yadin (Weiner), Shraga Friedman (Chairman)

PHEDRE (Altura) Producer, Nicole Stephane; Director, Pierre Jourdan; Screenplay, Jean Racine; Photography, Michel Kelber; Editor, Genevieve Winding; In color; 90 minutes; March release. CAST: Marie Bell (Phedre), Jean Chevrier (Theramene), Jacques Dacqmine (Theseus), Claud Giraud (Hippolyte), Tania Torrens (Aricie), Claudia Maurin (Ismene), Jean-Noel Sissia (Panope), Mary Marquet (Oenone)

FIVE FINGERS OF DEATH (Warner Bros.) Producer, Run Run Shaw; Director, Cheng Chang Ho; Screenplay, Chiang Yang; Photography, Wang Yunglung; In DeLuxe color; Rated R; 104 minutes; March release. CAST: Lo Lieh (Chao), Wang Ping (Sung), Wang Chin-Feng (Yen), Nan-Kung Hsun (Han), Tien Feng (Meng), Chao Hsiung (Okada), Tung Lin (Meng)

Paulo Jose in "The Priest
and the Girl"

Sally Kellerman, Sondra Locke, Robert Shaw
in "A Reflection of Fear"

205

"Soleil-O"

"Hunger for Love"

TOKOLOSHE (Artist International) Producer, Harry Shuster; Direction and Screenplay, Peter Prowse; Photography, Judex C. Viljoen; Editor, Mac Errington; Music, Sam Sklair; Designer, Tommy Askew; Assistant Director, Ray Frift; In Technicolor; Rated G; 81 minutes; March release. CAST: Saul Pelle (Boy), Sidney James (Blind Man), Chief Butelezei (Zulu Chief), Cy Sacks (Thief), Jimmy Sabe (Witchdoctor)

SOLEIL-O (New Yorker) Directed and written by Med Hondo; Photography, Francois Catonne; Editors, Michele Masnier, Clement Menuet; Music, Georges Anderson; In black and white; 104 minutes; March release. CAST: Robert Liensol, Theo Legitimus, Gabriel Glissand, Gregoire Germain, Mabousso Lo, Bernard Fresson, Gilles Segal

LOVE (Ajay) Director, Karoly Makk; Screenplay, Tibor Dery; Photography, Janos Toth; Music, Andras Mihaly; Editor, Gyorgy Sivo; a Mafilm production; 92 minutes; March release. CAST: Lili Darvas (Old Lady), Mari Torocsik (Luca), Ivan Darvas (Janos)

SUCH A GORGEOUS KID LIKE ME (Columbia) Executive Producer, Marcel Berbert; Director, Francois Truffaut; Screenplay, Jean-Loup Dabadie, Francois Truffaut; Based on novel by Henry Farrell; Photography, Pierre William Glenn; Art Director, Jean-Pierre Kohut; Music, Georges Delerue; Assistant Directors, Suzanne Schiffman, Bernard Cohn; Les Films du Carrosse production; Rated R; 98 minutes; March release. CAST: Bernadette Lafont (Camille), Claude Brasseur (Murene), Charles Denner (Arthur), Guy Marchand (Sam), Andre Dussollier (Stanislas), Philippe Leotard (Clovis), Anne Kreis (Helene), Gilbert Geniat (Isobel), Daniele Girard (Florence), Martine Ferriere (Secretary), Michel Delahaye (Marchal), Annick Fougerie (Teacher), Gaston Ouvrard Prison Guard), Jacob Weizbluth (Alphonse)

HUNGER FOR LOVE (Pathe Contemporary) Producers, Herbert Richers, Paulo Porto; Director, Nelson Pereira dos Santos; Photography, Dio Lufti; In Portugese with English subtitles; Black and white; 75 minutes; March release. CAST: Leila Diniz, Irene Stefania, Arduino Colasanti, Paulo Porto

COME HAVE COFFEE WITH US (Altura) Producer, Maurizio Lodi-Fe; Director, Alberto Lattuada; Screenplay, (Italian with English subtitles) Tulio Kezich, Alberto Lattuada, Adriano Baroco, Piero Chiara; Based on novel by Piero Chiara; Music, Fred Boggusto; 90 minutes; April release. CAST: Ugo Tognazzi (Emerenziano), Milena Vukotic (Tarsilia), Francesca Romana Coluzzi (Fortunata), Angela Goodwin (Camilla), Valentine (Caterina)

HOW TASTY WAS MY LITTLE FRENCHMAN (New Yorker) Producers, Nelson Pereira dos Santos, Luis Carlos Barreto; Direction and Screenplay, Nelson Pereira dos Santos; Photography, Dib Lufti; In Eastmancolor; 80 minutes; April release. CAST: Arduino Colasanti (Frenchman), Ana Maria Magalhaes (Girl), Ital Natur (Chief), and Eduardo Embassahy, Manfredo Colasanti, Jose Cleber

WEDDING IN WHITE (Avco Embassy) Producer, John Vidette; Direction and Screenplay, William Fruet; Photography, Richard Leiterman; Music, Milan Kymlicka; Art Director, Karen Bromley-Watkins; Editor, Tony Lower; Assistant Director, John Board; Costumes, Patty Unger; A Dermot Productions picture in Panavision and DeLuxe color; Rated R; 103 minutes; April release. CAST: Donald Pleasence (Jim), Carol Kane (Jeannie), Doris Petrie (Mary), Leo Phillips (Sandy), Paul Bradley (Jimmie), Doug McGrath (Billy), Christine Thomas (Sarah), Bonnie Carol Case (Dollie)

THE CHALLENGES, A TRILOGY (Selmier) Producer-Director, Dean Selmier; Screenplay, Jose Hernandez Miguel; Editor, Pablo G. del Amo; Music, Louis de Pablo; Photography, Luis Cuadrado; 96 minutes; April release. CAST: Francisco Rabal, Dean Selmier, Anuncion Balaguer, Teresa Rabal, Alfredo Mayo, Julia G. Caba, Barbara Deist, Fernando Polack, Julia Pena, Daysi Granados, Luis Suarez

Claude Brasseur, Bernadette Lafont
in "Such a Gorgeous Kid Like Me"

Leo Phillips, Carol Kane, Donald Pleasence,
Doris Petrie in "Wedding in White"

206

Richard Roundtree, Roy Thinnes
in "Charley-One-Eye"

Stig Engstrom
in "You're Lying"

CHARLEY-ONE-EYE (Paramount) Producer, James Swann; Director, Don Chaffey; Screenplay, Keith Leonard; Photography, Kenneth Talbot; Music, John Cameron; Editor, Mike Campbell; Assistant Director, Nick Granby; A David Paradine production; In Standard color; Rated R; 109 minutes; April release. CAST: Richard Roundtree (Black Man), Roy Thinnes (Indian), Nigel Davenport (Bounty Hunter), Jill Pearson (Officer's Wife), Aldo Sambrell (Mexican Driver), Luis Aller (Mexican Youth), Rafael Albaicin (Mexican Leader) Blood Suckers Alex Davion (Tony), Johnny Sekka (Bob), Madeline Hinde (Penelope), Patrick Mower (Richard), Imogen Hassall (Chris), Edward Woodward (Holstrom), William Mervyn (Honeydew), David Lodge (Colonel)

HEAD OF THE FAMILY (GGP) Producer, Turi Vasile; Director, Nanni Loy; In Eastmancolor; Rated GP; 105 minutes; April release. CAST: Leslie Caron (Paola), Nino Manfredi (Marco), Claudine Auger (Adriana), Ugo Tognazzi (Romeo)

SUBURBAN WIVES (Scotia International) Producer, Morton Lewis; Direction and Screenplay, Derek Ford; Photography, Bill Holland, Roy Poynter; Editor, Terry Keefe; Music, Terry Warr; In color; Rated R; 90 minutes; April release. CAST: Eva Whishaw (Sara), Maggie Wright (Irene), Peter May (John), Barry Linehan (His Boss), Nicola Austine (Jean), Claire Gordon (Sheila), James Donnelly (Bookmaker), Heather Chasen (Kathy), Dennis Hawthorne (Her Husband), Gabrielle Drake (Secretary), Yokki Rhodes (Yokki), Ian Sinclair (Instructor), Jane Cardew (Carole), Robin Culver (Photographer), Pauline Peart (Mavis), Richard Thorpe (Sara's Husband), Brian Miller (Husband's Friend), Sidonie Bond (Jill), Timothy Parkes (Her Husband), Mia Martin (Helen)

ONE ON TOP OF THE OTHER (GGP) Producer, Edmondo Amati; Director, Lucio Fulci; Screenplay, Lucio Fulci, Robert Gianviti; Music, Riz Ortolani; In color; 104 minutes; Rated R; April release. CAST: Marisa Mell (Susan), Jean Sorel (George), Elsa Martinelli (Jane), John Ireland (Detective), Alberto DeMendoza (Henry), Jean Sobieski (Benjamin), Faith Domergue (Sister-in-law)

MEMORIES OF UNDERDEVELOPMENT (Tricontinental) Direction and Screenplay, Tomas Gutierrez Alea; Based on novel by Edmundo Desnoes; Photography, Ramon Suarez; Editor, Nelson Rodriguez; Music, Leo Brower; 104 minutes; May release. CAST: Sergio Corrieri (Serge), Daisy Granados (Elena), Eslinda Nunez (Noemi), Beatriz Ponchora (Laura)

YOU'RE LYING (Grove Press) Producer, Goran Lindgren; Director, Vilgot Sjoman; In Swedish with English subtitles; An Evergreen film in black and white; 110 minutes; May release. CAST: Stig Engstrom (Lasse), Borge Ahlstedt (Bjorn), Siff Rund (Mother), Vilgot Sjoman (Himself)

HAPPINESS (New Yorker) Producer, Moskino Kombinat; Direction and Screenplay, Alexandre Medvedkine; Photography, Gleb Troianski; Music, Modeste Moussorgski; Designer, A. A. Outkine; In black and white; 70 minutes; May release. CAST: Piotr Zinoviev (Khmyr), Elena Egorova (Anna)

DEEP THRUST (American International) Producer, Raymond Chow; Director, Heang Feng; A Golden Harvest production presented by Hallmark Pictures; Rated R; 88 minutes; May release. CAST: Angelo Mao, Chang Yi, Pai Ying, June Wu, Anne Liu

FUNERAL PARADE OF ROSES (New Yorker) Producer, Mitsumu Kudo; Direction and Screenplay, Toshio Matsumoto; Photography, Tatsuo Suzuki; Art Director, Setsu Asakura; Music, Joji Yasa; Editor, Toshie Iwasa; An Evergreen film in black and white; 95 minutes; May release. CAST: Peter (Eddie), Toyosaburo Uchiyama (Guenvara), Don Madird (Tony), Emiko Azuma (Eddie's Mother), Yoshio Tsuchiya (Gonda)

"Happiness"

Angelo Mao
in "Deep Thrust"

Gian Maria Volonte
in "The Mattei Affair"

Ernest Borgnine, Yvette Mimieux, Ben Gazzara
in "The Neptune Factor"

THE HUNTERS ARE THE HUNTED (Radim) Producer, Rob Houwer; Director, Peter Fleischmann; Screenplay, Mr. Fleischmann; Based on play by Martin Sperr; Photography, Alain Derobe; Editors, Barbara Mondry, Jane Seitz; In color; 86 minutes; May release. CAST: Martin Sperr (Abram), Angela Winkler (Hannelore), Erika Wackernagel (Mayor's Wife), Else Quecke (Barbara), Hanna Schygulla (Paula), Maria Stadler (Butcher's Wife), Hans Elwenspoek (Priest)

THE OFFENSE (United Artists) Producer, Denis O'Dell; Director, Sidney Lumet; Screenplay, John Hopkins; Photography, Gerry Fisher; Editor, John Victor Smith; Art Director, John Clark; Assistant Director, Ted Sturgis; In color; Rated R; 112 minutes; May release. CAST: Sean Connery (Johnson), Trevor Howard (Cartwright), Vivien Merchant (Maureen), Ian Bannen (Baxter), Derek Newark (Jessard), John Hallam (Panton), Peter Bowles (Cameron), Ronald Radd (Lawson), Anthony Sagar (Hill), Howard Goorney (Lambeth), Richard Moore (Garrett), Maxine Gordon (Janie)

THE MATTEI AFFAIR (Paramount) Producer, Franco Cristaldi; Director, Francesco Rosi; Story and Screenplay, Francesco Rosi, Tonino Guerra, Nerio Minuzzo, Tito de Stafano; Editor, Ruggero Mastroianni; Music, Piero Piccioni; A cinema International presentation; Rated R; 118 minutes; May release. CAST: Gian Maria Volonte (Enrico Mattei), Luigi Equarzina (Journalist), Peter Baldwin (McHale), Renato Romano (Journalist), Franco Graziosi (Minister), Gianfranco Ombuen (Engineer), Elio Jotta (Official of Inquiry Commission), Edda Ferronao (Mrs. Mattei), Luciano Colitti (Bertuzzi)

AN AUTUMN AFTERNOON (New Yorker) Producer, Shizuo Yamanouchi; Director, Yasujiro Ozu; Photography, Yashun Atsuta; Editor, Yoshiyashu Hamamura; Screenplay, Kogo Noda, Yasujiro Ozu; Art Director, Tatsuo Hamada; Music, Takanobu Saito; A Shochiku Co. production in Agfacolor; 113 minutes; May release. Cast: Shima Iwashita (Michiko), Shin-Ichiro Mikami (Kazuo), Keiji Sada (Koichi), Mariko Okada (Akiko), Chishu Ryu (Shuhei), Nobuo Nakamura (Shuzo), Kuniko Miyake (Mobuko), Ryuji Kita (Susumu), Eijiro Tohno (Sakuma), Teruo Yoshida (Miura)

THE NEPTUNE FACTOR (20th Century-Fox) Producer, Sanford Howard; Director, Daniel Petrie; Executive Producers, David M. Perlmutter, Harold Greenberg; Screenplay, Jack DeWitt; Photography, Harry Makin; Music, Lalo Schifrin, William McCauley; Designers, Dennis Lynton Clark, Jack McAdam; Editor, Stan Cole; Assistant Directors, Frank Ernst, William Zborowsky; In Panavision and DeLuxe color; Rated G; 97 minutes; May release. CAST: Ben Gazzara (Blake), Yvette Mimieux (Leah), Walter Pidgeon (Andrews), Ernest Borgnine (Mack) Chris Wiggins (Captain), Donnelly Rhodes (Bob), Ed McGibbon (Norton), Michael J. Reynolds (Hal), David Yorston (Stephens), Stuart Gillard (Bradley), Mark Walker (Mounton), Kenneth Pogue (Thomas), Frank Perry (Sub Captain), Dan MacDonald (Hobbs), Leslie Carlson (Briggs), David Renton (Warrant Officer), Joan Gregson (Dobson), Dave Mann (Hawkes), Kay Fujiwara (Anita), Richard Whelan (Radio Officer)

HITLER: THE LAST TEN DAYS (Paramount) Executive Producer, John Heyman; Director, Ennio de Concini; Screenplay, Ennio de Concini, Marie Pia Fusco, Wolfgang Reinhardt; English screenplay adaption, Ivan Moffat; Based on Gerhard Boldt's "Last Days of the Chancellery"; Photography, Ennio Guarnieri; Music, Mischa Spoliansky; Editor, Kevin Connor; Art Director, Roy Walker; Assistant Director, Richard Dalton; A Wolfgang Reinhardt-West Films production; In Panavision and Technicolor; Rated PG; 106 minutes; May release. CAST: Alec Guinness (Hitler), Simon Ward (Hoffman), Adolfo Celi (Krebs), Diane Cilento (Hanna), Gabriele Ferzetti (Keitel), Eric Porter (Von Greim), Doris Kunstmann (Eva Braun), Joss Ackland (Burgdorf), John Barron (Dr. Stumpfegger), John Bennett (Goebbels), Sheila Gish (Frau Christian), Julian Glover (Fegelein), Michael Goodliffe (Weidling), John Hallam (Guensche), Barbara Jefford (Magda Goebbels), Mark Kingston (Bormann), Phyllida Law (Fraulein Manzialy), Ann Lynn (Fraulein Junge), Angela Pleasence (Trude), Andrew Sachs (Wagner), Philip Stone (Jodl), Timothy West (Gebhardt), William Abney (Voss), Kenneth Colley (Boldt), James Cossins (German Officer), Philip Locke (Hanske), Richard Fescud (Von Below), John Savident (Hewel)

Shin-Ichiro Mikami, Mariko Okada, Keiji Sadao,
Chishu Ryu in "An Autumn Afternoon"

Doris Kuntsmann, Alec Guinness
in "Hitler: The Last Ten Days"

Stefania Sabatini, Yveline Cery, Jean-Claude
Aimimi in "Adieu Philippine"

Sylva Koscina, Lando Buzzanca
in "Man of the Year"

AU PAIR GIRLS (Cannon) Producer, Guido Coen; Director, Val Guest; Music, Roger Webb; Screenplay, Val Guest, David Adnopoz; In color; May release. CAST: Gabrielle Drake, Astrid Frank, Me Me Lay, Richard O'Sullivan, Ferdy Mayne, Julian Barnes, John Standing, John LeMesurier, Rosalie Crutchley

AWOL (BFB) Producers, Arne Brandhild, Herb Freed; Executive Producer, Merrill S. Brody; Director, Herb Freed; Screenplay, Richard Z. Chesnoff, Herb Freed; Photography, Merrill Brody; Music, Rupert Holmes; In color; Rated R; 82 minutes; May release. CAST: Russ Thacker (Willy), Isabella Kaliff (Inga), Glynn Turman (Muhammed G.), Lenny Baker (Sidney), Dutch Miller (Cupp), Stefan Ekman (Sven)

ADIEU PHILLIPPINE (New Yorker) Producer, Unitec France; Director, Jacques Rozier; Screenplay, Jacques Rozier, Michel O'-Glor; Photography, Rene Mathelin; Editors, Monique Bonnot, Claude Durand; Music, Jacques Denjean; 111 minutes; May release. CAST: Yveline Cery (Liliane), Stefania Sabatini (Juliette), Jean-Claude Aimimi (Michel), Vittorio Caprioli (Pachala), Davide Tonelli (Horatio)

RED PSALM (Macmillan Audio Brandon) Director, Miklos Jansco; Screenplay, Gyula Hernadi; Photography, Janos Kende; Choreography, Ferenc Pesovar; In Eastmancolor; 88 minutes; June release. CAST: Andrea Drahota, Lajos Balazsovits, Andras Balint, Gyongyi Buros, Jozsef Madaras, Tibor Molnar, Tibor Orban, Bertalan Solti

INTERVAL (Avco Embassy) Producer, Merle Oberon; Director, Daniel Mann; Photography, Gabriel Figueroa; Screenplay, Gavin Lambert; Music, Armando Manzanero, Ruben Fuentes; Editor, Howard S. Deane; Costumes, Luis Estevez; Presented by Joseph E. Levine; In color; Rated PG; 84 minutes; June release. CAST: Merle Oberon (Serena), Robert Wolders (Chris), Claudio Brook (Armando), Russ Conway (Fraser), Charles Bateman (Husband), Britt Leach (Leonard), Peter Von Zerneck (Broch), Fernando Soler, Jr. (Waiter), Gloria Mestre (Rosalia), Christina Moreno (Jody), Betty Lyon (Ellie), Anel (Jackie)

A LIZARD IN A WOMAN'S SKIN (American International) Title changed to "Schizoid"; Direction and Screenplay, Lucio Fulci; Photography, Luigi Kurveiller; Art Director, Roman Calatayud; Editor, Jorge Serralonga; Music, Ennio Morricone; An Edmondo Amati production for Apollo Films; In Technicolor; Rated R; 96 minutes; June release. CAST: Florinda Bolkan (Carol), Stanley Baker (Corvin), Jean Sorel (Frank), Leo Genn (Edmund), Alberto De Mendoza (Detective), Silvia Monti (Julia), Penny Brown (Hippy)

MAN OF THE YEAR (Universal) Executive Producer, Alfonso Vicario; Producer-Director, Marco Vicario; Story and Screenplay, Piero Chiara, Marco Vicario; Photography, Tonino Delli Colli; Designer, Flavio Mogherini; Music, Armando Trovajoli; Sung by Nanni Svampa; Costumes, Mayer; Presented by Earl A. Glick and The Atlantica Cinematofrafica; In Eastmancolor; Rated R; 94 minutes; June release. CAST: Rossana Podesta (Coco), Lando Puzzanca (Michele), Luciano Salce (Achille), Adriana Asti (Marchesa), Ira Furstenberg (Signora Mezzini), Evi Marandi (Giusi), Brigitte Skay (Pina), Angela Luce (Amelia), Femi Benussi (Ersilia), Sandro Dori (Ambrogio), Bernard Skay (Pina), Angela Luce (Amelia), Femi Benussi (Ersilia), Sandro Dori (Ambrogio), Bernard Blier (Dr. Mezzini), Sylva Koscina (Carla)

JONATHAN (New Yorker) Direction and Screenplay, Hans W. Geissendorfer; Photography, Robby Muller; Editor, Wolfgang Hedinger; Music, Roland Kovac; Costumes, Ute Wilhelm; Art Director, Hans Gailling; An Iduna Films production; In Eastmancolor; 103 minutes; June release. CAST: Jurgen Jung (Jonathan), Hans Dieter Jendreyko (Josef), Paul Albert Krumm (Count), Thomas Astan (Thomas), Ilse Kunkele (Lena's mother), Eleonore Schminke (Lena), Oskar Von Schab (Professor), Ilone Grubel (Eleonore)

OPERATION LEONTINE (Macmillan Audio Brandon) Producer, Alain Poire; Director, Michel Audiard; Screenplay, Michel Audiard; Photography, Georges Barsky; In color; 85 minutes; June release. CAST: Francoise Rosay (Leontine), Marlene Jobert (Rita), Andre Pousse (Fred), Bernard Blier (Charles), Robert Dalban (Casmir), Paul Frankeur (Ruffin), Claude Rollet (Tiburce)

Robert Wolders, Merle Oberon
in "Interval"

Marlene Jobert
in "Operation Leontine"

Bud Spencer, Terence Hill
in "All the Way Boys"

Malcolm Tierney, Sandy Ratcliff
in "Family Life"

ALL THE WAY BOYS (Avco Embassy) Producer, Italo Zingarelli; Executive Producer, Roberto Palaggi; Direction and Screenplay, Giuseppe Colizzi; Music, Guido and Maurizio De Angelis; Photography, Marcello Masciocchi; A Joseph E. Levine presentation; In DeLuxe color; Rated G; 105 minutes; June release. CAST: Terence Hill (Plata), Bud Spencer (Salud), Cyril Cusack (Mad Man), Michel Antoine (Caveira), Rene Kolldehoff (Mr. Ears)

MAN FROM DEEP RIVER (Brenner) Producer, Giorgio Lenzi; Director, Umberto Lenzi; In Technicolor and Techniscope; Rated R; June release. CAST: Ivan Rassimov, Me Me Lay

PRISON GUARD (Filmaco) Producer, Novotny-Kubala; Direction and Screenplay, Ivan Renc; Film of America Corp. production; 90 minutes; July release. CAST: Jiri Hrzan (Pepa), Vera Tichanokova (Mother), Helene Vershurova (Mary), Karel Mares (Cervinka)

AND NOW THE SCREAMING STARTS (Cinerama) Producers, Milton Subotsky, Max J. Rosenberg; Director, Roy Ward Baker; Screenplay, Roger Marshall; Photography, Denys Coop; Editor, Peter Tanner; Art Director, Tony Curtis; Assistant Directors, Derek Whitehurst, Lindsey Vickers; An Amicus Films production; In color; Rated PG; 87 minutes; July release. CAST: Peter Cushing (Dr. Pope), Herbert Lom (Henry), Patrick Magee (Dr. Whittle), Ian Ogilvy (Charles), Stephanie Beacham (Catherine), Guy Rolfe (Maitland), Geoffrey Crutchley (Silas), Rosalie Crutchley (Mrs. Luke), Janet Key (Bridget), Gillian Lind (Aunt Edith), Sally Harrison (Sarah), Lloyd Lamble (Sir John), Norman Mitchell (Constable), Frank Forsyth (Servant)

BLOOD OF THE CONDOR (Tricontinental) Producer, Ricardo Rada; Director, Jorge Sanjines; Screenplay, Oscar Soria, Jorge Sanjines; Photography, Antonio Equino; A Ukamau Limitada production; In black and white; 74 minutes; July release. CAST: Marcelino Yanahuava (Ignacio), Benedicta Mendoza Huanca (Paulina), Vicente Salinas (Sixto)

FAMILY LIFE (Cinema 5) Producer, Tony Garnett; Director, Ken Loach; Screenplay, David Mercer; Associate Producer, Irving Teitelbaum; Editor, Roy Watts; Photography, Charles Stewart; Music, Marc Wilkinson; Art Director, William McCrow; Assistant Director, Sean Hudson; Executive Producer, Bob Blues; An Anglo/EMI production; Presented by Nat Cohen; In Technicolor; 108 minutes; July release. CAST: Sandy Ratcliff (Janice), Bill Dean (Baildon), Grace Cave (Mrs. Baildon), Malcolm Tierney (Tim), Hilary Martyn (Barbara), Michael Riddall (Dr. Donaldson), Alan MacNaughton (Carswell), Johnny Gee (Man in the garden)

THE ROWDYMAN (Crowley) Producer, Lawrence Z. Dane; Director, Peter Carter; Screenplay, Gordon Pinsent; Photography, Edmund Long; Music, Ben McPeak; Editor, Michael Manne; In color; 95 minutes; July release. CAST: Gordon Pinsent (Will), Frank Converse (Andrew), Will Geer (Stan), Linda Gorenson (Ruth), Ted Henley (Constable), Estelle Wall (Mary), Stuart Gillard (Bill), Austin Davis (Walt), Dawn Greenhaigh (Woman on train)

HOMO EROTICUS (CIDIF) Producer-Director, Marco Vicario; Screenplay, Piero Chiara, Marco Vicario; Photography, Tonino Delle Colli; Art Director, Flavio Mogherini; Editor, Sergio Montanari; Music, Armando Trovajoli; In color; Rated R; 112 minutes; July release. CAST: Lando Buzzanca (Michele), Rossana Podesta (Mrs. Coco), Luciano Salce (Coco), Adriana Asti (Marchesa), Sylva Koscina (Industrialist), Bernard Blier (Doctor), Ira Furstenberg (His wife), Brigitte Skay (Maid)

SIDDHARTHA (Columbia) Produced, Directed, and Adapted by Conrad Rooks; Based on novel by Hermann Hesse; Photography, Sven Nykvist; Art Director, Malcolm Golding; Music, Hemanta Kumar; Editor, Willy Kemplen; Costumes, Bhanu; In Panavision and Eastmancolor; July release. CAST: Shashi Kapoor (Siddhartha), Simi Garewal (Kamala), Romesh Sharma (Govinda), Pincho Kapoor (Kamaswami), Zul Vellani (Vasudeva), Amrik Singh (Siddhartha's father), Shanti Hiranand (Siddhartha's mother), Kunal Kapoor (Siddhartha's son)

Shashi Kapoor, Simi Garewal
in "Siddhartha"

Choei Takahashi, Sanae Cemi, Midori Tujita
in "Lake of Dracula"

Go Kato, Komaki Kurihara
in "The Long Darkness"

"1001 Danish Delights"

THE LONG DARKNESS (Toho) Executive Producers, Masayuki, Hideyuki; Director, Kei Kumai; Story, Tetsuro Miura; Screenplay, Keiji Hasebe, Kei Kumai; Photography, Kiyomi Kuroda; 120 minutes; July release. CAST: Go Kato (Tetsuro), Komaki Kurihara (Shino), with Uasushi Nagata, Kinzo Shin, Kaneko Iwasaki

DIARY OF A SHINJUKU BURGLAR (Grove) Producer, Masayumi Nakajimi; Director, Nagisa Oshima; Screenplay, Tsutomu Tamura, Mamoru Sasaki, Masao Adachi, Nagisa Oshima; Photography, Yasuhiro Yoshioka, Seizo Sergen; Editor, Nagisa Oshima; In color and black and white; 94 minutes; July release. CAST: Tadanori Tokoo (Birdey), Rie Yokoyama (Umeko), Molchi Tanabe, Tetsu Takahashi, Kei Sato, Fumio Watanabe, Mitsuhior Toura, Kara Juro

THE ADVERSARY (Audio Brandon) Producers, Nepal Dutte, Ahim Dutta; Direction and Screenplay, Satyajit Ray; Based on story by Sunil Ganguly; Photography, Soumendu Ray, Purmendu Base; Editor, Dulal Dutta; Music, Mr. Ray; A Priya Films production; 110 minutes; July release. CAST: Dhritiman Chatterjee (Siddhartha), Krishna Rose, Joyshree Roy, Kalyan Chatterjee, Debral Roy

LAKE OF DRACULA (Toho) Executive Producer, Fumio Tanaka; Director, Michio Yamamoto; In color; 82 minutes; August release. CAST: Midori Fujita (Akiko), Choei Takahashi (Sacki), Sanae Emi (Natsuoke), Mori Kishida

SWORD OF VENGEANCE (Toho) Producer, Shintaro Katsu; Director, Kenji Misumi; Story, Gozeki Kojima, Jazuo Koike; Screenplay, Kazuo Koike; Photography, Chishi Makiura; In color; 83 minutes; August release. CAST: Tomisaburo Wakayama, Fumio Watanabe, Yunosuka Ito, Shigeru Tsuyuguchi, Tomoko Mayama

THE DAY THE SUN ROSE (Shochiku) Producers, Nihon Eiga, Fukko Kyokai; Director, Tetsuya Yamanouchi; Screenplay, Hisayuki Suzuki, Kunio Shimizu; 123 minutes; August release. CAST: Kinnosuke Nakamura (Shinkichi), Toshiro Mifune (Kuma), Shima Iwashita (Ayame), Yunosuke Ito (Akamatsu)

LE SEX SHOP (Peppercorn-Wormser) Direction and Screenplay, Claude Berri; Photography, Pierre Lhomme; Editor, Sophie Coussein; Music, Serge Gainsbourg; In color; Rated X; 92 minutes; August release. CAST: Claude Berri (Claude), Juliet Berto (Isabelle), Jean-Pierre Marielle (Lucien), Nathalie Delon (Jacqueline), Beatrice Romand (Karin)

1001 DANISH DELIGHTS (Cambist) Director, Svend Methling; Screenplay, Bob Ramsing; Photography, Rolf Ronne; A Merry Films production; In color; Rated X; 85 minutes; August release. CAST: Dirch Passer (Count Axel), Axel Strobye (Baron Joachim), Lone Hertz (Inspector), Judy Gringer (Julie), Gertie Jung (Margaretha)

CAGED VIRGINS (Boxoffice International) Executive Producer, Sam Selsky; Director, Jean Rollins; A Harry Novak presentation; Rated R; August release. CAST: Marie Castel, Mireille D'Argent, Philippe Gaste, Dominique

WHEN WOMEN HAD TAILS (Film Ventures International) Director, Pasquale Festa Campanile; Music, Ennio Morricone; In Movielab color; Rated R; August release. CAST: Senta Berger, Giuliano Gemma, Frank Wolff, Paolo Borboni, Lando Buzzanca

THE HONG KONG CAT (American International) A Hallmark presentation in DeLuxe color; Rated R; August release. No other information available.

THE MILITARISTS (Toho) Director, Hiromichi Horikawa; Screenplay, Ryozo Kasahara; Photography, Kazuo Yamada; Art Directors, Iwao Akune, Shigekazu Ikuno; Music, Riichiro Manabe; In Panavision and Eastmancolor; 134 minutes; August release. CAST: Keiju Kobayashi (Tojo), Yuzo Kayama (Goro), Toshio Kurosawa (Pilot), and So Yamamura, Tatsuya Mihashi, Toshiro Mifune (Yamamoto)

ZATOICHI AT LARGE (Toho) Producer, Shintaro Katsu; Director, Kazuo Mori; Screenplay, Kinya Naoi; Story, Kan Shimozawa; Music, Hideakira Sakurai; In Eastmancolor; 88 minutes; September release. CAST: Shintaro Katsu, Hisaya Morishige, Naoko Otani, Etsushi Takahashi, Rentaro Mikuni

"Sword of Vengeance"

Keijiu Kobayashi
in "The Militarists"

211

Shintaro Katsu
in "Zatoichi at Large"

Richard Roundtree
in "Embassy"

THE ASSASSIN (Toho) Producer-Director, Masahiro Shinoda; Photography, Masao Kosugi; In black and white; No other credits; September release. CAST: Tetsuro Tanba (Hachiro)

DEADLY CHINA DOLL (MGM) Producer, Andrew G. Vagna; Director, Huang Feng; Screenplay, Ho Jen; Photography, Li Yiutang; Editor, Chiang Lung; Music, Joseph Koo; A Panasia production; Rated R; 94 minutes; September release. Cast: Angela Mao (Chin), Carter Huang (Pai), Yen I-feng (Han), Nan Kung-hsun (Hu), Ke Hsiang-ting (Chin)

TRIPLE IRONS (National General) Producers, Shaw Brothers; Director, Chang Cheh; Screenplay, I Kuang; Photography, Kung Mu-To; Art Director, Tsao Chuang-Sheng; Editor, Kuo Ting-Hung; Assistang Director, Li Kuo-Chiang; In color; Rated R: 115 minutes: September release. CAST: Li Ching (Pa), David Chiang (Lei), Ti Lung (Feng), Ku Feng (Lung), Chen Hsing (Chen), Wang Chung (Chin), Cheng Lei (Ho)

SCARLET CAMELLIA (Shiro Kido) Director, Yoshitaro Nomura; Screenplay, Masato Moida; Based on novel by Shugoro Yamamoto; Photoplay, Ko Kawamato; Music, Yasushi Akutagawa; Art Director, Takashi Matsuyama; In color; 117 minutes; September release. CAST: Shima Iwashita (Oshino), Yoshi Kato (Kihei), Sachiko Hidari (Osono), Elli Okada (General), Go Kato (Aoki)

QUE HACER (Impact) Producers, James Becket, Saul Landau; Direction and Screenplay, Saul Landau, Nina Serrano, Raul Ruiz; Photography, Gustavo Moris; Editor, Bill Yahraus; Music, Country Joe McDonald; A Lobo Films production; Rated R; 90 minutes; September release. CAST: Sandra Archer (Suzanne), Richard Stahl (Martin), Pablo de la Barra (Hugo), Anibal Reyna (Simon), Lucho Alarcon (Osvaldo), Jorge Yanez (Padre)

FISTS OF THE DOUBLE K (Cannon) In color; Rated R; No other details available; September release.

DEADLY CHINA DOLL (MGM) A Panasia Film; Rated R; No other details available; September release. Starring Angela Mao

EMBASSY (Hemdale) Director, Gordon Hessler; Screenplay, William Fairchild; Photography, Raoul Coutard; Editor, Willy Kemplen; Music, Jonathan Hodge; Song sung by Carl Douglas; In color; A K-Tel presentation; Rated PG; September release. CAST: Richard Roundtree (Shannon), Chuck Connors (Kesten), Marie-Jose Nat (Laure), Ray Milland (Ambassador), Broderick Crawford (Dunninger), Max von Sydow (Gorenko), David Bauer (Kadish), Larry Cross (Gamble), David Healy (Phelan), Karl Held (Rylands), Sara Marshall (Miss Harding), Dee Pollock (Stacy), Afif Boulos (Foreign Minister), Leila Buheiry (Leila), Gail Clymer (Switchboard operator), Edmond Rannania (Man in black), Mounir Maassri (Michel), Saladin Nader (Roge), David Parker (Tuler), Dean Turner (Clem), Peter Smith (Clerk)

KUNG FU THE INVISIBLE FIST (Mahler) A United International Film in color; Rated PG; No other details available; September release.

THE SHANGHAI KILLERS (American International) A Hallmark presentation in color; Rated R; No other details available; September release.

SEVEN BLOWS OF THE DRAGON (New World) A Shaw Brothers production; In Metrocolor; Rated R; September release. Starring David Chiang

LA GRANDE BOUFFE (ABKCO) Producer, Jean Pierre Rossau; Director, Marco Ferreri; Screenplay, Marco Ferreri, Rafael Azcona, Editors, Claudine Merlin, Gina Pignier; Photography, Mario Vulpiani, Pascuale Rachini; Music, Philippe Sarde; A Mara-Capitolina production; 125 minutes; September release. CAST: Marcello Mastroianni, Ugo Tognazzi, Michel Piccoli, Philippe Noiret, Andrea Ferreol

LADY KUNG-FU (National General) Producer, Raymond Chow; Director, Huang Feng; Photography, Li Yu Fang; Rated R; 99 minutes; September release. CAST: Angelo Mao, Carter Hunning, Pai Wing, Han Jae, Wei Ping Ao, Nancy Sit, Terio Yamane

Angelo Mao
in "Deadly China Doll"

Angelo Mao
in "Lady Kung-Fu"

Sharon Gurney, David Ladd
in "Raw Meat"

Tatsuya Nakadai, Keiju Kokayashi, Titsuro
Tamka in "Battle of Okinawa"

RAW MEAT (American International) Producer, Paul Maslansky; Director, Gary Sherman; Screenplay, Ceri Jones; Story, Gary Sherman; Photography, Alex Thomson; Music, Jeremy Rose, Wil Malne; Editor, Geoffrey Foot; Art Director, Dennis Gordon-Orr; In Technicolor; Rated R; 88 minutes; September release. CAST: Donald Pleasence (Inspector Calhoun), Norman Rossington (Det. Rogers), Christopher Lee (Stratton-Villers), David Ladd (Alex), Sharon Gurney (Patricia), Hugh Armstrong ("The Man"), June Turner ('The Woman")' James Cossins (Manfred), Clive Swift (Insp. Richardson), Heather Stoney (Alice), Hugh Dickson (Dr. Bacon), Jack Woolgar (Inspector), Ron Pember (Lift Operator), Colin McCormack, Gary Winkler (Constables), James Culliford (Publican), Suzanne Winkler (Prostitute), Gerry Crampton, Terry Plummer, Gordon Petrie (Tunnel Workers)

THE MAN CALLED NOON (National General) Producer, Euan Lloyd; Director, Peter Collinson; Screenplay, Scot Finch; Based on novel by Louis L'Amour; Photography, John Cabrera; Music, Luis Bacalov; Art Director, Jose Maria Tapiador; Assistant Director, Joe Ochoa; Editor, Alan Pattillo; A Frontier Films presentation; In Technicolor; Rated R; 97 minutes; September release. CAST: Richard Crenna (Noon), Stephen Boyd (Rimes), Rosanna Schiaffino (Fan), Farley Granger (Judge), Patty Shepard (Peg), Angel del Pozo (Janish), Howard Ross (Bayles), Aldo Sambrell (Kissling), Jose Jaspe (Henneker), Charley Bravo (Lang), Ricardo Palacios (Brakeman), Fernando Hilbeck (Ford), Jose Canalejas (Cherry), Cesar Burner (Charlie), Julian Ugarte (Cristobal), Barta Barri (Mexican), Adolfo Thous (Old Mexican), Bruce Fischer (Rancher)

SASUKE AGAINST THE WIND (Bijou) Producer, Shizuo Yamauchi; Director, Masahiro Shinoda; Screenplay, Yoshiyuki Fukuda; Based on novel by Koji Nakada; Photography, Massao Kosugi; Music, Mitsuru Takemitsu; In black and white; 99 minutes; September release. CAST: Kohil Takahashi (Sasuke), Mutsuhiro Toura (Mitsuaki), Misako Watanabe (Okiwa), Seiji Miyaguchi (Jinnai), Yasunori Irikawa (Yashiro), Minoru Hotaka (Genga), Tetsuro Tanha (Sakon), Jitsuko Yoshimura (Omiyo)

BATTLE OF OKINAWA (Toho) Executive Producers, Sanezumi Fujimoto, Hiroshi Haryu; Director, Kihachi Okamoto; Screenplay, Kaneto Shindo; Photography, Hiroshi Murai; Music, Masaru Sato; In Eastmancolor; 149 minutes; September release. CAST: Keiju Kobayashi, Yuzo Kayama, Tetsuro Tanba, Tatsuya Nakadai, Mayumi Ozora

WHAT? (Avco Embassy) Executive Producer, Andrew Graunsberg; Producer, Carlo Ponti; Director, Roman Polanski; Screenplay, Gerard Brach, Roman Polanski; Music, Claudio Gizzi; Photography, Marcello Gatti, Giuseppe Ruzzolini; Editor, Alastair McIntyre; In color; rated X; 112 minutes; October release. CAST: Marcello Mastroianni (Alex), Sydne Rome (Girl), Hugh Griffith (Villa Owner), Romolo Valli (Administrator), Guido Alberti (Priest), Giancarlo Piacentino (Stud), Roman Polanski (Zanzara), Roger Middleton (Jimmy)

SHADOW HUNTERS (Toho) Producer, Yujiro Ishihara; Director, Toshio Masuda; Screenplay, Takao Saito, Kanao Ikegami; In color; 89 minutes; October release. CAST: Yujiro Ishihara, Ryohei Uchida, Mikio Narita, Ruriko Asaoka

THE INHERITOR (Hera) Producer, Jacques E. Strauss; Direction and Screenplay, Philippe Labro; Photography, Jean Penzer; Editor, Claude Barrois; Music, Michel Colombier; Rated PG; 111 minutes; October release. CAST: Jean-Paul Belmondo (Bart), Carla Gravina (Liza), Jean Rochefort (Andre), Charles Denner (David), Maureen Kerwin (Lauren), Michel Beaune (Lambert), Jean Martin (Schneider), Jean De Sailly (Editor)

A TEAR IN THE OCEAN (Levitt-Pickman) Producer-Director, Henri Glaeser; Screenplay, Mr. Glaeser, A. P. Quince; From novel by Manes Sperber; Photography, Claude Lecomte; Music, Joseph Lemovitz; Syn-Frank Enterprises presentation in color; 86 minutes; October release. CAST: Alexandre Stere (Edi), Dominique Rollin (Bynie), Armand Abplanalp (Roman), Henri Glaeser (Rabbi), Dominique Zardi (Yanouch), Jacques Brafman (Mendel), Frantz Wolf (Commandant), Diane Lepvrier (Jadwiga)

Marcello Mastroianni
in "What?"

Jean-Paul Belmondo
in "The Inheritor"

Jack Hawkins (L), Donald Pleasence (C)
in "Tales That Witness Madness"

Woody Strode, Luciana Paluzzi, Henry Silva
in "The Italian Connection"

MASSACRE IN ROME (National General) Producer, Carlo Ponti; Director, George Pan Cosmatos; Screenplay, Robert Katz, Mr. Cosmatos; Based on "Death in Rome" by Robert Katz; Photography, Marcello Gatti; Editors, Francoise Bonnot, Robert Silvi; Music, Ennio Morricone; In color; Rated PG; 145 minutes; October release. CAST: Richard Burton (Kappler), Marcello Mastroianni (Father Pietro), Leo McKern (Maelzer), John Steiner (Dollmann), Robert Harris (Father Pancrazio), Della Boccardo (Elena)

TALES THAT WITNESS MADNESS (Paramount) Producer, Norman Priggen; Director, Freddie Francis; Screenplay, Jay Fairbank; Photography, Norman Warwick; Editor, Bernard Gribble; Music, Bernard Ebbinghouse; Art Director, Roy Walker; Assistant Director, Peter Saunders; A World Film production; In Eastmancolor; Rated R; 90 minutes; October release. CAST: Jack Hawkins (Nicholas), Donald Pleasence (Tremayne), Georgia Brown (Mother), Donald Houston (Father), Russell Lewis (Paul), David Wood (Tutor), Suzy Kendall (Ann/Beatrice), Peter McEnery (Timothy), Neil Kennedy, Richard Connaught (Moving Men), Beth Morris (Polly), Frank Forsyth (Uncle Albert), Joan Collins (Bella), Michael Jayston (Brian), Kim Novak (Auriol), Michael Petrovitch (Kimo), Mary Tamm (Ginny), Lesley Nunnerley (Vera), Leon Lissek (Keoki), Zohra Segal (Malia)

HISTORY LESSONS (New Yorker) Director, Jean-Marie Straub; Producer, Straub-Huillet; Screenplay, Jean-Marie Straub, Daniele Huillet; 85 minutes; October release. CAST: Gottfried Bold (Mummilius Spicer), Benedikt Zulauf (Young Man), Johann Unterpertinger (Peasant)

ANDREI RUBLEV (Columbia) Director, Andrei Tarkovsky; Screenplay, Andrei Mikhalkov-Kontchalovsky, Andrei Tarkovsky; Photography, Vadim Youssov; Editors, N. Beliaeva, L. Lararev; Music, Vlatcheslav Ovtichinnikov; A Mosfilm production; 146 minutes; October release. CAST: Anatoll Solonitzine (Andrei), Ivan Lapikov (Kiril), Nikolai Grinko (Daniel), Nikolai Sergueiev (Theophane), Irma Raouch (Simpleton), Nikolai Bourliaiev (Boriska), Youri Nasarov (Grand Duke)

THE ITALIAN CONNECTION (American International) Director, Fernando Di Leo; Screenplay, Augusto Finocchi, Ingo Hermess,Mr. Di Leo; A German-Italian Co-production in color; Rated R; 92 minutes; October release. Cast: Mario Adorf (Luca), Henry Silva (Dave), Woody Strode (Frank), Adolfo Celi (Don Vito), Luciana Paluzzi (Eva), Cyril Cusack (Corso)

THE PYX (Cinerama) Producers, Maxine Samuels, Julian Roffman; Director, Harvey Hart; Screenplay, Robert Schlitt; From novel by John Buell; Photography, Rene Vexier; Editor, Ron Wisman; Music, Harry Freedman; Songs composed and sung by Karen Black; In color; Rated R; 111 minutes; October release. CAST: Karen Black (Elizabeth), Christopher Plummer (Jim), Donald Pilon (Pierre), Jean-Louis Roux (Keerson), Yvette Brind'Amour (Meg), Jacques Godin (Superintendent), Lee Broker (Herbie), Terry Haig (Jimmy), Robin Gammell (Worther), Louise Rinfret (Sandra)

ANTONY AND CLEOPATRA (Rank) Producer, Peter Snell; Director, Charlton Heston; Photography, Rafael Pacheco; Editor, Eric Boyd-Perkins; Designer, Maurice Pelling; Music, John Scott; Additional Music, Augusto Algero; Assistant Director, Julio Sempere; In Technicolor and Todd AO35; Screenplay adapted from William Shakespeare's play by Charlton Heston; Rated G; 160 minutes; October release. CAST: Charlton Heston (Antony), Hildegard Neil (Cleopatra), Eric Porter (Enobarbus), John Castle (Octavius Caesar), Fernando Rey (Lepidus), Juan Luis Gallardo (Alexas), Carmen Sevilla (Octavia), Freddie Jones (Pompey), Peter Arno (Menas), Luis Barboo (Varrius), Fernando Bilbao (Menecrates), Warren Clarke (Scarus), Roger Delgado (Soothsayer), Julian Glover (Proculeius), Sancho Gracia (Canidius), Garrick Hagan (Eros), John Hallam (Thidias), Sergio Krumbel (Messenger), Jane Lapotaire (Charmian), Jose Manuel Martin (Guard), Joe Melia (Messenger), Manolo Otero (Sentry), Monica Peterson (Iras), Emiliano Redondo (Mardian), Aldo Sambrel (Ventidius), Felipe Solano (Soldier), Doug Wilmer (Agrippa)

Gottfried Bold
in "History Lessons"

Francine Moran, Christopher Plummer
in "The Pyx"

Lucretia Love, Lincoln Tate, Richard Widmark
in "Battle of the Amazons"

Kirk Douglas, Mark Lester, Lesley Anne Down
in "Scalawag"

SAMBIZANGA (New Yorker) Director, Sarah Maldoror; Screenplay, Mario de Andrade, Maurice Pons, Sarah Maldoror; From novel "La Vraie Vie de Domingos Xavier" by Luandino Vieira; Photography, Claude Agostini; In color; 102 minutes; November release. CAST: Domingos Oliviera (Domingos), Elisa Andrade (Maria), Dino Abelino (Zito), Jean M'Vondo (Petelo), Benoit Moutila (Chico), Talagongo (Miguel), Henriette Meya (Bebiana), Les Ombres

BATTLE OF THE AMAZONS (American International) Executive Producer, Sgenio Fiorentini; Producer, Riccardo Billi; Director, Al Bradley; Screenplay, Mario Amendola, Bruno Corbucci, Ferrando Izcaino Casas; Photography, Fausto Rossi; Music, Franco Micalizzi; Art Director, Bartolomeo Scavia; In Italian-Spanish Co-Production in Technicolor; Rated R; 92 minutes, November release. CAST: Lincoln Tate (Zeno), Lucretia Love (Eraglia), Robert Vidmark (Ilio), Solvy Stubing (Sinade), Paola Tedesco (Valeria), Mirta Miller (Melanippe), Benito Sefanelli (Erno), Genia Woods (Antiope), Gincarlo Bastianoni (Filodos), Luigi Ciavarro (Turone), Pilar Clement (Elperia), Sonia Ciuffi (Fara), Riccardo Pizzuti (Medonte), Marco Stefanelli (Medio), Franco Ukmar (Artemio)

SCREAMING TIGER (American International) In Chinese with English subtitles; In color; Rated R; 101 minutes; November release. CAST: Wang Yu (starred)

TIS PITY SHE'S A WHORE (Euro International) Producer, Silvio Clementelli; Director, Giuseppe Patroni Griffi; Screenplay, Patroni Griffi, Alfio Valdarnini, Carlo Carunchio; Based on John Ford play; Photography, Vittorio Storaro; Art Director, Mario Ceroli; Editor, Kim Arcalli; Music, Ennio Morricone; In Technicolor; Rated R; November release. CAST: Charlotte Rampling (Annabella), Oliver Tobias (Giovanni), Fabio Testi (Soranzo), Antonio Falsi (Bonaventura)

SCALAWAG (Paramount) Producer, Anne Douglas; Director, Kirk Douglas; Screenplay, Albert Maltz, Sid Fleishman; From story by Robert Louis Stevenson; Photography, Jack Cardiff; Editor, John Howard; Music, John Cameron; Art Director, Sjelko Senecic; Assistant Director, Bata Maricic; An Inex-Oceania/Bryna production; In Technicolor; Rated G; 93 minutes; November release. CAST: Kirk Douglas (Peg), Mark Lester (Jamie), Neville Brand (Brimstone/-Mudhook), George Eastman (Don Aragon), Don Stroud (Velvet), Lesley Anne Down (Lucy-Ann), Danny DeVito (Fly Speck), Mel Blanc (Barfly the Parrot), Phil Brown (Sandy), Davor Antolic (Rooster), Stole Arandjelovic (Beanbelly), Fabijan Sovagovic (Blackfoot), Shaft Douglas (Beau)

THE MERCHANT OF FOUR SEASONS (New Yorker) Executive Producer, Ingrid Fassbinder; Direction and Screenplay, Rainer Werner Fassbinder; Photography, Dietrich Lohmann; Editor, Rainer Werner Fassbinder; Costumes, Kurt Raab; In color; 88 minutes; November release. CAST: Irm Hermann (Irmgard), Hanna Schygulla (Erna), Hans Hirschmuller (Hans), Kurt Scheydt (Harry), Andrea Schober (Kurt's Wife)

THE SINFUL DWARF (Boxoffice International) Producer, Nicolas Poole; Director, Vidal Raski; Screenplay, William Mayo; Music, Ole Orsed; In color; 92 minutes; December release. Cast: Anne Sparrow, Tony Eades, Clara Keller, Torben, Werner Hedman, Gerda Madsen, Dale Robinson

FANTASTIC PLANET (New World) Director, Rene Laloux; Screenplay, Roland Topor, Rene Laloux; Based on novel by Stefan Wul; Graphic Direction, Joseph Kabri, Joseph Vania; Music, Alain Goraguer; Presented by Roger Corman; In color; Rated PG; 72 minutes; December release. An animated feature.

SCORE (Audubon) Producer-Director, Radley Metzger; Associate Producer, Ava Leighton; Screenplay, Jerry Douglas; Based on his play; Photography, Franjo Vodopivec; Editor, Doris Toumarkine; In Eastmancolor; 90 minutes; December release. CAST: Claire Wilbur (Elvira), Calvin Culver (Eddie), Lynn Lowry (Betsy), Gerald Grant (Jack), Carl Parker (Mike)

Wang Yu
in "Screaming Tiger"

Hans Hirschmuller
in "Merchant of Four Seasons"

215

Bibi Andersson

John Amos

Ursula Andress

Alan Arkin

Lauren Bacall

BIOGRAPHICAL DATA

(Name, real name, place and date of birth, school attended)

ABBOTT, JOHN: London, June 5, 1905.

ABEL, WALTER: St. Paul, Minn., June 6, 1898, AADA.

ADAMS, EDIE: (Elizabeth Edith Enke) Kingston, Pa., Apr. 16, 1931. Juilliard, Columbia.

ADAMS, JULIE: (Betty May) Waterloo, Iowa, Oct. 17, 1928. Little Rock Jr. College.

ADDAMS, DAWN: Felixstowe, Suffolk, Eng., Sept. 21, 1930. RADA.

ADRIAN, IRIS: (Iris Adrian Hostetter) Los Angeles, May 29, 1913.

AGAR, JOHN: Chicago, Jan. 31, 1921.

AHERNE, BRIAN: Worcestershire, Eng., May 2, 1902. Malvern College, U. of London.

AHN, PHILIP: Los Angeles, Mar. 29, 1911. U. of Calif.

AIMEE, ANOUK: Paris, Apr. 27, 1934. Bauer-Therond.

ALBERGHETTI, ANNA MARIA: Pesaro, Italy, May 15, 1936.

ALBERT, EDDIE: (Eddie Albert Heimberger) Rock Island, Ill, Apr. 22, 1908. U. of Minn.

ALBERT, EDWARD: Los Angeles, Feb. 20, 1951.

ALBERTSON, JACK: Rever, Mass.

ALBRIGHT, LOLA: Akron, Ohio, July 20, 1925.

ALDA, ALAN: NYC, Jan. 28, 1936, Fordham.

ALDA, ROBERT: (Alphonso D'Abruzzo) New York City, Feb. 26, 1914. NYU.

ALEJANDRO, MIGUEL: NYC, 1958.

ALEXANDER, JANE: Boston, Mass., Oct 28, 1939, Sarah Lawrence.

ALLBRITTON, LOUISE: Oklahoma City, July 3, 1920. U. of Okla.

ALLEN, STEVE: New York City, Dec. 26, 1921.

ALLEN, WOODY: Brooklyn, Dec. 1, 1935.

ALLENTUCK, KATHERINE: NYC, Oct. 16, 1954; Calhoun.

ALLYSON, JUNE: (Ella Geisman) Westchester, N.Y., Oct. 7, 1923.

AMECHE, DON: (Dominic Amichi) Kenosha, Wisc., May 31, 1908.

AMES, ED: Boston, July 9, 1929.

AMES, LEON: (Leon Wycoff) Portland, Ind., Jan. 20, 1903.

AMOS, JOHN: Newark, NJ., Dec. 27, Bronx Com. Col.

ANDERSON, JUDITH: Adelaide, Australia, Feb. 10, 1898.

ANDERSON, MICHAEL, JR.: London, Eng., 1943.

ANDERSSON, BIBI: Stockholm, Nov. 11, 1935, Royal Dramatic Sch.

ANDES, KEITH: Ocean City, N.J., July 12, 1920. Temple U., Oxford.

ANDRESS, URSULA: Switz., Mar. 19, 1936.

ANDREWS, DANA: Collins, Miss., Jan. 1, 1912. Sam Houston College.

ANDREWS, EDWARD: Griffin, Ga., Oct. 9, 1914. U. VA.

ANDREWS, HARRY: Tonbridge, Kent, Eng., Nov. 10, 1911.

ANDREWS, JULIE: (Julia Elizabeth Wells) Surrey, Eng. Oct. 1, 1935.

ANGEL, HEATHER: Oxford, Eng., Feb. 9, 1909. Wycombe Abbey School.

ANN-MARGRET: (Olsson) Valsjobyn, Sweden, Apr. 28, 1941. Northwestern U.

ANSARA, MICHAEL: Lowell, Mass., Apr. 15, 1922. Pasadena Playhouse.

ASTIN, JOHN: Baltimore, Md., Mar. 30, 1930, UMinn.

ANTHONY, TONY: Clarksburg, W. Va., Oct 16, 1937. Carnegie Tech.

ARCHER, JOHN: (Ralph Bowman) Osceola, Neb., May 8, 1915. U. of S. Calif.

ARDEN, EVE: (Eunice Quedens) Mill Valley, Calif., Apr. 30, 1912.

ARKIN, ALAN: NYC, Mar. 26, 1934. LACC.

ARLEN, RICHARD: Charlottesville, VA., Sept. 1, 1900. St. Thomas College.

ARNAZ, DESI: Santiago, Cuba, Mar. 2, 1917, Colegio de Dolores.

ARNESS, JAMES: (Aurness) Minneapolis, Minn., May 26, 1923. Beloit College.

ARTHUR, BEATRICE: (Frankel) NYC, May 13, 1926, New School.

ARTHUR, JEAN: NYC, Oct. 17, 1908.

ARTHUR, ROBERT: (Robert Arthaud) Aberdeen, Wash., June 18. U. of Wash.

ASHLEY, ELIZABETH: Ocala, Fla., Aug. 30, 1939.

ASTAIRE, FRED: (Fred Austerlitz) Omaha, Neb., May 10, 1899.

ASTOR, MARY: (Lucile V. Langhanke) Quincy, Ill., May 3, 1906. Kenwood-Loring School.

ATHERTON, WILLIAM: New Haven, Conn., July 30, 1947, Carnegie Tech.

ATTENBOROUGH, RICHARD: Cambridge, Eng., Aug. 29, 1923. RADA.

AUBERJONOIS, RENE: NYC, June 1, 1940, Carnegie.

AUGER, CLAUDINE: Paris, Apr. 26, Dramatic Cons.

AULIN, EWA: Stockholm, Sweden, Feb. 14, 1950.

AUMONT, JEAN PIERRE: Paris, Jan. 5, 1913. French Nat'l School of Drama.

AUTRY, GENE: Tioga, Texas, Sept. 29, 1907.

AVALON, FRANKIE: (Francis Thomas Avallone) Philadelphia, Sept. 18, 1940.

AYLMER, FELIX: Corsham, Eng., Feb. 21, 1889. Oxford.

AYRES, LEW: Minneapolis, Minn., Dec. 28, 1908.

AZNAVOUR, CHARLES: (Varenagh Aznourian) Paris, May 22, 1924.

BACALL, LAUREN: (Betty Perske) NYC, Sept. 16, 1924. AADA.

BACKUS, JIM: Cleveland, Ohio, Feb. 25, 1913. AADA.

BADDELEY, HERMIONE: Shropshire, Eng., Nov. 13, 1908. Margaret Morris School.

BAILEY, PEARL: Newport News, Va., March 29, 1918.

BAIN, BARBARA: Chicago, Sept. 13, 1934. U. Ill.

BAKER, CARROLL: Johnstown, Pa., May 28, 1931. St. Petersburg Jr. College.

BAKER, DIANE: Hollywood, Calif, Feb. 25, USC

BAKER, STANLEY: Glamorgan, Wales, Feb. 28, 1928.

BALABAN, ROBERT: Chicago, Aug. 16, 1945, Colgate.

BALIN, INA: Brooklyn, Nov. 12, 1937. NYU.

BALL, LUCILLE: Jamestown, N.Y., Aug. 6, 1911. Chatauqua Musical Inst.

BALSAM, MARTIN: NYC Nov. 4, 1919. Actors Studio.

Dirk Benedict   Marisa Berenson   Helmut Berger   Judi Bowker   Scott Brady

BANCROFT, ANNE: (Anna Maria Italiano) Bronx, N.Y., Sept. 17, 1931. AADA.

BANNEN, IAN: Airdrie, Scot., June 29, 1928.

BARDOT, BRIGITTE: Paris, Sept. 28, 1934.

BARRIE, WENDY: London, May 8, 1919.

BARRON, KEITH: Mexborough, Eng., Aug. 8, 1936. Sheffield Playhouse.

BARRY, DONALD: (Donald Barry de Acosta) Houston, Tex. Texas School of Mines.

BARRY, GENE: (Eugene Klass) NYC, June 14, 1921.

BARRYMORE, JOHN BLYTH: Beverly Hills, Calif., June 4, 1932. St. John's Military Academy.

BARTHOLOMEW, FREDDIE: London, Mar. 28, 1924.

BASEHART, RICHARD: Zanesville, Ohio, Aug. 31, 1914.

BATES, ALAN: Allestree, Derbyshire, Eng., Feb. 17, 1934. RADA.

BAXTER, ALAN: East Cleveland, Ohio, Nov. 19, 1911. Williams U.

BAXTER, ANNE: Michigan City, Ind., May 7, 1923, Ervine School of Drama.

BAXTER, KEITH: South Wales, Apr. 29, 1933, RADA.

BEAL, JOHN: (J. Alexander Bliedung) Joplin, Mo., Aug. 13, 1909. Pa. U.

BEATTY, ROBERT: Hamilton, Ont., Can., Oct. 19, 1909. U. of Toronto.

BEATTY, WARREN: Richmond, Virginia, March 30, 1937.

BEERY, NOAH, JR.: NYC, Aug. 10, 1916. Harvard Military Academy.

BELAFONTE, HARRY: NYC, Mar. 1, 1927.

BELASCO, LEON: Odessa, Russia, Oct. 11, 1902.

BEL GEDDES, BARBARA: NYC, Oct. 31, 1922.

BELL, TOM: Liverpool, Eng., 1932.

BELLAMY, RALPH: Chicago, June 17, 1905.

BELMONDO, JEAN PAUL: Paris, Apr. 9, 1933.

BENEDICT, DIRK: Montana, 1945, Whitman Col.

BENJAMIN, RICHARD: NYC, May 22, 1938, Northwestern U.

BENNETT, BRUCE: (Herman Brix) Tacoma, Wash., U. of Wash.

BENNETT, JILL: Penang, Malay, Dec. 24, 1931.

BENNETT, JOAN: Palisades, N.J., Feb. 27, 1910. St. Margaret's School.

BENNY, JACK: (Jack Kubelsky) Waukegan, Ill., Feb. 14, 1894.

BENSON, ROBBY: Dallas, Tex., Jan. 21, 1956.

BERENSON, MARISSA: NYC, 1947.

BERGEN, CANDICE: Los Angeles, May. 8, 1946.

BERGEN, EDGAR: Chicago, Feb. 16, 1903. Northwestern U.

BERGEN, POLLY: Knoxville, Tenn., July 14, 1930. Compton Jr. College.

BERGER, HELMUT: Salzburg, Aus., 1945.

BERGER, WILLIAM: Austria, Jan. 20, 1928, Columbia.

BERGERAC, JACQUES: Biarritz, France, May 26, 1927. Paris U.

BERGMAN, INGRID: Stockholm, Sweden, Aug. 29, 1917. Royal Dramatic Theatre School.

BERLE, MILTON: (Milton Berlinger) NYC, July 12, 1908. Professional Children's School.

BERLIN, JEANNIE: Los Angeles, Nov. 1, 1949.

BERLINGER, WARREN: Brooklyn, Aug. 31, 1937. Columbia.

BEST, JAMES: Corydon, Ind., July 26, 1926.

BETTGER, LYLE: Philadelphia, Feb. 13, 1915. Anada.

BETZ, CARL: Pittsburgh, Mar. 9. Duquesne, Carnegie Tech.

BEYMER, RICHARD: Avoca, Iowa, Feb. 21, 1939.

BIKEL, THEODORE: Vienna, May 2, 1924. RADA.

BISHOP, JOEY: (Joseph Abraham Gottlieb) Bronx, N.Y., Feb. 3, 1918.

BISHOP, JULIE: (formerly Jacqueline Wells) Denver, Colo., Aug. 30, 1917. Westlake School.

BISSET, JACQUELINE: Waybridge, Eng., Sept. 13, 1944.

BIXBY, BILL: San Francisco, Jan. 22, 1934. U. Cal.

BLACK, KAREN: (Ziegler) Park Ridge, Ill., July 1, 1942. Northwestern.

BLAINE, VIVIAN: (Vivian Stapleton) Newark, N.J., Nov. 21, 1924.

BLAIR, BETSY: (Betsy Boger) NYC, Dec. 11.

BLAIR, JANET: (Martha Jane Lafferty) Blair, Pa., Apr. 23, 1921.

BLAKE, AMANDA: (Beverly Louise Neill) Buffalo, N.Y., Feb. 20.

BLAKE, ROBERT: (Michael Gubitosi) Nutley, N.J., Sept. 18, 1933.

BLONDELL, JOAN: NYC, Aug. 30, 1909.

BLOOM, CLAIRE: London, Feb. 15, 1931. Badminton School.

BLUE, BEN: Montreal, Can., Sept. 12, 1901.

BLYTHE, ANN: Mt. Kisco, N.Y., Aug. 16, 1928. New Wayburn Dramatic School.

BOGARDE, DIRK: London, Mar. 28, 1921. Glasgow & Univ. College.

BOLGER, RAY: Dorchester, Mass., Jan. 10, 1906.

BOND, DEREK: Glasgow, Scot., Jan. 26, 1920. Askes School.

BONDI, BEULAH: Chicago, May 3, 1892.

BOONE, PAT: Jacksonville, Fla., June 1, 1934. Columbia U.

BOONE, RICHARD: Los Angeles. June 18, 1917, Stanford U.

BOOTH, SHIRLEY: NYC, Aug. 30, 1907.

BORGNINE, ERNEST: (Borgnino) Hamden, Conn., Jan. 24, 1918. Randall School.

BOWER, JUDI: Shawford, Eng., Apr. 6, 1954.

BOWMAN, LEE: Cincinnati, Dec. 28, 1914. AADA.

BOYD, STEPHEN: (William Miller) Belfast, Ire., July 4, 1928.

BOYER, CHARLES: Figeac, France, Aug. 28, 1899. Sorbonne U.

BOYLE, PETER: Philadelphia, Pa., 1937, LaSalle Col.

BRACKEN, EDDIE: NYC, Feb. 7, 1920. Professional Children's School.

BRADY, SCOTT: (Jerry Tierney) Brooklyn, Sept. 13, 1924. Bliss-Hayden Dramatic School.

BRAND, NEVILLE: Kewanee, Ill., Aug. 13, 1921.

BRANDO, JOCELYN: San Francisco, Nov. 18, 1919. Lake Forest College. AADA.

BRANDO, MARLON: Omaha, Neb., Apr. 3, 1924. New School of Social Research.

BRASSELLE, KEEFE: Elyria, Ohio, Feb. 7.

BRAZZI, ROSSANO: Bologna, Italy, 1916. U. of Florence.

BRENNAN, WALTER: Swampscott, Mass., July 25, 1894.

BRENT, GEORGE: Dublin, Ire., Mar. 15, 1904. Dublin U.

BRENT, ROMNEY: (Romulo Larralde) Saltillo, Mex., Jan. 26, 1902.

BRIAN, DAVID: NYC, Aug. 5, 1914. CCNY.

BRIDGES, BEAU: Los Angeles, Dec. 9, 1941. UCLA.

BRIDGES, JEFF: Los Angeles, Dec. 4, 1949.

| Barry Brown | Catherine Burns | Edd Byrnes | Rosalind Cash | Jean-Pierre Cassel |

BRIDGES, LLOYD: San Leandro, Calif., Jan. 15, 1913.

BRITT, MAY: (Maybritt Wilkins) Sweden, March 22, 1936.

BRODIE, STEVE: (Johnny Stevens) Eldorado, Kan., Nov. 25, 1919.

BROMFIELD, JOHN: (Farron Bromfield) South Bend, Ind., June 11, 1922. St. Mary's College.

BRONSON, CHARLES: (Buchinsky) Ehrenfeld, Pa., Nov. 3, 1922.

BROOKS, GERALDINE: (Geraldine Stroock) NYC, Oct. 29, 1925. AADA.

BROWN, BARRY: San Jose, Cal., Apr. 19, 1951, LACC.

BROWN, JAMES: Desdemona, Tex., Mar. 22, 1920. Baylor U.

BROWN, JIM: Manhasset, L.I., N.Y., Feb. 17, 1935 Syracuse U.

BROWN, Tom: NYC, Jan. 6, 1913. Professional Children's School.

BROWNE, CORAL: Melbourne, Aust., July 23, 1913.

BRUCE, VIRGINIA: Minneapolis, Sept. 29, 1910

BRYNNER, YUL: Sakhalin Island, Japan, July 11, 1915.

BUCHHOLZ, HORST: Berlin, Ger., Dec. 4, 1933. Ludwig Dramatic School.

BUETEL, JACK: Dallas, Tex., Sept. 5, 1917.

BUJOLD, GENEVIEVE: Montreal, Can., July 1, 1942.

BURKE, PAUL: New Orleans, July 21, 1926. Pasadena Playhouse.

BURNETT, CAROL: San Antonio, Tex., Apr. 26, 1933. UCLA.

BURNS, CATHERINE: NYC, Sept. 25, 1945, AADA.

BURNS, GEORGE: (Nathan Birnbaum) NYC, Jan. 20, 1896.

BURR, RAYMOND: New Westminster, B.C., Can., May 21, 1917. Stanford, U. of Cal., Columbia.

BURTON, RICHARD (Richard Jenkins) Pontrhydyfen, S. Wales, Nov. 10, 1925. Oxford.

BUTTONS, RED: (Aaron Chwatt) NYC, Feb. 5, 1919.

BUZZI, RUTH: Wequetequock, R.I., July 24, 1936. Pasadena Playhouse.

BYGRAVES, MAX: London, Oct. 16, 1922. St. Joseph's School.

BYRNES, EDD: NYC, July 30, 1933. Haaren High

CAAN, JAMES: Bronx, NY, Mar. 26, 1939.

CABOT, SUSAN: Boston, July 6, 1927.

CAESAR, SID: Yonkers, N.Y., Sept. 8, 1922.

CAGNEY, JAMES: NYC, July 1, 1904. Columbia.

CAGNEY, JEANNE: NYC, Mar. 25, 1919. Hunter.

CAINE, MICHAEL: (Maurice Michelwhite) London, Mar. 14, 1933.

CALHOUN, RORY: (Francis Timothy Durgin) Los Angeles, Aug. 8, 1923.

CALLAN, MICHAEL: (Martin Calinieff) Philadelphia, Nov. 22, 1935.

CALVERT, PHYLLIS: London, Feb. 18, 1917. Margaret Morris School.

CALVET, CORRINE: (Corrine Dibos) Paris, Apr. 30. U. Of Paris.

CAMBRIDGE, GODFREY: NYC, Feb. 26, 1933. CCNY.

CAMERON, ROD: (Rod Cox) Calgary, Alberta, Can., Dec. 7, 1912.

CAMPBELL, GLEN: Delight, Ark. Apr. 22, 1935

CANALE, GIANNA MARIA: Reggio Calabria, Italy, Sept. 12.

CANNON, DYAN: (Samille Diane Friesen) Jan. 4, 1929, Tacoma, Wash.

CANOVA, JUDY: Jacksonville, Fla., Nov. 20, 1916.

CAPERS, VIRGINIA: Sumter, SC, 1925, Juilliard.

CAPUCINE: (Germaine Lefebvre) Toulon, France, Jan. 6, 1935.

CARDINALE, CLAUDIA: Tunis, NAfrica, Apr. 15, 1939; College Paul Cambon.

CAREY, HARRY, JR,: Saugus, Calif., May 16, Black Fox Military Academy.

CAREY, MACDONALD: Sioux City, Iowa, Mar. 15, 1913. U. of Wisc., U. of Iowa.

CAREY, PHILIP: Hackensack, N.J., July 15, 1925. U. of Miami.

CARMICHAEL, HOAGY: Bloomington, Ind., Nov. 22, 1899. Ind. U.

CARMICHAEL, IAN: Hull, Eng., June 18, 1920. Scarborough College.

CARNE, JUDY: (Joyce Botterill) Northampton, Eng., 1939. Bush-Davis Theatre School.

CARNEY, ART: Mt. Vernon, N.Y., Nov. 4, 1918.

CARON, LESLIE: Paris, July 1, 1931. Nat'l Conservatory, Paris.

CARR, VIKKI: (Florence Cardona) July 19, 1942. San Fermardo, Col.

CARRADINE, DAVID: Hollywood, Dec. 8, 1936. San Francisco State.

CARRADINE, JOHN: NYC, Feb. 5, 1906.

CARREL, DANY: Tourane, Indochina, Sept. 20, 1936. Marseilles Cons.

CARROLL, DIAHANN: (Johnson) NYC, July 17, 1935. NYU.

CARROLL, JOHN: (Julian LaFaye) New Orleans.

CARROLL, MADELEINE: West Bromwich, Eng., Feb. 26, 1906. Birmingham U.

CARROLL, PAT: Shreveport, La., May 5, 1927. Catholic U.

CARSON, JOHNNY: Corning, Iowa, Oct. 23, 1925. U. of Neb.

CARSTEN, PETER: (Ransenthaler) Weissenberg, Bavaria, Apr. 30, 1929; Munich Akademie for Actors.

CASH, ROSALIND: Atlantic City, NJ, Dec. 31, 1938, CCNY.

CASON, BARBARA: Memphis, Tenn., Nov. 15, 1933, UIowa.

CASS, PEGGY: (Mary Margaret) Boston, May 21, 1925.

CASSAVETES, JOHN: NYC, Dec. 9, 1929. Colgate College, Academy of Dramatic Arts.

CASSEL, JEAN-PIERRE: Paris, 1932.

CASSIDY, DAVID: NY C, Apr. 12, 1950.

CASSIDY, JOANNA: Camden, NJ, 1944, Syracuse U.

CASTELLANO, RICHARD: Bronx, NY, Sept. 3, 1934.

CAULFIELD, JOAN: Orange, N.J., June 1. Columbia U.

CELI, ADOLFO: Sicily, July 27, 1922, Rome Academy.

CHAKIRIS, GEORGE: Norwood, O., Sept. 16, 1933.

CHAMBERLAIN, RICHARD: Beverly Hills, Cal., March 31, 1935. Pomona.

CHAMPION, GOWER: Geneva, Ill., June 22, 1921.

CHAMPION, MARGE: Los Angeles, Sept. 2, 1926.

CHANNING, CAROL: Seattle, Jan. 31, 1921. Bennington.

CHAPLIN, CHARLES: London, Apr. 16, 1889.

CHAPLIN, GERALDINE: Santa Monica, Cal. July 31, 1944. Royal Ballet.

CHAPLIN, SYDNEY: Los Angeles, Mar. 31, 1926. Lawrenceville.

CHARISSE, CYD: (Tula Ellice Finklea) Amarillo, Tex., Mar. 3, 1923. Hollywood Professional School.

CHASE, ILKA: NYC, Apr. 8, 1905.

CHER: (Cheryl La Piere) 1946.

CHIARI, WALTER: Verona, Italy, 1930.

Ellen Corby   John Cullum   Joan Collins   Joseph Cotten   Blythe Danner

CHRISTIAN, LINDA: (Blanca Rosa Welter) Tampico, Mex., Nov. 13, 1923.

CHRISTIE, JULIE: Chukua, Assam, India, Apr. 14, 1941.

CHRISTOPHER, JORDAN: Youngstown, O., Oct. 23, 1940. Kent State.

CHURCHILL, SARAH: London, Oct. 7, 1916.

CILENTO, DIANE: Queensland, Australia, Oct. 5, 1933. AADA.

CLARK, DANA: NYC, Feb. 18, 1915. Cornell, Johns Hopkins U.

CLARK, DICK: Mt. Vernon, N.Y., Nov. 30, 1929, Syracuse University.

CLARK, PETULA: Epsom England, Nov. 15, 1932.

CLARK, MAE: Philadelphia, Aug. 16, 1910.

CLEMENTS, STANLEY: Long Island, N.Y., July 16, 1926.

CLOONEY, ROSEMARY: Maysville Ky., May 23, 1928.

COBB, LEE J.: NYC, Dec. 8, 1911. CCNY.

COBURN, JAMES: Laurel, Neb., Aug. 31, 1928. LACC.

COCA, IMOGENE: Philadelphia, Nov. 18, 1908.

COCO, JAMES: NYC, Mar. 21, 1929.

CODY, KATHLEEN: Bronx, NY, Oct. 30, 1953.

COLBERT, CLAUDETTE: (Claudette Chauchoin) Paris, Sept. 13, 1907. Art Students League.

COLE, GEORGE: London, Apr. 22, 1925.

COLLINS, JOAN: London, May 23, 1933. Francis Holland School.

COMER, ANJANETTE: Dawson, Tex., Aug. 7, 1942. Baylor, Tex. U.

CONANT, OLIVER: NYC, Nov. 15, 1955; Dalton.

CONNERY, SEAN: Edinburgh, Scot. Aug. 25, 1930.

CONNORS, CHUCK: (Kevin Joseph Connors) Brooklyn, Apr. 10, 1924. Seton Hall College.

CONRAD, WILLIAM: Louisville, Ky., Sept. 27, 1920.

CONTE, RICHARD: (Nicholas Conte) NYC, Mar. 24, 1914. Neighborhood Playhouse.

COOGAN, JACKIE: Los Angeles, Oct. 26, 1914. Villanova College.

COOK, ELISHA, JR.: San Francisco, Dec. 26, 1907. St. Albans.

COOPER, BEN,: Hartford, Conn., Sept. 30. Columbia U.

COOPER, JACKIE: Los Angeles, Sept. 15, 1921.

COOTE, ROBERT: London, Feb. 4, 1909. Hurstpierpont College.

CORBY, ELLEN: (Hansen) Racine, Wisc., June 13, 1914.

CORCORAN, DONNA: Quincy, Mass., Sept. 29.

CORD, ALEX: (Viespi) Floral Park, L.I., Aug. 3, 1931. NYU, Actors Studio.

CORDAY, MARA: (Marilyn Watts) Santa Monica, Calif., Jan. 3, 1932.

COREY, JEFF: NYC, Aug. 10, 1914. Fagin School.

CORRI, ADRIENNE: Glasgow, Scot., Nov. 13, 1933. RADA.

CORTESA, VALENTINA: Milan, Italy, Jan. 1, 1925.

COSBY, BILL: Philadelphia, 1937. Temple U.

COTTEN, JOSEPH: Petersburg, Va., May 13, 1905.

COURTENAY, TOM: Hull, Eng., Feb. 25, 1937. RADA.

CORLAN, ANTHONY: Cork City, Ire., May 9, 1947; Birmingham School of Dramatic Arts.

COURTLAND, JEROME: Knoxville, Tenn., Dec. 27, 1926.

CRABBE, BUSTER (LARRY): (Clarence Linden) Oakland, Calif., U. of S. Cal.

CRAIG, JAMES: (James H. Meador) Nashville, Tenn., Feb. 4, 1912. Rice Inst.

CRAIG, MICHAEL: India in 1929.

CRAIN, JEANNE: Barstow, Cal., May 25, 1925.

CRAWFORD, BRODERICK: Philadelphia, Dec. 9, 1911.

CRAWFORD, JOAN: (Billie Cassin) San Antonio, Tex., Mar. 23, 1908.

CRENNA, RICHARD: Los Angeles, Nov. 30, 1927. USC.

CRISTAL, LINDA: (Victoria Moya) Buenos Aires, 1935.

CROSBY, BING: (Harry Lillith Crosby) Tacoma, Wash., May 2, 1904. Gonzaga College.

CROWLEY, PAT: Olyphant, Pa., Sept. 17, 1933.

CULLUM, JOHN: Knoxville, Tenn., Mar. 2, 1930, UTenn.

CULP, ROBERT: Berkeley, Calif., Aug. 16, 1930. U. Wash.

CUMMINGS, CONSTANCE: Seattle, Wash., May 15, 1910.

CUMMINGS, ROBERT: Joplin, Mo., June 9, 1910. Carnegie Tech.

CUMMINS, PEGGY: Prestatyn, N. Wales, Dec. 18, 1926. Alexandra School.

CURTIS, KEENE: Salt Lake City, U., Feb. 15, 1925, U. Utah.

CURTIS, TONY: (Bernard Schwartz) NYC, June 3, 1925.

CUSHING, PETER: Kenley, Surrey, Eng., May 26, 1913.

CUTTS, PATRICIA: London, July 20, 1927. RADA.

DAHL, ARLENE: Minneapolis, Aug. 11, 1927. U. Minn.

DALLESANDRO, JOE: Pensacola, Fla., Dec. 31, 1948.

DALTON, TIMOTHY: Wales, 1945; RADA.

DAMONE, VIC: (Vito Farinola) Brooklyn, June 12, 1928.

DANIELS, WILLIAM: Bklyn, Mar. 31, 1927. Northwestern

DANNER, BLYTHE: Philadelphia, Pa., Bard Col.

DANO, ROYAL: NYC, Nov. 16, 1922, NYU.

DANTINE, HELMUT: Vienna, Oct. 7, 1918. U. Calif.

DANTON, RAY: NYC, Sept. 19, 1931. Carnegie Tech.

DARBY, KIM: (Deborah Zerby) North Hollywood, Cal., July 8, 1948.

DARCEL, DENISE: (Denise Billecard) Paris, Sept. 8, 1925. U. Dijon.

DARREN, JAMES: Philadelphia, June 8, 1936. Stella Adler School.

DARRIEUX, DANIELLE: Bordeaux, France, May 1, 1917. Lycee LaTour.

DA SILVA, HOWARD: Cleveland, Ohio, May 4, 1909. Carnegie Tech.

DAUPHIN, CLAUDE: Corbeil, France, Aug. 19, 1903. Beaux Arts School.

DAVIDSON, JOHN: Pittsburgh, Dec. 13, 1941. Denison U.

DAVIES, RUPERT: Liverpool, Eng., 1916.

DAVIS, BETTE: Lowell, Mass., Apr. 5, 1908. John Murray Anderson Dramatic School.

DAVIS, OSSIE: Cogdell, Ga., Dec. 18, 1917. Howard U.

DAVIS, SAMMY, JR.: NYC, Dec. 8, 1925.

DAY, DENNIS: (Eugene Dennis McNulty) NYC, May 21, 1917. Manhattan College.

DAY, DORIS: (Doris Kappelhoff) Cincinnati, Apr. 3, 1924.

DAY, LARAINE: (Johnson) Roosevelt, Utah, Oct. 13, 1920.

DAYAN, ASSEF: Israel, 1945. U. Jerusalem.

DEAN, JIMMY: Plainview, Tex., Aug. 10, 1928.

DE CARLO, YVONNE: (Peggy Yvonne Middleton) Vancouver, B.C., Can., Sept. 1, 1924. Vancouver School of Drama.

DEE, FRANCES: Los Angeles, Nov. 26, 1907. Chicago U.

DEE, JOEY: (Joseph Di Nicola) Passaic, N.J., June 11, 1940. Patterson State College.

| Ruby Dee | Robert Duvall | Isobel Elsom | Michael Enserro | Shelley Fabares |

DEE, RUBY: Cleveland, O., Oct. 27, Hunter Col.

DEE, SANDRA: (Alexandra Zuck) Bayonne, N.J., Apr. 23, 1942.

DE FORE, DON: Cedar Rapids, Iowa, Aug. 25, 1917. U. Iowa.

DE HAVEN, GLORIA: Los Angeles, July 23, 1925.

DE HAVILLAND, OLIVIA: Tokyo, Japan, July 1, 1916. Notre Dame Convent School.

DELL, GABRIEL: Barbados, BWI, Oct. 7, 1930.

DELON, ALAIN: Sceaux, Fr., Nov. 8, 1935.

DEL RIO, DOLORES: (Dolores Ansunsolo) Durango, Mex., Aug. 3, 1905. St. Joseph's Convent.

DE NIRO, ROBERT: NYC, Aug. 17, 1943, Stella Adler.

DENISON, MICHAEL: Doncaster, York, Eng., Nov. 1, 1915. Oxford.

DENEUVE, CATHERINE: Paris, Oct. 22, 1943.

DENNIS, SANDY: Hastings, Neb., Apr. 27, 1937. Actors Studio.

DEREK, JOHN: Hollywood, Aug. 12, 1926.

DERN, BRUCE: Chicago, June 4, 1936, UPa.

DE SICA, VITTORIO: Sora, Caserta, Italy, July 7, 1902.

DEVINE, ANDY: Flagstaff, Ariz., Oct. 7, 1905. Ariz. State College.

DEWHURST, COLLEEN: Montreal, June 3, 1926, Lawrence U.

DEXTER, ANTHONY: (Walter Reinhold Alfred Fleischmann) Talmadge, Neb., Jan. 19, 1919. U. Iowa.

DICKINSON, ANGIE: Kulm, N. Dak., Sept. 30, 1932. Glendale College.

DIETRICH, MARLENE: (Maria Magdalene von Losch) Berlin, Ger., Dec. 27, 1904. Berlin Music Academy.

DIFFRING, ANTON: Loblenz, Ger. Berlin Dramatic Art School.

DILLER, PHYLLIS: Lima, O., July 17, 1917. Bluffton College.

DILLMAN, BRADFORD: San Francisco, Apr. 14, 1930.

DOBSON, TAMARA: Baltimore, Md., 1947, Md. Inst. of Art.

DOMERGUE, FAITH: New Orleans, June 16, 1925.

DONAHUE, TROY: (Merle Johnson) NYC, Jan. 27, 1937. Columbia U.

DONNELL, JEFF: (Jean Donnell) South Windham, Me., July 10, 1921. Yale Drama School.

DONNELLY, RUTH: Trenton, N.J., May 17, 1896.

DORS, DIANA: Swindon, Wilshire, Eng., Oct. 23, 1931. London Academy of Music.

D'ORSAY, FIFI: Montreal, Can., Apr. 16, 1904.

DOUGLAS, KIRK: Amsterdam, N.Y., Dec. 9, 1916. St. Lawrence U.

DOUGLAS, MELVYN: (Melvyn Hesselberg) Macon, Ga., Apr. 5, 1901.

DOUGLAS, MICHAEL: Hollywood, Sept. 25, 1944, U. Cal.

DOWN, LESLEY ANN: London, Mar. 17, 1954.

DRAKE, BETSY: Paris, Sept. 11, 1923.

DRAKE, CHARLES: (Charles Ruppert) NYC, Oct. 2, 1914. Nichols College.

DREW, ELLEN: (formerly Terry Ray) Kansas City, Mo., Nov. 23, 1915.

DRIVAS, ROBERT: Chicago, Oct. 7, 1938. U. Chi.

DRU, JOANNE: (Joanne LaCock) Logan, W. Va., Jan. 31, 1923. John Robert Powers School.

DUFF, HOWARD: Bremerton, Wash., Nov. 24, 1917.

DUKE, PATTY: NYC, Dec. 14, 1946.

DULLEA, KEIR: Cleveland, N.J., May 30, 1936. Neighborhood Playhouse, SF State Col.

DUNAWAY, FAYE: Bascom, Fla., Jan, 14, 1941. Fla. U.

DUNCAN, SANDY: Henderson, Tex., Feb. 20, 1946; Len Morris Col.

DUNNE, IRENE: Louisville, Ky., Dec. 20, 1904. Chicago College of Music.

DUNNOCK, MILDRED: Baltimore, Jan. 25, 1906. Johns Hopkins and Columbia U.

DURANTE, JIMMY: NYC, Feb. 10, 1893.

DURNING, CHARLES: Highland Falls, NY, Feb. 28, 1933, NYU.

DUVALL, ROBERT: San Diego, Cal., 1930, Principia Col.

DVORAK, ANN: (Ann McKim) NY C, Aug. 2, 1912.

EASTON, ROBERT: Milwaukee, Nov. 23, 1930. U. of Texas.

EASTWOOD, CLINT: San Francisco, May 31, 1930 LACC.

EATON, SHIRLEY: London, 1937. Aida Foster School.

EDEN, BARBARA: (Moorhead) Tucson, Ariz., 1934.

EDWARDS, VINCE: NYC, July 9, 1928. AADA.

EGAN, RICHARD: San Francisco, July 29, 1923. Stanford U.

EGGAR, SAMANTHA: London, Mar. 5, 1939.

EKBERG, ANITA: Malmo, Sweden, Sept. 29, 1931.

ELLIOTT, DENHOLM: London, May 31, 1922. Malvern College.

ELSOM, ISOBEL: Cambridge, Eng., Mar. 16, 1894.

ELY, RON: (Ronald Pierce) Hereford, Tex. June 21, 1938.

EMERSON, FAYE: Elizabeth, La., July 8, 1917. San Diego State College.

ENSERRO, MICHAEL: Soldier, Pa., Oct. 5, 1918. Allegheny Col.

ERDMAN, RICHARD: Enid, Okla., June 1, 1925.

ERICKSON, LEIF: Alameda, Calif., Oct. 27, 1911. U. of Calif.

ERICSON, JOHN: Dusseldorf, Ger., Sept. 25, 1926. AADA.

ESMOND, CARL: Vienna, June 14, 1906. U. of Vienna.

EVANS, DALE: (Francis Smith) Uvalde, Texas, Oct. 31, 1912.

EVANS, EDITH: London, Feb. 8, 1888.

EVANS, GENE: Holbrook, Ariz., July 11, 1922.

EVANS, MAURICE: Dorchester, Eng., June 3, 1901.

EVERETT, CHAD: (Ray Cramton) South Bend, Ind., June 11, 1936.

EWELL, TOM: (Yewell Tompkins) Owensboro, Ky., Apr. 29, 1909. U. of Wisc.

FABARES, SHELLEY: Los Angeles, Jan. 19, 1944.

FABIAN: (Fabian Forte) Philadelphia, Feb. 6, 1940.

FABRAY, NANETTE: (Ruby Nanette Fabares) San Diego, Oct. 27, 1920.

FAIRBANKS, DOUGLAS JR.: NYC, Dec. 9, 1909, Collegiate School.

FALK, PETER: NYC, Sept. 16, 1927, New School.

FARENTINO, JAMES: Brooklyn, Feb. 24, 1938.

FARR, FELICIA: Westchester, N.Y., Oct. 4, 1932. Penn State College.

FARRELL, CHARLES: Onset Bay, Mass., Aug. 9, 1901. Boston U.

FARROW, MIA: Los Angeles, Feb. 9, 1945.

FAULKNER, GRAHAM: London, Sept. 26, 1947, Webber-Douglas Acad.

FAYE, ALICE: (Ann Leppert) NYC, May 5, 1915.

FELDON, BARBARA: (Hall) Pittsburgh, Mar. 12, 1941. Carnegie Tech.

FELLOWS, EDITH: Boston, May 20, 1923.

Robert Forster Rhonda Fleming Al Freeman, Jr. Joan Greenwood John Gavin

FERRER, JOSE: Santurce, P.R., Jan. 8, 1912. Princeton U.

FERRER, MEL: Elberon, N.J., Aug. 25, 1917. Princeton U.

FERRIS, BARBARA: London 1943.

FIELD, SALLY: Pasadena, Cal., Nov. 6, 1946.

FIGUEROA, RUBEN: NYC 1958.

FINCH, PETER: London, Sept. 28, 1916.

FINNEY, ALBERT: Salford, Lancashire, Eng., May 9, 1936. RADA.

FISHER, EDDIE: Philadelphia, Aug. 10, 1928.

FITZGERALD, GERALDINE: Dublin, Ire., Nov. 24, 1914. Dublin Art School.

FLEMING, RHONDA: (Marilyn Louis) Los Angeles, Aug. 10, 1922.

FLEMYNG, ROBERT: Liverpool, Eng., Jan. 3, 1912. Haileybury College.

FLYNN, JOE: Youngstown, O., Nov. 8, 1924; Notre Dame.

FOCH, NINA: Leyden, Holland, Apr. 20, 1924.

FONDA, HENRY: Grand Island, Neb., May 16, 1905. Minn. U.

FONDA, JANE: NYC, Dec. 21, 1937. Vassar.

FONDA, PETER: NYC, Feb. 23, 1939. U. of Omaha.

FONTAINE, JOAN: Tokyo, Japan, Oct. 22, 1917.

FORD, GLENN: (Gwyllyn Samuel Newton Ford) Quebec, Can., May 1, 1916.

FORD, PAUL: Baltimore, Nov. 2, 1901. Dartmouth.

FOREST, MARK: (Lou Degni) Brooklyn, Jan. 1933.

FORREST, STEVE: Huntsville, Tex., Sept. 29. UCLA.

FORSTER, ROBERT: (Foster, Jr.) Rochester, N.Y., July 13, 1941. Rochester U.

FORSYTHE, JOHN: Penn's Grove, N.J., Jan. 29, 1918.

FOX, EDWARD: London, 1937, RADA.

FOX, JAMES: London, 1939.

FRANCIS, CONNIE: (Constance Franconero) Newark, N.J., Dec. 12, 1938.

FRANCIOSA, ANTHONY: NYC, Oct. 25, 1928.

FRANCIS, ANNE: Ossining, N.Y., Sept. 16.

FRANCIS, ARLENE: (Arlene Kazanjian) Boston, Oct. 20, 1908. Finch School.

FRANCISCUS, JAMES: Clayton, Mo., Jan. 31. 1934, Yale.

FRANCKS, DON: Vancouver, Can., Feb. 28, 1932.

FRANZ, ARTHUR: Perth Amboy, N.J., Feb. 29, 1920. Blue Ridge College.

FRANZ, EDUARD: Milwaukee, Wisc., Oct. 31, 1902.

FREEMAN, AL, JR.: San Antonio, Texas, 1934. CCLA.

FREEMAN, MONA: Baltimore, Md., June 9, 1926.

FREY, LEONARD: Brooklyn, Sept. 4, 1938, Neighborhood Playhouse.

FURNEAUX, YVONNE: Lille, France, 1928. Oxford U.

GABEL, MARTIN: Philadelphia, June 19, 1912. AADA.

GABIN, JEAN: Villette, France, May 17, 1904.

GABOR, EVA: Budapest, Hungary, Feb. 11, 1925.

GABOR, ZSA ZSA: (Sari Gabor) Budapest, Hungary, Feb. 6, 1923.

GAM, RITA: Pittsburgh, Pa., Apr. 2, 1928.

GARBER, VICTOR: Montreal, Can., Mar. 16, 1949.

GARBO, GRETA: (Greta Gustafson) Stockholm, Sweden, Sept. 18, 1906.

GARDENIA, VINCENT: Naples, Italy, Jan. 7, 1922.

GARDINER, REGINALD: Wimbledon, Eng., Feb. 1903. RADA.

GARDNER, AVA: Smithfield, N.C., Dec. 24, 1922. Atlantic Christian College.

GARNER, JAMES: (James Baumgarner) Norman, Okla., Apr. 7, 1928. Okla. U.

GARNER, PEGGY ANN: Canton, Ohio, Feb. 3, 1932.

GARRETT, BETTY: St. Joseph, Mo., May 23, 1919. Annie Wright Seminary.

GARRISON, SEAN: NYC, Oct. 19, 1937.

GARSON, GREER: Ireland, Sept. 29, 1908.

GASSMAN, VITTORIO: Genoa, Italy, Sept. 1, 1922. Rome Academy of Dramatic Art.

GAVIN, JOHN: Los Angeles, Apr. 8, 1935. Stanford U.

GAYNOR, JANET: Philadelphia, Oct. 6, 1906.

GAYNOR, MITZI: (Francesca Marlene Von Gerber) Chicago, Sept. 4, 1930.

GAZZARA, BEN: NYC, Aug. 28, 1930.

GEER, WILL: Frankfort, Ind., Mar. 9, 1902. Columbia.

GEESON, JUDY: Arundel, Eng., Sept. 10, 1948, Corona.

GENN, LEO: London, Aug. 9, 1905. Cambridge.

GIELGUD, JOHN: London, Apr. 14, 1904. RADA.

GILLMORE, MARGALO: London, May 31, 1897. AADA.

GILMORE, VIRGINIA: (Sherman Poole) Del Monte, Calif., July 26, 1919. U. of Calif.

GINGOLD, HERMIONE: London, Dec. 9, 1897.

GISH, LILLIAN: Springfield, Ohio, Oct. 14, 1896.

GLEASON, JACKIE: Brooklyn, Feb. 26, 1916.

GODDARD, PAULETTE: (Levy) Great Neck, N.Y., June 3, 1911.

GONZALES-GONZALEZ, PEDRO: Aguilares, Tex., Dec. 21, 1926.

GORDON, GALE: (Aldrich) NYC, Feb. 2, 1906.

GORDON, RUTH: Wollaston, Mass., Oct. 30, 1896. AADA.

GORING, MARIUS: Newport, Isle of Wright; 1912; Cambridge; Old Vic.

GORMAN, CLIFF: Jamaica, NY, Oct. 13, 1936, NYU.

GOULD, ELLIOTT: (Goldstein); Bklyn, Aug. 29, 1938. Columbia U.

GOULET, ROBERT: Lawrence, Mass., Nov. 26, 1933. Edmonton School.

GRAHAME, GLORIA: (Gloria Grahame Hallward) Los Angeles, Nov. 28, 1929.

GRANGER, FARLEY: San Jose, Calif., July 1, 1925.

GRANGER, STEWART: (James Stewart) London, May 6, 1913. Webber-Douglas School of Acting.

GRANT, CARY: (Archibald Alexander Leach) Bristol, Eng., Jan. 18, 1904.

GRANT, KATHRYN: (Olive Grandstaff) Houston, Tex., Nov. 25, 1933. UCLA.

GRANT, LEE: NYC, Oct. 31, 1929, Juilliard.

GRANVILLE, BONITA: NYC, Feb. 2, 1923.

GRAVES, PETER: (Aurness) Minneapolis, Mar. 18, 1926. U. of Minn.

GRAY, COLEEN: (Doris Jensen) Staplehurst, Neb., Oct. 23, 1922. Hamline U.

GRAYSON, KATHRYN: (Zelma Hedrick) Winston-Salem, N.C., Feb. 9, 1923.

GREENE, LORNE: Ottawa, Can., Feb. 12, 1915.

GREENE, RICHARD: Plymouth, Eng., Aug. 25, 1918. Cardinal Vaughn School.

GREENWOOD, JOAN: London, 1919. RADA.

GREER, JANE: Washington, D.C., Sept. 9, 1924.

Virginia Grey   Steven Hill   Anne Heywood   Ken Howard   Katharine Houghto

GREER, MICHAEL: Galesburg, Ill., Apr. 20, 1943.

GREY, JOEL: (Katz) Cleveland, O., Apr. 11, 1932.

GREY, VIRGINIA: Los Angeles, Mar. 22, 1923.

GRIFFITH, ANDY: Mt. Airy, N.C., June 1, 1926. U.N.C.

GRIFFITH, HUGH: Marian Glas, Anglesey, N. Wales, May 30, 1912.

GRIMES, GARY: San Francisco, June 2, 1955.

GRIMES, TAMMY: Lynn, Mass., Jan. 30, 1934, Stephens Col.

GRIZZARD, GEORGE: Roanoke Rapids, N.C., Apr. 1, 1928, U.N.C.

GRODIN, CHARLES: Pittsburgh, Pa., Apr. 21, 1935.

GUARDINO, HARRY: Brooklyn, Dec. 23, 1925, Haaren High.

GUINNESS, ALEC: London, Apr. 2, 1914. Pembroke Lodge School.

HACKETT, BUDDY: (Leonard Hacker) Brooklyn, Aug. 31, 1924.

HACKETT, JOAN: NYC, May 1, Actors Studio.

HACKMAN, GENE: San Bernardino, Jan. 30, 1931.

HADDON, DALE: Montreal, Can., May 26, 1949, Neighborhood Playhouse.

HALE, BARBARA: DeKalb, Ill., Apr. 18, 1922. Chicago Academy of Fine Arts.

HAMILTON, GEORGE: Memphis, Tenn., Aug. 12, 1939. Hackley School.

HAMILTON, MARGARET: Cleveland, Ohio, Dec. 9, 1902. Hathaway-Brown School.

HAMILTON, NEIL: Lynn, Mass., Sept. 9, 1899.

HAMPSHIRE, SUSAN: London, May 12, 1941.

HARDIN, TY: (Orison Whipple Hungerford II) NYC, 1930.

HARDING, ANN: (Dorothy Walton Gatley) Fort Sam Houston, Texas, Aug. 17, 1904.

HARRINGTON, PAT: NYC, Aug. 13, 1929, Fordham U.

HARRIS, BARBARA: (Sandra Markowitz) Evanston, Ill., 1937.

HARRIS, JULIE: Grosse Pointe, Mich., Dec. 2, 1925. Yale Drama School.

HARRIS, RICHARD: Limerick, Ire., Oct. 1, 1930. London Acad.

HARRIS, ROSEMARY: Ashby, Eng., Sept. 19, 1930. RADA

HARRISON, NOEL: London, Jan. 29, 1936.

HARRISON, REX: Huyton, Cheshire, Eng., Mar. 5, 1908.

HARTMAN, ELIZABETH: Youngstown, O., Dec. 23, 1941. Carnegie Tech.

HAVER, JUNE: Rock Island, Ill., June 10, 1926.

HAVOC, JUNE: (June Hovick) Seattle, Wash., Nov. 8, 1916.

HAWN, GOLDIE: Washington, DC, Nov. 21, 1945.

HAYDEN, LINDA: Stanmore, Eng., Aida Foster School.

HAYDEN, STERLING; (John Hamilton) Montclair, N.J., March 26, 1916.

HAYES, HELEN: (Helen Brown) Washington, D.C., Oct. 10, 1900. Sacred Heart Convent.

HAYES, MARGARET: (Maggie) Baltimore, Dec. 5, 1925.

HAYWARD, SUSAN: (Edythe Marrener) Brooklyn, June 30, 1919.

HAYWORTH, RITA: (Margarita Cansino) NYC, Oct. 17, 1919.

HEATHERTON, JOEY: NYC, Sept. 14, 1944.

HECKART, EILEEN: Columbus, Ohio, Mar. 29, 1919. Ohio State U.

HEDISON, DAVID: Providence, R.I., May 20, 1929. Brown U.

HEMMINGS, DAVID: Guilford, Eng.; Nov. 18, 1938.

HENDERSON, MARCIA: Andover, Mass., July 22, 1932. AADA.

HENDRIX, WANDA: Jacksonville, Fla., Nov. 3, 1928.

HENREID, PAUL: Trieste, Jan. 10, 1908.

HENRY, BUCK: (Zuckerman) NYC, 1931; Dartmouth.

HEPBURN, AUDREY: Brussels, Belgium, May 4, 1929.

HEPBURN, KATHARINE: Hartford, Conn., Nov. 8, 1909. Bryn Mawr.

HESTON, CHARLTON: Evanston, Ill., Oct. 4, 1924. Northwestern U.

HEYWOOD, ANNE: (Violet Pretty) Birmingham, Eng., Dec. 11, 1933.

HICKMAN, DARRYL: Hollywood, Cal., July 28, 1933. Loyola U.

HICKMAN, DWAYNE: Los Angeles, May 18, 1934. Loyola.

HILL, STEVEN: Seattle, Wash., Feb. 24, 1922. U. Wash.

HILL, TERENCE: (Mario Giotti) Venice, Italy, 1941, URome.

HILLER, WENDY: Bramhall, Cheshire, Eng., Aug. 15, 1912. Winceby House School.

HOFFMAN, DUSTIN: Los Angeles, Aug. 8, 1937. Pasadena Playhouse.

HOLBROOK, HAL: (Harold) Cleveland, O., Feb. 17, 1925. Denison.

HOLDEN, WILLIAM: O'Fallon, Ill., Apr. 17, 1918. Pasadena Jr. Coll.

HOLLIMAN, EARL: Tennasas Swamp, Delhi, La., Sept. 11. UCLA.

HOLLOWAY, STANLEY: London, Oct. 1, 1890.

HOLM, CELESTE: NYC, Apr. 29, 1919.

HOMEIER, SKIP: (George Vincent Homeier) Chicago, Oct. 5, 1930. UCLA.

HOMOLKA, OSCAR: Vienna, Aug. 12, 1898. Vienna Dramatic Academy.

HOOKS, ROBERT: Washington, D.C., Apr. 18, 1937. Temple.

HOPE, BOB: London, May 26, 1904.

HOPPER, DENNIS: Dodge City, Kan., May 17, 1936.

HORNE, LENA: Brooklyn, June 30, 1917.

HORTON, ROBERT: Los Angeles, July 29, 1924. UCLA.

HOUGHTON, KATHARINE: Hartford, Conn., Mar. 10, 1945. Sarah Lawrence.

HOUSER, JERRY: Los Angeles, July 14, 1952; Valley Jr. Col.

HOUSEMAN, JOHN: Bucharest, Sept. 22, 1902.

HOWARD, KEN: El Centro, Cal., Mar. 28, 1944, Yale.

HOWARD, RON: Duncan, Okla., Mar. 1, 1954.

HOWARD, RONALD: Norwood, Eng., Apr. 7, 1918. Jesus College.

HOWARD, TREVOR: Kent, Eng., Sept. 29, 1916. RADA.

HOWES, SALLY ANN: London, July 20, 1934.

HUDSON, ROCK: (Roy Scherer Fitzgerald) Winnetka, Ill., Nov. 17, 1925.

HUGHES, BARNARD: Bedford Hills, NY, July 16, 1915, Manhattan Col.

HUNNICUTT, ARTHUR: Gravelly, Ark., Feb. 17, 1911. Ark. State.

HUNNICUT, GAYLE: Ft. Worth, Tex., Feb. 6, 1943, UCLA.

HUNT, MARSHA: Chicago, Oct. 17, 1917.

HUNTER, IAN: Cape Town, S.A., June 13, 1900. St. Andrew's College.

HUNTER, KIM: (Janet Cole) Detroit, Nov. 12, 1922.

HUNTER, TAB: (Arthur Galien) NYC, July 11, 1931.

| Robert Hutton | Sally Kellerman | Page Johnson | Doris Kunstmann | Aron Kincaid |

HUSSEY, RUTH: Providence, R.I., Oct. 30, 1917. U. of Mich.

HUSTON, JOHN: Nevada, Mo., Aug. 5, 1906.

HUTTON, BETTY: (Betty Thornberg) Battle Creek, Mich., Feb. 26, 1921.

HUTTON, LAUREN: (Mary): Charleston, S.C., Nov. 17, 1943. Newcomb Col.

HUTTON, ROBERT: (Winne) Kingston, N.Y., June 11, 1920. Blair Academy.

HYDE-WHITE, WILFRID: Gloucestershire, Eng., May 12, 1903. RADA.

HYER, MARTHA: Fort Worth, Tex., Aug. 10, 1930. Northwestern U.

IRELAND, JOHN: Vancouver, B.C., Can., Jan. 30, 1915.

IVES, BURL: Hunt Township, Ill., June 14, 1909. Charleston Ill. Teachers College.

JACKSON, ANNE: Alleghany, Pa., Sept. 3, 1926. Neighborhood Playhouse.

JACKSON, GLENDA: Birkenhead, Eng., May 9, 1936. RADA.

JACOBI, LOU: Toronto, Can., Dec. 28, 1913.

JACOBY, SCOTT: Chicago, Nov. 19, 1956.

JAECKEL, RICHARD: Long Beach, N.Y., Oct. 10, 1926.

JAFFE, SAM: NYC, Mar. 8, 1898.

JAGGER, DEAN: Lima, Ohio, Nov. 7, 1903. Wabash College.

JANSSEN, DAVID: (David Meyer) Naponee, Neb., Mar. 27, 1930.

JARMAN, CLAUDE, JR.: Nashville, Tenn., Sept. 27, 1934.

JASON, RICK: NYC, May 21, 1926. AADA.

JEAN, GLORIA: (Gloria Jean Schoonover) Buffalo, N.Y. Apr. 14, 1928.

JEFFREYS, ANNE: (Carmichael) Goldsboro, N.C., Jan. 26, 1923. Anderson College.

JEFFRIES, LIONEL: London, 1927, RADA.

JERGENS, ADELE: Brooklyn, Nov. 26, 1922.

JESSEL, GEORGE: NYC, Apr. 3, 1898.

JOHNS, GLYNIS: Durban, S. Africa, Oct. 5, 1923.

JOHNSON, CELIA: Richmond, Surrey, Eng., Dec. 18, 1908. RADA.

JOHNSON, PAGE: Welch, W. Va., Aug. 25, 1930. Ithaca.

JOHNSON, RAFER: Hillsboro, Tex., Aug. 18, 1935. UCLA.

JOHNSON, RICHARD: Essex, Eng., 1927. RADA.

JOHNSON, VAN: Newport, R.I., Aug. 28, 1916.

JONES, CAROLYN: Amarillo, Tex., Apr. 28, 1933.

JONES, CHRISTOPHER: Jackson, Tenn., Aug. 18, 1941, Actors Studio.

JONES, DEAN: Morgan County, Ala., Jan. 25, 1936. Ashburn College.

JONES, JACK: Bel-Air, Calif., Jan. 14, 1938.

JONES, JAMES EARL: Arkabutla, Miss., Jan. 17, 1931. U. Mich.

JONES, JENNIFER: (Phyllis Isley) Tulsa, Okla., Mar. 2, 1919. AADA.

JONES, SHIRLEY: Smithton, Pa., March 31, 1934.

JONES, TOM: (Thomas Jones Woodward) Pontypridd, Wales, June 7, 1940.

JORDAN, RICHARD: NYC, July 19, 1938, Harvard.

JORY, VICTOR: Dawson City, Can., Nov. 28, 1902, CalU.

JOURDAN, LOUIS: Marseilles, France, June 18, 1921.

JURADO, KATY: (Maria Christina Jurado Garcia) Guadalajara, Mex., 1927.

KAHN, MADELINE: Boston, Mass., Sept. 29, 1942, Hofstra U.

KANE, CAROL: Cleveland, O., 1952.

KASZNAR, KURT: Vienna, Aug. 12, 1913. Gymnasium, Vienna.

KAUFMANN, CHRISTINE: Lansdorf, Graz, Austria, Jan. 11, 1945.

KAYE, DANNY: (David Daniel Kominski) Brooklyn, Jan. 18, 1913.

KAYE, STUBBY: NYC, Nov. 11, 1918.

KEACH, STACY: Savannah, Ga., June 2, 1941; UCal., Yale.

KEDROVA, LILA: Greece, 1918.

KEEL, HOWARD: (Harold Keel) Gillespie, Ill., Apr. 13, 1919.

KEELER, RUBY: (Ethel) Halifax, N.S. Aug. 25, 1909.

KEITH, BRIAN: Bayonne, N.J., Nov. 14, 1921.

KELLERMAN, SALLY: Long Beach, Cal., June 2, 1938; Actors Studio West.

KELLY, GENE: Pittsburgh, Aug. 23, 1912. U. of Pittsburgh.

KELLY, GRACE: Philadelphia, Nov. 12, 1929. AADA.

KELLY, JACK: Astoria, N.Y., Sept. 16, 1927. UCLA.

KELLY, NANCY: Lowell, Mass., Mar. 25, 1921. Bentley School.

KEMP, JEREMY: Chesterfield, Eng., 1935, Central Sch.

KENNEDY, ARTHUR: Worcester, Mass., Feb. 17, 1914. Carnegie Tech.

KENNEDY, GEORGE: NYC, Feb. 18, 1925.

KERR, DEBORAH: Helensburg, Scot., Sept. 30, 1921. Smale Ballet School.

KERR, JOHN: NYC, Nov. 15, 1931. Harvard and Columbia.

KIDDER, MARGOT: Yellow Knife, Can., Oct. 17, 1948; UBC.

KILEY, RICHARD: Chicago, Mar. 31, 1922. Loyola.

KINCAID, ARON: (Norman Neale Williams III) Los Angeles, June 15, 1943. UCLA.

KING, ALAN: (Irwin Kniberg) Brooklyn, Dec. 26, 1927.

KITT, EARTHA: North, S.C., Jan. 26, 1928.

KLEMPERER, WERNER: Cologne, Mar. 22, 1920.

KNIGHT, ESMOND: East Sheen, Eng., May 4, 1906.

KNIGHT, SHIRLEY: Goessel, Kan., July 5. Wichita U.

KNOWLES, PATRIC: (Reginald Lawrence Knowles) Horsforth, Eng., Nov. 11, 1911.

KNOX, ALEXANDER: Strathroy, Ont., Can., Jan. 16, 1907.

KNOX, ELYSE: Hartford, Conn., Dec. 14, 1917. Traphagen School.

KOHNER, SUSAN: Los Angeles, Nov. 11, 1936. U. of Calif.

KORVIN, CHARLES: (Geza Korvin Karpathi) Czechoslovakia, Nov. 21. Sorbonne.

KOSLECK, MARTIN: Barkotzen, Ger., Mar. 24, 1914. Max Reinhardt School.

KOTTO, YAPHET: NYC, Nov. 15, 1937.

KREUGER, KURT: St. Moritz, Switz., July 23, 1917. U. of London.

KRUGER, HARDY: Berlin, Ger., Apri. 12, 1928.

KRUGER, OTTO: Toledo, Ohio, Sept. 6, 1885. Michigan and Columbia U.

KUNTSMANN, DORIS: Hamburg, 1944

KWAN, NANCY: Hong Kong, May 19, 1939. Royal Ballet.

LACY, JERRY: Sioux City, I., Mar. 27, 1936, LACC.

LAMARR, HEDY: (Hedwig Kiesler) Vienna, Sept. 11, 1915.

LAMAS, FERNANDO: Buenos Aires, Jan. 9, 1920.

LAMB, GIL: Minneapolis, June 14, 1906. U. of Minn.

LAMOUR, DOROTHY: Dec. 10, 1914. Spence School.

| Elsa Lanchester | William Marshall | Michele Lee | Ron Leibman | Janet Margolin |

LANCASTER, BURT: NYC, Nov. 2, 1913. NYU.

LANCHESTER, ELSA: (Elsa Sullivan) London, Oct. 28, 1902.

LANE, ABBE: Brooklyn, Dec. 14, 1935.

LANGAN, GLENN: Denver, Colo., July 8, 1917.

LANGE, HOPE: Redding Ridge, Conn., Nov. 28, 1933. Reed College.

LANGTON, PAUL: Salt Lake City, Apr. 17, 1913. Travers School of Theatre.

LANSBURY, ANGELA: London, Oct. 16, 1925. London Academy of Music.

LANSING, ROBERT: (Brown) San Diego, Cal., June 5.

LASSER, LOUISE: NYC. Brandeis U.

LAURIE, PIPER: (Rosetta Jacobs) Detroit, Jan. 22, 1932.

LAW, JOHN PHILLIP: Hollywood, Sept. 7, 1937. Neighborhood Playhouse., UHawaii.

LAWFORD, PETER: London, Sept. 7, 1923.

LAWRENCE, BARBARA: Carnegie, Okla., Feb. 24, 1930. UCLA.

LAWRENCE, CAROL: (Laraia) Melrose Park, Ill., Sept. 5, 1935.

LAWSON, LEIGH: Atherston, Eng., July 21, 1945, RADA.

LEACHMAN, CLORIS: Des Moines, Iowa, Apr. 30, 1930. Northwestern U.

LEDERER, FRANCIS: Karlin, Prague, Czechoslovakia, Nov. 6, 1906.

LEE, CHRISTOPHER: London, May 27, 1922. Wellington College.

LEE, MICHELE: (Dusiak) Los Angeles, June 24, 1942. LACC.

LEIBMAN, RON: NYC, Oct. 11, 1937, Ohio Wesleyan.

LEIGH, JANET: (Jeanette Helen Morrison) Merced, Calif., July 6, 1927. College of Pacific.

LEIGHTON, MARGARET: Barnt Green, Worcestershire, Eng., Feb. 26, 1922. Church of England Col.

LEMBECK, HARVEY: Brooklyn, Apr. 15, 1923. U. of Ala.

LEMMON, JACK: Boston, Feb. 8, 1925. Harvard.

LENZ, RICK: Springfield, Ill., Nov. 21, 1939. U. Mich.

LEONARD, SHELDON: (Bershad) NYC, Feb. 22, 1907, Syracuse U.

LESLIE, BETHEL: NYC, Aug. 3, 1929. Breaney School.

LESLIE, JOAN: (Joan Brodell) Detroit, Jan. 26, 1925. St. Benedict's.

LESTER, MARK: Oxford, Eng., July 11, 1958.

LETTIERI, AL: NYC, Feb. 24, Actors Studio.

LEVENE, SAM: NYC, 1907.

LEWIS, JERRY: Newark, N.J., Mar. 16, 1926.

LIGON, TOM: New Orleans, La., Sept. 10, 1945.

LILLIE, BEATRICE: Toronto, Can., May 29, 1898.

LINCOLN, ABBEY: (Anna Marie Woolridge) Chicago, Aug. 6, 1930.

LINDFORS, VIVECA: Uppsala, Sweden, Dec. 29, 1920. Stockholm Royal Dramatic School.

LISI, VIRNA: Rome, 1938.

LITTLE, CLEAVON: Chickasha, Okla., June 1, 1939, San Diego State.

LIVESEY, ROGER: Barry, Wales, June 25, 1906. Westminster School.

LOCKE, SONDRA: Shelbyville, Tenn., 1947.

LOCKHART, JUNE: NYC, June 15, 1925. Westlake School.

LOCKWOOD, GARY: Van Nuys, Cal., 1937.

LOCKWOOD, MARGARET: Karachi, Pakistan, Sept. 15, 1916. RADA.

LOLLOBRIGIDA, GINA: Subiaco, Italy, 1928. Rome Academy of Fine Arts.

LOM, HERBERT: Prague, Czechoslovakia, 1917. Prague U.

LONDON, JULIE: (Julie Peck) Santa Rosa, Calif., Sept. 26, 1926.

LONG, RICHARD: Chicago, Dec. 17, 1927.

LOPEZ, PERRY: NYC, July 22, 1931. NYU.

LORD, JACK: (John Joseph Ryan) NYC, Dec. 30, 1928. NYU.

LOREN, SOPHIA: (Sofia Scicolone) Rome, Italy, Sept. 20, 1934.

LOUISE, TINA: (Blacker) NYC, Feb. 11, 1934, Miami U.

LOY, MYRNA: (Myrna Williams) Helena, Mont., Aug. 2, 1905. Westlake School.

LUND, JOHN: Rochester, N.Y., Feb. 6, 1913.

LUNDIGAN, WILLIAM: Syracuse, N.Y., June 12, 1914. Syracuse U.

LUPINO, IDA: London, Feb. 4, 1918. RADA.

LYNDE, PAUL: Mt. Vernon, Ohio, June 13, 1926. Northwestern U.

LYNLEY, CAROL: NYC, Feb. 13, 1942.

LYNN, JEFFREY: Auburn, Mass., 1910. Bates College.

LYON, SUE: Davenport, Iowa, July 10, 1946.

LYONS, ROBERT F.: Albany, N.Y.; AADA.

MacARTHUR, JAMES: Los Angeles, Dec. 8, 1937. Harvard.

MacGINNIS, NIALL: Dublin, Ire., Mar. 29, 1913. Dublin U.

MacGRAW, ALI: NYC, Apr. 1, 1939, Wellesley.

MacLAINE, SHIRLEY: (Beatty) Richmond, Va., Apr. 24, 1934.

MacMAHON, ALINE: McKeesport, Pa., May 3, 1899. Barnard College.

MacMURRAY, FRED: Kankakee, Ill., Aug. 30, 1908. Carroll College.

MACNEE, PATRICK: London, Feb. 1922.

MacRAE, GORDON: East Orange, N.J., Mar. 12, 1921.

MADISON, GUY: (Robert Moseley) Bakersfield, Calif., Jan. 19, 1922. Bakersfield Jr. College.

MAHARIS, GEORGE: Astoria, N.Y., Sept. 1, 1928. Actors Studio.

MAHONEY, JOCK: (Jacques O'Mahoney) Chicago, Feb. 7, 1919. U. of Iowa.

MALDEN, KARL: (Malden Sekulovich) Gary, Ind., Mar. 22, 1914.

MALONE, DOROTHY: Chicago, Jan. 30, 1925. S. Methodist U.

MARAIS, JEAN: Cherbourg, France, Dec. 11, 1913. St. Germain.

MARCH, FREDRIC: (Frederick McIntyre Bickel) Racine, Wisc., Aug. 31, 1897. U. of Wisc.

MARGO: (Maria Marguerita Guadalupe Boldoay Castilla) Mexico City, May 10, 1918.

MARGOLIN, JANET: NYC, July 25, 1943. Walden School.

MARLOWE, HUGH: (Hugh Hipple) Philadelphia, Jan. 30, 1914.

MARSHALL, BRENDA: (Ardis Anderson Gaines) Isle of Negros, P.I., Sept. 29. 1915. Texas State College.

MARSHALL, E. G.: Owatonna, Minn., June 18, 1910. U. of Minn.

MARSHALL, WILLIAM: Gary, Ind., Aug. 19, 1924, NYU.

MARTIN, DEAN: (Dino Crocetti) Steubenville, Ohio, June 17, 1917.

MARTIN, MARY: Weatherford, Tex., Dec. 1, 1914. Ward-Belmont School.

MARTIN, STROTHER: Kokomo, Ind., 1919, UMich.

MARTIN, TONY: (Alfred Norris) Oakland, Cal., Dec. 25, 1913. St. Mary's College.

MARVIN, LEE: NYC, Feb. 19, 1924.

MARX, GROUCHO: (Julius Marx) NYC, Oct. 2, 1895.

MASON, JAMES: Huddersfield, Yorkshire, Eng., May 15, 1909. Cambridge.

MASON, MARSHA: St. Louis, Mo., Apr. 3, 1942, Webster Col.

David McCallum   Vera Miles   Toshiro Mifuni   Yvette Mimieux   Greg Morris

MASON, PAMELA: (Pamela Kellino) Westgate, Eng., Mar. 10, 1918.

MASSEN, OSA: Copenhagen, Den., Jan. 13, 1916.

MASSEY, DANIEL: London, Oct. 10, 1933. Eaton and King's Colleges.

MASSEY, RAYMOND: Toronto, Can., Aug. 30, 1896. Oxford.

MASTROIANNI, MARCELLO: Fontana Liri, Italy, Sept. 28, 1924.

MATTHAU, WALTER: (Matuschanskayasky) NYC, Oct. 1, 1920.

MATURE, VICTOR: Louisville, Ky., Jan. 29, 1916.

MAY, ELAINE: (Berlin) Philadelphia, Apr. 21, 1932.

MAYEHOFF, EDDIE: Baltimore, July 7, Yale.

McCALLUM, DAVID: Scotland, Sept. 19, 1933. Chapman Coll.

McCAMBRIDGE, MERCEDES: Joliet, Ill., March 17, 1918, Mundelein College.

McCARTHY, KEVIN: Seattle, Wash., Feb. 15, 1914. Minn. U.

McCLORY, SEAN: Dublin, Ire., March 8, 1924. U. of Galway.

McCLURE, DOUG: Glendale, Calif., May 11, 1938. UCLA.

McCOWEN, ALEC: Tunbridge Wells, Eng., May 26, 1925, RADA.

McCREA, JOEL: Los Angeles, Nov. 5, 1905. Pomona College.

McDERMOTT, HUGH: Edinburgh, Scot., Mar. 20, 1908.

McDOWALL, RODDY: London, Sept. 17, 1928. St. Joseph's.

McDOWELL, MALCOLM: (Taylor) Leeds, Eng., June 13, 1943.

McENERY, PETER: Walsall, Eng., Feb. 21, 1940.

McGAVIN, DARREN: Spokane, Wash., May 7, 1922. College of Pacific.

McGIVER, JOHN: NYC, Nov. 5, 1915. Fordham, Columbia U.

McGUIRE, BIFF: New Haven, Conn., Oct. 25, 1926, Mass State Col.

McGUIRE, DOROTHY: Omaha, Neb., June 14, 1919.

McKAY, GARDNER: NYC, June 10, 1932. Cornell.

McKENNA, VIRGINIA: London, June 7, 1931.

McKUEN, ROD: Oakland, Cal., Apr. 29, 1933.

McLERIE, ALLYN ANN: Grand Mere, Can., Dec. 1, 1926.

McNAIR, BARBARA: Chicago, March 4, 1939. UCLA.

McNALLY, STEPHEN: (Horace McNally) NYC, July 29, Fordham U.

McNAMARA, MAGGIE: NYC, June 18. St. Catherine.

McQUEEN, BUTTERFLY: Tampa, Fla., Jan. 8, 1911. UCLA.

McQUEEN, STEVE: Slater, Mo., Mar. 24, 1932.

MEADOWS, AUDREY: Wuchang, China, 1924. St. Margaret's.

MEADOWS, JAYNE: (formerly, Jayne Cotter) Wuchang, China, Sept. 27, 1923. St. Margaret's.

MEDFORD, KAY: (Maggie O'Regin) NYC, Sept. 14, 1920.

MEDWIN, MICHAEL: London, 1925. Instut Fischer.

MEEKER, RALPH: (Ralph Rathgeber) Minneapolis, Nov. 21, 1920. Northwestern U.

MELL, MARISA: Vienna, Austria, 1942.

MERCOURI, MELINA: Athens, Greece, Oct. 18, 1915.

MEREDITH, BURGESS: Cleveland, Ohio, Nov. 16, 1909. Amherst.

MEREDITH, LEE: (Judi Lee Sauls) Oct. 1947. AADA.

MERKEL, UNA: Covington, Ky., Dec. 10, 1903.

MERMAN, ETHEL: (Ethel Zimmerman) Astoria, N.Y., Jan. 16, 1909.

MERRILL, DINA: (Nedinia Hutton) NYC, Dec. 9, 1925. AADA.

MERRILL, GARY: Hartford, Conn., Aug. 2, 1915. Bowdoin, Trinity.

MICHELL, KEITH: Adelaide, Aus., Dec. 1, 1926.

MIFUNE, TOSHIRO: Tsingtao, China, Apr. 1, 1920.

MILES, SARAH: Ingatestone, Eng., Dec. 31, 1943.

MILES, SYLVIA: NYC, Sept. 9, 1932.

MILES, VERA: (Ralston) Boise City, Okla., Aug. 23, 1929, UCLA.

MILLAND, RAY: (Reginald Truscott-Jones) Neath, Wales, Jan. 3, 1908. King's College.

MILLER, ANN: (Lucille Ann Collier) Chireno, Tex., Apr. 12, 1919. Lawler Professional School.

MILLER, JASON: Long Island City, NY, Apr. 22, 1939, Catholic U.

MILLER, MARVIN: St. Louis, July 18, 1913. Washington U.

MILLS, HAYLEY: London, Apr. 18, 1946. Elmhurst School.

MILLS, JOHN: Suffolk, Eng., Feb. 22, 1908.

MILNER, MARTIN: Detroit, Mich., 1933.

MIMIEUX, YVETTE: Los Angeles, Jan. 8, 1941. Hollywood High.

MINEO, SAL: NYC, Jan. 10, 1939. Lodge School.

MINNELLI, LIZA: Los Angeles, Mar. 12, 1946.

MIRANDA, ISA: (Ines Sampietro) Milan, Italy, July 5, 1917.

MITCHELL, CAMERON: Dalastown, Pa., Nov. 1918. N.Y. Theatre School.

MITCHELL, JAMES: Sacramento, Calif., Feb. 29, 1920. LACC.

MITCHUM, ROBERT: Bridgeport, Conn., Aug. 6, 1917.

MONTALBAN, RICARDO: Mexico City, Nov. 25, 1920.

MONTAND, YVES: (Yves Montand Livi) Mansummano, Tuscany, Oct. 13, 1921.

MONTGOMERY, BELINDA; Winnipeg, Can., July 23, 1950.

MONTGOMERY, ELIZABETH: Los Angeles, Apr. 15, 1933. AADA.

MONTGOMERY, GEORGE: (George Letz) Brady, Mont., Aug. 29, 1916. U. of Mont.

MONTGOMERY, ROBERT: (Henry, Jr.) Beacon, N.Y., May 21, 1904.

MOOR, BILL: Toledo, O., July 13, 1931, Northwestern.

MOORE, CONSTANCE: Sioux City, Iowa, Jan. 18, 1922.

MOORE, DICK: Los Angeles, Sept. 12, 1925.

MOORE, KIERON: County Cork, Ire., 1925. St. Mary's College.

MOORE, MARY TYLER: Brooklyn, Dec. 29, 1937.

MOORE, ROGER: London, Oct. 14, 1927. RADA.

MOORE, TERRY: (Helen Koford) Los Angeles, Jan. 7, 1929.

MOOREHEAD, AGNES: Clinton, Mass., Dec. 6, 1906. AADA.

MOORE, KENNETH: Gerrards Cross, Eng., Sept. 20, 1914. Victoria College.

MOREAU, JEANNE: Paris, Jan. 3, 1928.

MORENO, RITA: (Rosita Alverio) Humacao, P.R., Dec. 11, 1931.

MORGAN, DENNIS: (Stanley Morner) Prentice, Wisc., Dec. 10, 1920. Carroll College.

MORGAN, HARRY (HENRY): (Harry Bratsburg) Detroit, Apr. 10, 1915. U. of Chicago.

MORGAN, MICHELE: (Simone Roussel) Paris, Feb. 29, 1920. Paris Dramatic School.

MORIARTY, MICHAEL: Detroit, Mich., Apr. 5, 1941. Dartmouth.

MORISON, PATRICIA: NYC, 1919.

MORLEY, ROBERT: Wiltshire, Eng., May 26, 1908. RADA.

MORRIS, GREG: Cleveland, O., 1934. Ohio State.

Robert Morse   Kim Novak   Don Nute   Nancy Olson   Dennis Patrick

MORRIS, HOWARD: NYC, Sept. 4, 1919. NYU.

MORROW, VIC: Bronx, N.Y., Feb. 14, 1932. Fla. Southern College.

MORSE, ROBERT: Newton, Mass., May 18, 1931.

MOSTEL, ZERO: Brooklyn, Feb. 28, 1915. CCNY.

MULLIGAN, RICHARD: NYC, Nov. 13, 1932.

MURPHY, GEORGE: New Haven, Conn., July 4, 1902. Yale.

MURRAY, DON: Hollywood, July 31, 1929. AADA.

MURRAY, KEN: (Don Court) NYC, July 14, 1903.

NADER, GEORGE: Pasadena, Calif., Oct. 19, 1921. Occidental College.

NAPIER, ALAN: Birmingham, Eng., Jan. 7, 1903. Birmingham University.

NATWICK, MILDRED: Baltimore, June 19, 1908. Bryn Mawr.

NAUGHTON, JAMES: Middletown, Conn., Dec. 6, 1945. Yale.

NEAL, PATRICIA: Packard, Ky., Jan. 20, 1926. Northwestern U.

NEFF, HILDEGARDE: (Hildegard Knef) Ulm, Ger., Dec. 28, 1925. Berlin Art Academy.

NELSON, BARRY: (Robert Nielsen) Oakland, Cal., 1925.

NELSON, DAVID: NYC, Oct. 24, 1936. USC.

NELSON, GENE: (Gene Berg) Seattle, Wash., Mar. 24, 1920.

NELSON, HARRIET HILLIARD: (Peggy Lou Snyder) Des Moines, Iowa, July 18.

NELSON, LORI: (Dixie Kay Nelson) Santa Fe, N.M., Aug. 15, 1933.

NELSON, OZZIE: (Oswald) Jersey City, N.J., Mar. 20, 1907. Rutgers U.

NELSON, RICK: (Eric Hilliard Nelson) Teaneck, N.J., May 8, 1940.

NESBITT, CATHLEEN: Cheshire, Eng., Nov. 24, 1889. Victoria College.

NEWLEY, ANTHONY: Hackney, London, Sept. 21, 1931.

NEWMAN, PAUL: Cleveland, Ohio, Jan. 26, 1925. Yale.

NEWMAR, JULIE: (Newmeyer) Los Angeles, Aug. 16, 1935.

NICHOLS, MIKE: (Michael Igor Peschkowsky) Berlin, Nov. 1931. U. Chicago.

NICHOLSON, JACK: Neptune, N.J., Apr. 22, 1937.

NICOL, ALEX: Ossining, N.Y., Jan. 20, 1919. Actors Studio.

NIELSEN, LESLIE: Regina, Saskatchewan, Can., Feb. 11, 1926.
226 Neighborhood Playhouse.

NIVEN, DAVID: Kirriemuir, Scot., Mar. 1, 1910. Sandhurst College.

NOLAN, LLOYD: San Francisco, Aug. 11, 1902. Stanford U.

NORRIS, CHRISTOPHER: NYC, Oct. 7, 1943; Lincoln Square Acad.

NORTH, HEATHER: Pasadena, Cal., Dec. 13, 1950; Actors Workshop.

NORTH, SHEREE: (Dawn Bethel) Los Angeles, Jan. 17, 1933. Hollywood High.

NOVAK, KIM: (Marilyn Novak) Chicago, Feb. 18, 1933. LACC.

NUGENT, ELLIOTT: Dover, Ohio, Sept. 20, 1900. Ohio State U.

NUTE, DON: Connellsville, Pa., Mar. 13. Denver U.

NUYEN, FRANCE: (Vannga) Marseilles, France, July 31, 1939. Beaux Arts School.

OATES, WARREN: Depoy, Ky., July 5, 1928.

OBERON, MERLE: (Estelle Merle O'Brien Thompson) Tasmania, Feb. 19, 1911.

O'BRIAN, HUGH: (Hugh J. Krampe) Rochester, N.Y., Apr. 19, 1928. Cincinnati U.

O'BRIEN, CLAY: Ray, Ariz., May 6, 1961.

O'BRIEN, EDMOND: NYC, Sept. 10, 1915. Fordham, Neighborhood Playhouse.

O'BRIEN, MARGARET: (Angela Maxine O'Brien) Los Angeles, Jan. 15, 1937.

O'BRIEN, PAT: Milwaukee, Nov. 11, 1899. Marquette U.

O'CONNELL, ARTHUR: NYC, Mar. 29, 1908. St. John's.

O'CONNOR, CARROLL: Bronx, N.Y., Aug. 2, 1925; Dublin National Univ.

O'CONNOR, DONALD: Chicago, Aug. 28, 1925.

O'CONNOR, GLYNNIS: NYC, Nov. 19, 1956, NYSU.

O'HARA, MAUREEN: (Maureen FitzSimons) Dublin, Ire., Aug. 17, 1921. Abbey School.

O'HERLIHY, DAN: Wexford, Ire., May 1, 1919. National U.

OLIVIER, LAURENCE: Dorking, Eng., May 22, 1907. Oxford.

OLSON, NANCY: Milwaukee, Wisc., July 14, UCLA.

O'NEAL, PATRICK: Ocala, Fla., Sept. 26, 1927. U. of Fla.

O'NEAL, RON: Utica, NY, Sept. 1, 1937, Ohio State.

O'NEAL, RYAN: Los Angeles, Apr. 20, 1941.

O'NEAL, TATUM: Los Angeles, Nov. 5, 1963.

O'NEIL, TRICIA: Shreveport, La., Mar. 11, 1945, Baylor U.

O'NEILL, JENNIFER: Rio de Janeiro, Feb. 20, 1949; Neighborhood Playhouse.

O'SULLIVAN, MAUREEN: Byle, Ire., May 17, 1911. Sacred Heart Convent.

O'TOOLE, PETER: Connemara, Ireland, Aug. 2, 1932. RADA.

OWEN, REGINALD: Wheathampstead, Eng., Aug. 5, 1887. Tree's Academy.

PACINO, AL: NYC, Apr. 25, 1940.

PAGE, GERALDINE: Kirksville, Mo., Nov. 22, 1924. Goodman School.

PAGET, DEBRA: (Debralee Griffin) Denver, Aug. 19, 1933.

PAIGE, JANIS: (Donna Mae Jaden) Tacoma, Wash., Sept. 16, 1922.

PALANCE, JACK: Lattimer, Pa., Feb. 18, 1920. U. N. C.

PALMER, BETSY: East Chicago, Ind., Nov. 1, 1929. DePaul U.

PALMER, GREGG: (Palmer Lee) San Francisco, Jan. 25, 1927. U. Utah.

PALMER, LILLI: Posen, Austria, May 24, 1914. Ilka Gruning School.

PALMER, MARIA: Vienna, Sept. 5, 1924. College de Bouffement.

PAPAS, IRENE: Chiliomodion, Greece, 1929.

PARKER, ELEANOR: Cedarville, Ohio, June 26, 1922. Pasadena Playhouse.

PARKER, FESS: Fort Worth, Tex., Aug. 16, 1927. USC.

PARKER, JEAN: (Mae Green) Deer Lodge, Mont., Aug. 11, 1918.

PARKER, SUZY: (Cecelia Parker) San Antonio, Tex. Oct. 28, 1933.

PARKER, WILLARD: (Worster Van Eps) NYC, Feb. 5, 1912.

PARKINS, BARBARA: Vancouver, Can., May 22, 1945.

PARSONS, ESTELLE: Lynn, Mass. Nov. 20, 1927. Boston U.

PATRICK, DENNIS: Philadelphia, Mar. 14, 1918.

PATRICK, NIGEL: London, May 2, 1913.

PATTERSON, LEE: Vancouver, Can., 1929. Ontario College of Art.

PAVAN, MARISA: (Marisa Pierangeli) Cagliari, Sardinia, June 19, 1932. Torquado Tasso College.

PEACH, MARY: Durban, S. Africa, 1934.

PEARSON, BEATRICE: Denison, Tex., July 27, 1920.

PECK, GREGORY: La Jolla, Calif., Apr. 5, 1916. U. of Calif

PEPPARD, GEORGE: Detroit, Oct. 1, 1933. Carnegie Tech.

Bernadette Peters   Anthony Perkins   Alice Playten   Rex Reed   Debbie Reynolds

PERKINS, ANTHONY: NYC, Apr. 14, 1932. Rollins College.

PERREAU, GIGI: (Ghislaine) Los Angeles, Feb. 6, 1941.

PETERS, BERNADETTE: Jamaica, NY, Feb. 28, 1948.

PETERS, BROCK: NYC, July 2, 1927, CCNY.

PETERS, JEAN: (Elizabeth) Canton, Ohio, Oct. 15, 1926. Ohio State U.

PETTET, JOANNA: London, Nov. 16, 1944; Neighborhood Playhouse.

PHILLIPS, MICHELLE: (Holly Gilliam) NJ, June 4, 1944.

PICERNI, PAUL: NYC, Dec. 1, 1922. Loyola U.

PICKENS, SLIM: (Louis Bert Lindley, Jr.) Kingsberg, Calif., June 29, 1919.

PICKFORD, MARY: (Gladys Mary Smith) Toronto, Can., Apr. 8, 1893.

PIDGEON, WALTER: East St. John, N.B., Can., Sept. 23, 1898.

PINE, PHILLIP: Hanford, Calif., July 16, 1925. Actors' Lab.

PLAYTEN, ALICE: NYC, Aug. 28, 1947, NYU.

PLEASENCE, DONALD: Workshop, Eng, Oct. 5, 1919. Sheffield School.

PLESHETTE, SUZANNE: NYC, Jan. 31, 1937. Syracuse U.

PLUMMER, CHRISTOPHER: Toronto, Can., Dec. 13, 1927.

PODESTA, ROSSANA: Tripoli, June 20, 1934.

POITIER, SIDNEY: Miami, Fla., Feb. 20, 1924.

POLLARD, MICHAEL J.: Pacific, N.J., May 30, 1939.

PORTER, ERIC: London, Apr. 8, 1928, Wimbledon Col.

POWELL, ELEANOR: Springfield, Mass., Nov. 21, 1913.

POWELL, JANE: (Suzanne Burce) Portland, Ore., Apr. 1, 1929.

POWELL, WILLIAM: Pittsburgh, July 29, 1892. AADA.

POWERS, MALA: (Mary Ellen) San Francisco, Dec. 29, 1921. UCLA.

PRENTISS, PAULA: (Paula Ragusa) San Antonio, Tex., Mar. 4, 1939. Northwestern U.

PRESLE, MICHELINE: (Micheline Chassagne) Paris, Aug. 22, 1922. Rouleau Drama School.

PRESLEY, ELVIS: Tupelo, Miss., Jan. 8, 1935.

PRESNELL, HARVE: Modesto, Calif., Sept. 14, 1933. USC.

PRESTON, ROBERT: (Robert Preston Meservey) Newton Highlands, Mass., June 8, 1913. Pasadena Playhouse.

PRICE, VINCENT: St. Louis, May 27, 1911. Yale.

PRINCE, WILLIAM: Nicholas, N.Y., Jan. 26, 1913. Cornell U.

PRINCIPAL, VICTORIA: Tokyo, Jan. 3, 1945, Dade Jr. Col.

PROVINE, DOROTHY: Deadwood, S.D., Jan. 20, 1937. U. of Wash.

PROWSE, JULIET: Bombay, India, Sept. 25, 1936.

PRYOR, RICHARD: Peoria, Ill., 1940.

PURCELL, LEE: Cherry Point, N.C., 1947; Stephens.

PURCELL, NOEL: Dublin, Ire., Dec. 23, 1900. Irish Christian Brothers.

PURDOM, EDMUND: Welwyn Garden City, Eng., Dec. 19, St. Ignatius College.

QUAYLE, ANTHONY: Lancashire, Eng., Sept. 7, 1913. Old Vic School.

QUINN, ANTHONY: Chihuahua, Mex., Apr. 21, 1915.

RAFFERTY, FRANCES: Sioux City, Iowa, June 16, 1922. UCLA.

RAFT, GEORGE: NYC, 1903.

RAINES, ELLA: (Ella Wallace Rains Olds) Snoqualmie Falls, Wash., Aug. 6, 1921. U. of Wash.

RAMSEY, LOGAN: Long Beach, Cal., Mar. 21, 1921; St. Joseph.

RANDALL, TONY: Tulsa, Okla., Feb. 26, 1920. Northwestern U.

RANDELL, RON: Sydney, Australia, Oct. 8, 1920. St. Mary's College.

RASULALA, THALMUS: (Jack Crowder) Miami, Fla., Nov. 15, 1939. U. Redlands.

RAY, ALDO: (Aldo DeRe) Pen Argyl, Pa. Sept. 25, 1926. UCLA.

RAYE, MARTHA: (Margie Yvonne Reed) Butte, Mont., Aug. 27, 1916.

RAYMOND, GENE: (Raymond Guion) NYC, Aug. 13, 1908.

REAGAN, RONALD: Tampico, Ill., Feb. 6, 1911. Eureka College.

REASON, REX: Berlin, Ger., Nov. 30, 1928. Pasadena Playhouse.

REDFORD, ROBERT: Santa Monica, Calif., Aug. 18, 1937. AADA.

REDGRAVE, CORIN: London, July 16, 1939.

REDGRAVE, LYNN: London, Mar. 8, 1943.

REDGRAVE, MICHAEL: Bristol, Eng., Mar. 20, 1908. Cambridge.

REDGRAVE, VANESSA: London, Jan. 30, 1937.

REDMAN, JOYCE: County Mayo, Ire., 1919. RADA.

REED, DONNA: (Donna Mullenger) Denison, Iowa, Jan. 27, 1921. LACC.

REED, OLIVER: Wimbledon, Eng., Feb. 13, 1938.

REED, REX: Ft. Worth, Tex., Oct. 2, 1939, LSU.

REEVES, STEVE: Glasgow, Mont., Jan. 21, 1926.

REID, ELLIOTT: NYC, Jan. 16, 1920.

REINER, CARL: NYC, Mar. 20, 1922. Georgetown.

REINER, ROBERT: NYC, 1945, UCLA.

REMICK, LEE: Quincy, Mass., Dec. 14, 1935. Barnard College.

RETTIG, TOMMY: Jackson Heights, N.Y., Dec. 10, 1941.

REVILL, CLIVE: Wellington, NZ, Apr. 18, 1930.

REYNOLDS, BURT: West Palm Beach, Fla. Feb. 11, 1936. Fla. State U.

REYNOLDS, DEBBIE: (Mary Frances Reynolds) El Paso, Tex., Apr. 1, 1932.

REYNOLDS, MARJORIE: Buhl, Idaho, Aug. 12, 1921.

RHOADES, BARBARA: Poughkeepsie, N.Y., 1947.

RICH, IRENE: Buffalo, N.Y., Oct. 13, 1897. St. Margaret's School.

RICHARDS, JEFF: (Richard Mansfield Taylor) Portland, Ore., Nov. 1. USC.

RICHARDSON, RALPH: Cheltenham, Eng., Dec. 19, 1902.

RICKLES, DON: NYC, May 8, 1926. AADA.

RIGG, DIANA: Doncaster, Eng., July 20, 1938. RADA'

ROBARDS, JASON: Chicago, July 26, 1922. AADA.

ROBERTS, TONY: NYC, Oct. 22, 1939, Northwestern U.

ROBERTS, RACHEL: Llanelly, Wales, Sept. 20, 1927, RADA.

ROBERTS, RALPH: Salisbury, NC, Aug. 17, 1922, UNC.

ROBERTSON, CLIFF: La Jolla, Calif., Sept. 9, 1925. Antioch College.

ROBSON, FLORA: South Shields, Eng., Mar. 28, 1902. RADA.

ROCHESTER: (Eddie Anderson) Oakland, Calif., Sept. 18, 1905.

ROGERS, CHARLES "BUDDY": Olathe, Kan., Aug. 13, 1904. U. of Kan.

ROGERS, GINGER: (Virginia Katherine McMath) Independence, Mo., July 16, 1911.

ROGERS, ROY: (Leonard Slye) Cincinnati, Nov. 5, 1912.

ROLAND, GILBERT: (Luis Antonio Damaso De Alonso) Juarez, Mex., Dec. 11, 1905. **227**

Ayn Ruymen   Robert Stack   Jennifer Salt

ROMAN, RUTH: Boston, Dec. 23. Bishop Lee Dramatic School.

ROMERO, CESAR: NYC, Feb. 15, 1907. Collegiate School.

ROONEY, MICKEY: (Joe Yule, Jr.) Brooklyn, Sept. 23, 1920.

ROSS, DIANA: Detroit, Mich., Mar. 26, 1945.

ROSS, KATHARINE: Hollywood, Jan. 29, 1943.

ROTH, LILLIAN: Boston, Dec. 13, 1910.

ROUNDS, DAVID: Bronxville, NY, Oct. 9, 1938, Denison U.

ROUNDTREE, RICHARD: New Rochelle, N.Y., Sept. 7, 1942. Southern Ill.

ROWLANDS, GENA: Cambria, Wisc., June 19, 1936.

RULE, JANICE: Cincinnati, Aug. 15, 1931.

RUSH, BARBARA: Denver, Colo., Jan. 4. U. of Calif.

RUSSELL, JANE: Bemidji, Minn., June 21, 1921. Max Reinhardt School.

RUSSELL, JOHN: Los Angeles, Jan. 3, 1921. U. of Calif.

RUSSELL, KURT: Springfield, Mass., March 17, 1951.

RUSSELL, ROSALIND: Waterbury, Conn., June 4, 1911. AADA.

RUTHERFORD, ANN: Toronto, Can., 1924.

RUYMEN, AYN: Brooklyn, July 18, 1947, HB Studio.

SAINT, EVA MARIE: Newark, N.J., July 4, 1924. Bowling Green State U.

ST. JACQUES, RAYMOND: (James Arthur Johnson) Conn.

ST. JOHN, BETTA: Hawthorne, Calif., Nov. 26, 1929.

ST. JOHN, JILL: (Jill Oppenheim) Los Angeles, Aug. 19, 1940.

SALT, JENNIFER: Los Angeles, Sept. 4, 1944. Sarah Lawrence Col.

SANDS, TOMMY: Chicago, Aug. 27, 1937.

SAN JUAN, OLGA: NYC, Mar. 16, 1927.

SARGENT, RICHARD: (Richard Cox) Carmel, Cal., 1933. Stanford U.

SARRAZIN, MICHAEL: Quebec City, Can., May 22, 1940.

SAVALAS, TELLY: (Aristotle) Garden City, N.Y., Jan. 21, 1925. Columbia.

SAXON, JOHN: (Carmen Orrico) Brooklyn, Aug. 5, 1935.

SCHEIDER, ROY: Orange, N.J., Nov. 10, 1935, Franklin-Marshall.

SCHELL, MARIA: Vienna, Jan. 15, 1926.

SCHELL, MAXIMILIAN: Vienna, Dec. 8, 1930.

SCHNEIDER, MARIA: Paris, Mar. 27, 1952.

SCHNEIDER, ROMY: Vienna, Sept. 23, 1938.

SCOFIELD, PAUL: Hurstpierpoint, Eng., Jan. 21, 1922. London Mask Theatre School.

SCOTT, GEORGE C.: Wise, Va., Oct. 18, 1927. U. of Mo.

SCOTT, GORDON: (Gordon M. Werschkul) Portland, Ore., Aug. 3, 1927. Oregon U.

SCOTT, MARTHA: Jamesport, Mo., Sept. 22, 1914. U. of Mich.

SCOTT, RANDOLPH: Orange County, Va., Jan. 23, 1903. U. of N.C.

SEAGULL, BARBARA HERSHEY: (Herzstein) Hollywood, Feb. 5, 1948.

SEARS, HEATHER: London, 1935.

SEBERG, JEAN: Marshalltown, Iowa, Nov. 13, 1938. Iowa U.

SECOMBE, HARRY: Swansea, Wales, Sept. 8, 1921.

SEGAL, GEORGE: NYC, Feb. 13, 1934. Columbia.

SELLERS, PETER: Southsea, Eng., Sept. 8, 1925. Aloysius College.

SELWART, TONIO: Watenberg, Ger., June 9, 1906. Munich U.

SERNAS, JACQUES: Lithuania, July 30, 1925.

SEYLER, ATHENE: (Athene Hannen) London, May 31, 1889.

SEYMOUR, ANNE: NYC, Sept. 11, 1909. American Laboratory Theatre.

SHARIF, OMAR: (Michel Shalboub) Alexandria, Egypt, Oct. 10, 1932. Victoria Col.

SHATNER, WILLIAM: Montreal, Can., Mar. 22, 1931. McGill U.

SHAW, ROBERT: Orkney Isles, Scot., Aug. 9, 1927, RADA.

SHAW, SEBASTIAN: Holt, Eng., May 29, 1905. Gresham School.

SHAWLEE, JOAN: Forest Hills, N.Y., Mar. 5, 1929.

SHAWN, DICK: (Richard Shulefand) Buffalo, N.Y., Dec. 1. U. of Miami.

SHEARER, MOIRA: Dunfermline, Scot., Jan. 17, 1926. London Theatre School.

SHEARER, NORMA: Montreal, Can., Aug. 10, 1904.

SHEEN, MARTIN: (Ramon Estevez) Dayton, O., Aug. 3, 1940.

SHEFFIELD, JOHN: Pasadena, Calif., Apr. 11, 1931. UCLA.

SHEPHERD, CYBILL: Memphis, Tenn., 1950. Hunter, NYU.

SHORE, DINAH: (Frances Rose Shore) Winchester, Tenn., Mar. 1, 1917. Vanderbilt U.

SHOWALTER, MAX: (formerly Casey Adams) Caldwell, Kan., June 2, 1917. Pasadena Playhouse.

SIDNEY, SYLVIA: NYC, Aug. 8, 1910. Theatre Guild School.

SIGNORET, SIMONE: (Simone Kaminker) Wiesbaden, Ger., Mar. 25, 1921. Solange Sicard School.

SILVERS, PHIL: (Philip Silversmith) Brooklyn, May 11, 1912.

SIM, ALASTAIR: Edinburg, Scot., 1900.

SIMMONS, JEAN: London, Jan. 31, 1929. Aida Foster School.

SIMON, SIMONE: Marseilles, France, Apr. 23, 1914.

SINATRA, FRANK: Hobokan, N.J., Dec. 12, 1917.

SKELETON, RED: (Richard) Vincennes, Ind., July 18, 1913.

SLEZAK, WALTER: Vienna, Austria, May 3, 1902.

SMITH, ALEXIS: Penticton, Can., June 8, 1921. LACC.

SMITH, JOHN: (Robert E. Van Orden) Los Angeles, Mar. 6, 1931. UCLA.

SMITH, KATE: (Kathryn Elizabeth) Greenville, Va., May 1, 1909.

SMITH, KENT: NYC, Mar. 19, 1907. Harvard U.

SMITH, MAGGIE: Ilford, Eng., Dec. 28, 1934.

SMITH, ROGER: South Gate, Calif., Dec. 18, 1932. U. of Ariz.

SNODGRESS, CARRIE: Chicago, Oct. 27, 1946. UNI.

SOMMER, ELKE: Berlin, Nov. 5, 1941.

SONNY: (Salvatore Bono) 1935.

SORDI, ALBERTO: Rome, Italy, 1925.

SORVINO, PAUL: NYC, 1939, AMDA.

SOTHERN, ANN: (Harriet Lake) Valley City, N.D., Jan. 22, 1909. Washington U.

STACK, ROBERT: Los Angeles, Jan. 13, 1919. USC.

STADLEN, LEWIS J.: Brooklyn, Mar. 7, 1947, Neighborhood Playhouse.

STAMP, TERENCE: London, 1940.

STANDER, LIONEL: NYC, Jan 11, 1908, UNC.

STANG, ARNOLD: Chelsea, Mass., Sept. 28, 1925.

STANLEY, KIM: (Patricia Reid) Tularosa, N.M., Feb. 11, 1921. U. of Tex.

STANWYCK, BARBARA: (Ruby Stevens) Brooklyn, July 16, 1907.

STAPLETON, MAUREEN: Troy, N.Y., June 21, 1925.

STEEL, ANTHONY: London, May 21, 1920. Cambridge.

STEELE, TOMMY: London, Dec. 17, 1936.

STEIGER, ROD: Westhampton, N.Y., Apr. 14, 1925.

STERLING, JAN: (Jane Sterling Adriance) NYC, Apr. 3, 1923. Fay Compton School.

STERLING, ROBERT: (Robert Sterling Hart) Newcastle, Pa., Nov. 13, 1917. U. of Pittsburgh.

STEVENS, CONNIE: (Concetta Ann Ingolia) Brooklyn, Aug. 8, 1938. Hollywood Professional School.

STEVENS, KAYE: (Catherine) Pittsburgh, July 21, 1933.

STEVENS, MARK: (Richard) Cleveland, Ohio, Dec. 13, 1922.

(gleston) Hot Coffee, Miss., Oct. 1, 1936.

STEWART, ALEXANDRA: Montreal, Can., June 10. Louvre.

STEWART, ELAINE: Montclair, N.J., May 31, 1929.

STEWART, JAMES: Indiana, Pa., May 20, 1908. Princeton

STEWART, MARTHA: (Martha Haworth) Bardwell, Ky., Oct. 7, 1922.

STOCKWELL, DEAN: Hollywood, March 5.

STORM, GALE: (Josephine Cottle) Bloomington, Tex., Apr. 5, 1922.

STRASBERG, SUSAN: NYC, May 22, 1938.

STRAUD, DON: Hawaii, 1943.

STRAUSS, ROBERT: NYC, Nov. 8, 1913.

STREISAND, BARBRA: Brooklyn, Apr. 24, 1942.

STRODE, WOODY: Los Angeles, 1914.

STRUDWICK, SHEPPERD: Hillsboro, N.C., Sept. 22, 1907. U. of N.C.

STRUTHERS, SALLY: Portland, Ore., July 28, 1948, Pasadena Playhouse.

SULLIVAN, BARRY: (Patrick Barry) NYC, Aug. 29, 1912. NYU.

SULLY, FRANK: (Frank Sullivan) St. Louis, 1910. St. Teresa's College.

SUTHERLAND, DONALD: St. John, New Brunswick, July 17, 1934. U. Toronto.

SWANSON, GLORIA: (Josephine May Swenson) Chicago, Mar. 27, 1898. Chicago Art Inst.

SWINBURNE, NORA: Bath, Eng., July 24, 1902. RADA.

SWIT, LORETTA: Passaic, NJ, Nov. 4, AADA.

SYLVESTER, WILLIAM: Oakland, Calif., Jan. 31, 1922. RADA.

SYMS, SYLVIA: London, 1934. Convent School.

TABORI, KRISTOFFER: Los Angeles, Aug. 4, 1952.

TALBOT, LYLE: (Lysle Hollywood) Pittsburgh, Feb. 8, 1904.

TALBOT, NITA: NYC, Aug. 8, 1930. Irvine Studio School.

TAMBLYN, RUSS: Los Angeles, Dec. 30.

TANDY, JESSICA: London, June 7, 1909. Dame Owens' School.

TAYLOR, DON: Freeport, Pa., Dec. 13, 1920. Penn State U.

TAYLOR, ELIZABETH: London, Feb. 27, 1932. Byron House School.

TAYLOR, KENT: (Louis Weiss) Nashua, Iowa, May 11, 1907.

TAYLOR, ROD: (Robert) Sydney, Aust., Jan. 11, 1930.

TAYLOR-YOUNG, LEIGH: Wash., D.C., Jan. 25, 1945. Northwestern.

TEAGUE, ANTHONY SKOOTER: Jacksboro, Tex., Jan. 4, 1940.

TEAL, RAY: Grand Rapids, Mich., Jan. 12, 1902. Pasadena Playhouse.

TEMPLE, SHIRLEY: Santa Monica, Calif., Apr. 23, 1928.

TERRY-THOMAS: (Thomas Terry Hoar Stevens) Finchley, London, July 14, 1911. Ardingly College.

Woody Strode

Lurene Tuttle

TERZIEFF, LAURENT: Paris, 1935.

THACKER, RUSS: Washington, DC, June 23, 1946, Montgomery Col.

THATCHER, TORIN: Bombay, India, Jan. 15, 1905. RADA.

THAXTER, PHYLLIS: Portland, Me., Nov. 20, 1921. St Genevieve School.

THOMAS, DANNY: (Amos Jacobs) Deerfield, Mich., Jan. 6, 1914.

THOMAS, MARLO: (Margaret) Detroit, Nov. 21, 1943. USC.

THOMAS, RICHARD: NYC, June 13, 1951. Columbia.

THOMPSON, MARSHALL: Peoria, Ill., Nov. 27, 1925. Occidental College.

THOMPSON, REX: NYC, Dec. 14, 1942.

THOMPSON, SADA: Des Moines, Io., Sept. 27, 1929, Carnegie Tech.

THORNDIKE, SYBIL: Gainsborough, Eng., Oct. 24, 1882. Guild Hall School of Music.

THULIN, INGRID: Solleftea, Sweden, Jan. 27, 1929, Royal Drama Theatre.

TIERNEY, GENE: Brooklyn, Nov. 20, 1920. Miss Farmer's School.

TIERNEY, LAWRENCE: Brooklyn, Mar. 15, 1919. Manhattan College.

TIFFIN, PAMELA: (Wonso) Oklahoma City, Oct. 13, 1942.

TODD, RICHARD: Dublin, Ire., June 11, 1919. Shrewsbury School.

TOPOL: (Chaim Topol) Tel-Aviv, Israel, Sept. 9, 1935.

TORN, RIP: Temple, Tex., Feb. 6, 1931. U. Tex.

TOTTER, AUDREY: Joliet, Ill., Dec. 20.

TRAVERS, BILL: Newcastle-on-Tyne, Eng., Jan. 3, 1922.

TRAVIS, RICHARD: (William Justice) Carlsbad, N.M., Apr. 17, 1913.

TREACHER, ARTHUR: (Veary) Brighton, Eng., July 2, 1894.

TREMAYNE, LES: London, Apr. 16, 1913. Northwestern Columbia, UCLA.

TRINTIGNANT, JEAN-LOUIS: Pont-St. Esprit, France, Dec. 11, 1930. Dullin-Balachova Drama School.

TRYON, TOM: Hartford, Conn., Jan. 14, 1926. Yale.

TSOPEI, CORINNA: Athens, Greece, June 21, 1944.

TUCKER, FORREST: Plainfield, Ind., Feb. 12, 1919. George Washington U.

TURNER, LANA: (Julia Jean Mildred Frances Turner) Wallace, Idaho, Feb. 8, 1920.

Kristoffer Tabori

TUSHINGHAM, RITA: Liverpool, Eng., 1942.

TUTTLE, LURENE: Pleasant Lake, Ind., Aug. 20, 1906, USC.

TWIGGY: (Lesley Hornby) London, Sept. 19, 1949.

TYLER, BEVERLY: (Beverly Jean Saul) Scranton, Pa., July 5, 1928.

TYSON, CICELY: NYC, Dec. 19.

UGGAMS, LESLIE: NYC, May 25, 1943.

ULLMAN, LIV: Tokyo, Dec. 19, 1939, Webber-Douglas Acad.

URE, MARY: Glasgow, Scot., 1934. Central School of Drama.

USTINOV, PETER: London, Apr. 16, 1921. Westminster School.

VACCARO, BRENDA: Brooklyn, Nov. 18, 1939. Neighborhood Playhouse.

VALLEE, RUDY: (Hubert) Island Pond, Vt., July 28, 1901. Yale.

VALLI, ALIDA: Pola, Italy, May 31, 1921. Rome Academy of Drama.

VAN, BOBBY: NYC, Dec. 6, 1930.

VAN CLEEF, LEE: Somerville, N.J., Jan. 9, 1925.

VAN DEVERE, TRISH: (Patricia Dressel) Englewood Cliffs, NJ, Mar. 9, 1945, Ohio Wesleyan.

VAN DOREN, MAMIE: (Joan Lucile Olander) Rowena, S.D., Feb. 6, 1933.

VAN DYKE, DICK: West Plains, Mo., Dec. 13, 1925.

VAN FLEET, JO: Oakland, Cal., 1922.

VAN PATTEN, DICK: NYC, Dec. 9, 1928.

VAN PATTEN, JOYCE: NYC, Mar. 9, 1934.

VAN ROOTEN, LUIS: Mexico City, Nov. 29, 1906. U. of Pa.

VAUGHN, ROBERT: NYC, Nov. 22, 1932. USC.

VENUTA, BENAY: San Francisco, Jan. 27, 1911.

VERA-ELLEN (Rohe): Cincinnati, Feb. 16, 1926.

VERDON, GWEN: Culver City, Calif., Jan. 13, 1925.

VINCENT, JAN-MICHAEL: Denver, Col., July 15, Ventura Col.

VIOLET, ULTRA: (Isabelle Collin-Dufresne) Grenoble, France.

VITALE, MILLY: Rome, Italy, July 16, 1938. Lycee Chateaubriand.

VOIGHT, JON: Yonkers, N.Y., Dec. 29, 1938. Catholic U.

VOLONTE, GIAN MARIA: Milan, Italy, Apr. 9, 1933.

VON SYDOW, MAX: Lund, Swed., July 10, 1929, Royal Drama Theatre.

VYE, MURVYN: Quincy, Mass., July 15, 1913. Yale.

Ruth Warrick   Christopher Walken   Gwen Welles   Robert Young   Mai Zetterling

WAGNER, ROBERT: Detroit, Feb. 10, 1930.

WALKEN, CHRISTOPHER: Astoria, NY, Mar. 31, 1943, Hofstra U.

WALKER, CLINT: Hartfold, Ill., May 30, 1927. USC.

WALKER, NANCY: (Ann Myrtle Swoyer) Philadelphia, May 10, 1921.

WALLACH, ELI: Brooklyn, Dec. 7, 1915. CCNY, U. of Tex.

WALLIS, SHANI: London, Apr. 5, 1941.

WALSTON, RAY: New Orleans, Nov. 22, 1918. Cleveland Playhouse.

WALTER, JESSICA: Brooklyn, NY, Jan. 31, Neighborhood Playhouse.

WANAMAKER, SAM: Chicago, 1919. Drake.

WARD, BURT: (Gervis) Los Angeles, July 6, 1945.

WARDEN, JACK: Newark, N.J., Sept. 18, 1920.

WARREN, LESLEY ANN: NYC, Aug., 16, 1946.

WARRICK, RUTH: St. Joseph, Mo., June 29, UMo.

WASHBOURNE, MONA: Birmingham, Eng., Nov. 27, 1903.

WATERS, ETHEL: Chester, Pa., Oct. 31, 1900.

WATERSTON, SAM: Cambridge, Mass., Nov. 15, 1940. Yale.

WATLING, JACK: London, Jan. 13, 1923. Italia Conti School.

WATSON, DOUGLASS: Jackson, Ga., Feb. 24, 1921, UNC.

WAYNE, DAVID: (Wayne McKeehan) Travers City, Mich., Jan. 30, 1916. Western Michigan State U.

WAYNE, JOHN: (Marion Michael Morrison) Winterset, Iowa, May 26, 1907. USC.

WEAVER, DENNIS: Joplin, Mo., June 4, 1925. U. Okla.

WEAVER, MARJORIE: Crossville, Tenn., Mar. 2, 1913. Indiana U.

WEBB, ALAN: York, Eng., July 2, 1906. Dartmouth.

WEBB, JACK: Santa Monica, Calif. Apr. 2, 1920.

WEBBER, ROBERT: Santa Ana, Cal., Oct. 14, Compton Jr. Col.

WELCH, RAQUEL: (Tejada) Chicago, Sept. 5, 1940.

WELD, TUESDAY: (Susan) NYC, Aug. 27, 1943. Hollywood Professional School.

WELDON, JOAN: San Francisco, Aug. 5, 1933. San Francisco Conservatory.

WELLES, GWEN: NYC, Mar. 4.

WELLES, ORSON: Kenosha, Wisc., May 6, 1915. Todd School.

WERNER, OSKAR: Vienna, Nov. 13, 1922.

WEST, MAE: Brooklyn, Aug. 17, 1892.

WHITAKER, JOHNNY: Van Nuys, Cal., Dec. 13, 1959.

WHITE, CAROL: London, Apr. 1, 1944.

WHITE, CHARLES: Perth Amboy, NJ, Aug. 29, 1920, Rutgers U.

WHITE, JESSE: Buffalo, N.Y., Jan. 3, 1919.

WHITMAN, STUART: San Francisco, Feb. 1, 1929. CCLA.

WHITMORE, JAMES: White Plains, NY, Oct. 1, 1922. Yale.

WIDDOES, KATHLEEN: Wilmington, Del., Mar. 21, 1939.

WIDMARK, RICHARD: Sunrise, Minn., Dec. 26, 1914. Lake Forest U.

WILCOX-HORNE, COLIN: Highlands N.C., Feb. 4, 1937. U. Tenn.

WILCOXON, HENRY: British West Indies, Sept. 8, 1905.

WILDE, CORNEL: NYC, Oct. 13, 1915. CCNY, Columbia.

WILDER, GENE: Milwaukee, Wis., 1935, U Iowa.

WILDING, MICHAEL: Westcliff, Eng., July 23, 1912. Christ's Hospital.

WILLIAMS, BILLY DEE: NYC, Apr. 6, 1937.

WILLIAMS, EMLYN: Mostyn, Wales, Nov. 26, 1905. Oxford.

WILLIAMS, ESTHER: Los Angeles, Aug. 8, 1923.

WILLIAMS, GRANT: NYC, Aug. 18, 1930. Queens College.

WILLIAMS, JOHN: Chalfont, Eng., Apr. 15, 1903. Lancing College.

WILLIAMSON, FRED: Gary, Ind., 1938, Northwestern.

WILSON, DEMOND: NYC, Oct. 13, 1946, Hunter Col.

WILSON, FLIP: (Clerow Wilson) Jersey City, N.J., Dec. 8, 1933.

WILSON, NANCY: Chillicothe, O., Feb. 20, 1937.

WILSON, SCOTT: Atlanta, Ga., 1942.

WINDOM, WILLIAM: NYC, Sept. 28, 1923, Williams Col.

WINDSOR, MARIE: (Emily Marie Bertelson) Marysvale, Utah, Dec. 11, 1924. Brigham Young U.

WINFIELD, PAUL: Los Angeles, 1940, UCLA.

WINN, KITTY: Wash., D.C., 1944. Boston U.

WINTERS, JONATHAN: Dayton Ohio, Nov. 11, 1925. Kenyon College.

WINTERS, ROLAND: Boston, Nov. 22, 1904.

WINTERS, SHELLEY: (Shirley Schrift) St. Louis, Aug. 18, 1922. Wayne U.

WINWOOD, ESTELLE: Kent, Eng., Jan. 24, 1883. Lyric Stage Academy.

WITHERS, GOOGIE: Karachi, India, Mar. 12, 1917. Italia Conti School.

WOOD, NATALIE: (Natasha Gurdin) San Francisco, July 20, 1938.

WOOD, PEGGY: Brooklyn, Feb. 9, 1894.

WOODLAWN, HOLLY: (Harold Ajzenberg) Juana Diaz, PR, 1947.

WOODS, JAMES: Vernal, U., Apr. 18, 1947, MIT.

WOODWARD, JOANNE: Thomasville, Ga., Feb. 27, 1931. Neighborhood Playhouse.

WOOLAND, NORMAN: Dusseldorf, Ger., Mar. 16, 1910. Edward VI School.

WRAY, FAY: Alberta, Can., Sept. 10, 1907.

WRIGHT, TERESA: NYC, Oct. 27, 1918.

WYATT, JANE: Campgaw, N.J., Aug. 10, 1912. Barnard College.

WYMAN, JANE: (Sarah Jane Fulks) St. Joseph, Mo., Jan. 4, 1914.

WYMORE, PATRICE: Miltonvale, Kan., Dec. 17, 1927.

WYNN, KEENAN: NYC, July 27, 1916. St. John's.

WYNN, MAY: (Donna Lee Hickey) NYC, Jan. 8, 1930.

WYNTER, DANA: London, June 8, Rhodes U.

YORK, DICK: Fort Wayne, Ind., Sept. 4, 1928. De Paul U.

YORK, MICHAEL: Fulmer, Eng., Mar. 27, 1942. Oxford.

YORK, SUSANNAH: London, Jan. 9, 1941, RADA.

YOUNG, ALAN: (Angus) North Shield, Eng., Nov. 19, 1919.

YOUNG, GIG: (Byron Barr) St. Cloud, Minn., Nov. 4, 1913. Pasadena Playhouse.

YOUNG, LORETTA: (Gretchen) Salt Lake City, Jan. 6, 1913. Immaculate Heart College.

YOUNG, ROBERT: Chicago, Feb. 22, 1907.

ZETTERLING, MAI: Sweden, May 27, 1925. Ordtuery Theatre School.

ZIMBALIST, EFREM, JR.: NYC, Nov. 30, 1923. Yale.

ADRIAN, MAX, 69, versatile Irish-born actor on film, state, and tv, died Jan. 19, 1973 in his Surrey, Eng. home. Among his films are "Primrose Path," "Henry V," "Deadly Affair," "Young Mr. Pitt," "Pickwick Papers," "Her Favorite Husband," "Music Lovers," and "The Devils." No reported survivors.

ALLEGRET, MARC, 73, director, died in his Paris home Nov. 3, 1973. He had directed over 50 films, including "Mamzelle Nitouche," "Gribouille," "Lentree des Artistes," "Fanny," "Futures Vedettes," and his last "Le Bal du Comte D'Orgel" in 1970. Surviving are his director brother, Yves, and a daughter.

APPLEWHITE, ERIC, 76, character actor, died May 29, 1973 in Miami, Fla. He had appeared in many films but was best known for the TV series "Flipper" in which he was the sheriff, and "Gentle Ben" as the doctor. His wife, a daughter, and son survive.

ARCHER, EUGENE, 42, Texas-born former film reviewer for the NY Times, died of natural causes in his Los Angeles apartment Jan. 30, 1973. He was currently teaching at UCLA. He had appeared in "La Collectioneuse," and co-authored "Ten Days Wonder." His mother survives.

ARMSTRONG, ROBERT, 82, film, stage, and tv actor, died Apr. 20, 1973 in Santa Monica, Cal. During his 50 year career, he had appeared in over 100 films, including "King Kong," "Son of Kong," "Mighty Joe Young," "Main Event," "Blood under the Sun," "Sea of Grass," "Paleface," "The Fugitive," and "Public Enemy's Wife." He had been in retirement for 10 years. Surviving is his widow.

AUERBACH, GEORGE, 68, film and stage writer, died in Nov. 1973 in Exeter, NH. Among his credits for MGM and Paramount are "His Brother's Wife," "She Asked for It," and "Blossoms on Broadway." Five daughters survive.

BANNER, JOHN, 63, film, stage, and TV actor, died of an abdominal hemorrhage on Jan. 28, 1973 in his native Vienna. Among his films are "The Blue Angel," "The Interns," "Fallen Sparrow," "Seven Miles from Alcatraz," "The Juggler," "Story of Ruth," "Once upon a Honeymoon," "36 Hours," "The Moon Is Down," and "Wicked Dreams of Paula Schultz." For 6 years he was Sgt. Shultz on TV's "Hogan's Heroes." He and his wife, who survives, had been living in France for several years.

BARKER, LEX, 54, film and stage actor, collapsed and died on a NYC street May 11, 1973. Best known as the tenth actor to portray Tarzan, he eventually became a top western star in Germany. His films include "Farmer's Daughter," "Mr. Blandings Builds His Dream House," "Velvet Touch," "Tarzan's Magic Touch," "Tarzan and the Slave Girl," "Tarzan's Peril," "Tarzan and the She-Devil," "War Drums," "Girl in the Kremlin," "The Boy Cried Murder," and "Apache Gold." A son and his fifth wife survive.

BEAL, SCOTT, 83, pioneer actor and assistant director, died of cancer July 10, 1973 in Hollywood. Began career in 1910, and among his credits are "Dracula," "Back Street," and "Imitation of Life." Surviving is a sister.

BOREL, LOUIS, 67, Dutch actor, died in Apr. 1973 in Amsterdam where he retired in 1949. He had appeared in numerous Hollywood films. No reported survivors.

BORG, VEDA ANN, 58, Boston-born film actress, died Aug. 16, 1973 in Hollywood. Her credits include "Three Cheers for Love," "Mother Wore Tights," "Big Jim McLain," and "Guys and Dolls." Surviving are her mother, and a son, Andrew McLaglen, Jr. She was divorced from director McLaglen.

BRADFORD, LANE, 50, film and tv actor, died June 7, 1973 of a cerebral hemorrhage in Honolulu. He appeared in many Monogram and Republic westerns, and tv's "Lone Ranger," "Death Valley Days," "Bonanza," "Gunsmoke," and "District Attorney." His wife survives.

BRADSHAW, GEORGE, 64, writer, died while in a taxi near his home in NYC on Nov. 11, 1973. Many of his stories were adapted for films, including "Memorial to a Bad Man," "When Winter Comes," "How to Steal a Million," and "Second Fiddle." No survivors reported.

BLACKMER, SIDNEY, 78, stage and film actor, died of cancer Oct. 5, 1973 in NYC. His film career began in "The Perils of Pauline" in 1914 and ended with "Rosemary's Baby" in 1968. He had appeared in over 200 pictures, including "Billion Dollar Mystery," "Count of Monte Cristo," "Little Colonel," "In Old Chicago," "Duel in the Sun," "Saturday's Hero," "The High and the Mighty," "High Society," "Tammy and the Bachelor," "How to Murder Your Wife," and "Joy in the Morning." Two sons and his second wife, former actress Suzanne Kaaren, survive.

Max Adrian (1964)

Robert Amstrong (1936)

Lex Barker (1964)

Sidney Blackmer (1968)

Joe E. Brown (1951)

Lon Chaney (1964)

BREAKSTON, GEORGE P., 53, child actor who became a director, screenwriter, and producer, died May 21, 1973 in Paris where he had been living for some years. His film credits as an actor include "No Greater Glory," "Wild Boys of the Road," "Great Expectations," "It Happened One Night," "Return of Peter Grimm," "Dark Angel," "Hangover Square" and several films of the Andy Hardy series. Surviving is his wife.

BROWN, JOE E., 80, Ohio-born film and stage comedian, died July 6, 1973 after a long illness in his Brentwood, Cal., home. Noted for his elastic mouth and slapstick antics, his film career began in 1928 in "Crooks Can't Win." He subsequently appeared in over 50 pictures, including "The Gladiator," "Wide Open Faces," "Sons o' Fun," "Six Day Bike Rider," "Going Wild," "Sit Tight," "Circus Clown," "You Said a Mouthful," "Chatterbox," "Pin Up Girl," "Hollywood Canteen," "Elmer the Great," "Hold Everything," "Midsummer Night's Dream," and "Some Like it Hot." He leaves his wife and two daughters.

BUFFINGTON, ADELE, 73, western screen writer, died Nov. 23, 1973 of arteriosclerosis in Woodland Hills, Cal. She had written more than 150 westerns for such stars as Tom Mix, Buck Jones, and Tim McCoy. Among her credits are "Bullwhip," "Cow Country," "Streets of San Francisco," "Beyond the Great Divide," and "Flame of the West."

BUTLER, ROYAL, 80, western character actor, died July 28, 1973 in Desert Hot Springs, Cal. He had appeared in many films with Gene Autry and Johnny Mack Brown before retiring in 1955. His wife and son survive.

CARNEY, ALAN, 63, Brooklyn-born film and stage comedian, died of a heart attack May 2, 1973 in Van Nuys, Cal. Credits include "Mr. Lucky," "Li'l Abner," "Convoy," "In which We Serve," "Step Lively," "Radio Stars on Parade," "Master Mind," "Zombies on Broadway," "The Pretender," and "Its a Mad, Mad, Mad, Mad World." A brother and sister survive.

CARR, MARY, 99, actress, died June 24, 1973 in Woodland Hills, Cal. She appeared in films for more than 50 years, including roles in "Over the Hill to the Poor House," and "Friendly Persuasion." Surviving are two sons and two daughters.

CASTLE, PEGGIE, 46, Virginia-born film and tv actress, was found dead of cirrhosis of the liver in her Hollywood home on Aug. 11, 1973. Her film debut was in 1950 in "Mr. Belvedere Goes to College," followed by "Overland Pacific," "Wagons West," "Miracle in the Rain," "Son of Belle Starr," "White Orchid," "Target Zero," "Seven Hills of Rome," and "I, the Jury." She was a regular in the tv series "The Lawman," and "The Outlaws." Her third husband died earlier in the year.

CAVETT, FRANK, 67, Ohio-born screenwriter, died Mar. 25, 1973 in Santa Monica, Cal. He won two "Oscars" for his collaboration on "Going My Way" and "The Greatest Show on Earth." He had also worked on "Angelica," "Tom Brown's School Days," "Second Chorus," "Syncopation," and "The Corn Is Green." Survivors include two sons and a daughter.

CHANEY, LON, JR., 67, Oklahoma-born character acter, died after a long illness on July 12, 1973 in San Clemente, Cal. As with his father, he became known as an interpreter of "monster" roles, including Dracula, The Wolf Man, and Frankenstein's monster. Other films were "Of Mice and Men," "Northwest Mounted Police," "One Million B.C.," "My Favorite Brunette," "Pardners," "High Noon," "Billy the Kid," and "Cobra Woman." During the early part of his career he was known as Creighton Chaney. Surviving are two sons by his first marriage, and his second wife.

COOPER, MELVILLE, 76, English-born film and stage character actor, died Mar. 29, 1973 of cancer in Woodland Hills, Cal. Made film debut in 1934 and appeared in numerous pictures, including "13 Rue Madeleine," "Father of the Bride," "Lady Eve," "Pride and Prejudice," "Rebecca," "It Should Happen to You," "Love Happy," and "Baby Makes Three," A daughter survives.

COOPER, MERIAN, 78, Florida-born film director, producer, and author, died of cancer Apr. 21, 1973 in San Diego, Cal. His 1938 creation of "King Kong" made him known throughout the world. Among his other films were "Grass," "Chang," "Four Feathers," "Little Women," "Northwest Passage," "Flying down to Rio," "Last Days of Pompeii," "Lost Patrol," "Fort Apache," "She Wore a Yellow Ribbon," "Wagon Master," "Rio Grande," and "The Quiet Man." His widow, former actress Dorothy Jordan, a son, and two daughters survive.

COWARD, NOEL, 73, English-born actor, playwright, composer, director, and wit, died of a heart attack Mar. 26, 1973 in his Jamaica, W.I., villa. His film career began in 1918 in "Hearts of the World," subsequently appearing in "The Scoundrel," "In Which We Serve" which he wrote and directed, "The Astonished Heart," "Meet Me Tonight," "Around the World in 80 Days," "Our Man in Havana," "Boom," "Bunny Lake Is Missing," and "The Italian Job." He also wrote or adapted for films "Cavalcade," "Blithe Spirit," "Brief Encounter," "This Happy Breed." He was knighted by Queen Elizabeth in 1970. He was never married, and had no close relatives. He was buried in Jamaica.

CRANE, NORMA, 42, film, stage, and tv actress, died of cancer Sept. 28, 1973 in Los Angeles. She had appeared in "Tea and Sympathy," "Penelope," "They Call Me Mr. Tibbs," "Fiddler on the Roof," and "Double Solitaire." She left no immediate survivors.

CROSSE, RUPERT, 45, film and tv actor, died of cancer Mar. 5, 1973 in Nevis, W.I. He was nominated for an "Oscar" as best supporting actor in "The Reivers" in 1968. He also co-starred in tv's series "Partners." His widow and son survive.

DALLIMORE, MAURICE, character acter in his 70's, died Feb. 20, 1973 in Hollywood. He had appeared in many films, including "The Collector." Two brothers survive.

DARIN, BOBBY, 37, Bronx-born singer and actor, died in Los Angeles, Dec. 20, 1973 after open-heart surgery. After becoming a top nightclub star, he appeared in such films as "Come September," "Too Late Blues," "Hell Is for Heroes," "If a Man Answers," "Point Blank," "Happy Mother's Day, Love, George." He was nominated for an "Oscar" for his role in "Capt. Newman, M.D." He leaves a son by his first wife, actress Sandra Dee. His body was donated to medical science for research.

DE CORDOVA, ARTURO, 66, Mexican actor, died Nov. 3, 1973 in Mexico City. He had appeared in over 100 films, including "For Whom the Bell Tolls," "Hostages," "Frenchman's Creek," "Masquerade in Mexico," "Sword of Gascony," "A Medal for Benny," and "Incendiary Blonde." No reported survivors.

DELGADO, ROGER, 53, British-born actor, was killed June 19, 1973 in a car accident while working on a film in Turkey. He had appeared in, among many others, "Star," "Khartoum," "Road to Hong Kong," and "Antony and Cleopatra." His wife survives.

DODD, CLAIRE, age not reported, one of the 1930's most beautiful film actresses, died Nov. 23, 1973 after a long illness in Beverly Hills, Cal. Appeared on Broadway before going to Hollywood for such films as "Footlight Parade," "Hard to Handle," "Elmer the Great," "Roberta," "Babbitt," "Gambling Lady," "Glass Key," "Three Loves Has Nancy," several Perry Mason films, "An American Tragedy," "Road to Reno," "Up Pops the Devil," "If I Had My Way," "Slightly Honorable," "Black Cat," "In the Navy," and "Mississippi Gambler." She retired in 1942 after her second marriage. Surviving are her husband, four sons, and a daughter.

DUNN, MICHAEL, 39, Oklahoma-born stage and film actor, died of undetermined causes in London on Aug. 29, 1973, where he was filming "The Abdication." He had appeared in "You're a Big Boy Now," "Madigan," "No Way to Treat a Lady," "Justine," "Werewolf of Washington," and "Ship of Fools" for which he received an Academy Award nomination for supporting actor. He was separated from his wife, Joy Talbot.

ELLIS, ROBERT, 40, former child star, died of kidney failure Nov. 23, 1973 in Los Angeles. He began his career at 5 and subsequently appeared in over 50 films, including the Henry Aldrich series. No reported survivors.

ESSLER, FRED, 77, character actor, died Jan. 17, 1973 in Woodland Hills, Cal. He had appeared in numerous films, including "The Unsinkable Molly Brown," and on tv's "77 Sunset Strip," "Perry Mason," and "Life of Riley." His widow survives.

FIELD, BETTY, 55, Boston-born film and stage actress, died Sept. 13, 1973 of a cerebral hemorrhage in Hyannis, Mass. Her film debut was in 1939 in "What a Life!," followed by "Of Mice and Men," "Seventeen," "Victory," "Shepherd of the Hills," "Blues in the Night," "Kings Row," "Are Husbands Necessary?," "Flesh and Fantasy," "Tomorrow the World," "Great Moment," "The Southerner," "Great Gatsby," "Picnic," "Bus Stop," "Peyton Place," "Bird Man of Alcatraz," "Seven Women," "How to Save a Marriage," "Coogan's Bluff." Surviving are her third husband, artist Raymond Olivere, two sons and a daughter by her first marriage to playwright Elmer Rice.

Noel Coward (1959)

Claire Dodd (1934)

Betty Field (1958)

Minna Gombell (1937)

Betty Grable (1967)

William Haines (1930)

FORD, JOHN, 78, one of America's greatest directors, died Aug. 31, 1973 of cancer in his Palm Desert, Cal., home. He had directed over 140 films, and received "Oscars" for "The Informer," "Grapes of Wrath," "How Green Was My Valley," "The Quiet Man," and for a WWII documentary, "The Battle of Midway." Among his other pictures are "Stagecoach," "Lost Patrol," "Young Mr. Lincoln," "The Fugitive," "Arrowsmith," "Three Godfathers," "Tobacco Road," "Hurricane," "Long Voyage Home," "My Darling Clementine," "She Wore a Yellow Ribbon," "What Price Glory?," "Sgt. Rutledge," "Donovan's Reef," and "Seven Women." He is survived by his wife, a son and a daughter.

FRASCA, MARY, also known as La Sorrentina, age unreported, singer and actress, died July 24, 1973 in NYC. Among the films in which she had appeared were "The Gang That Couldn't Shoot Straight," "Lovers and Other Strangers," and "The Godfather." Her husband survives.

FREED, ARTHUR, 78, song writer and film producer, died Apr. 12, 1973 of a heart attack in Hollywood. He was the industry's most active producer of musicals, and received "Oscars" for "An American in Paris," and "Gigi." Among his songs are "Pagan Love Song," "You Are My Lucky Star," "Fit as a Fiddle," "All I Do Is Dream of You," "Temptation," and "Singin' in the Rain." His pictures include "Strike up the Band," "Lady Be Good," "For Me and My Gal," "Cabin in the Sky," "Girl Crazy," "Meet Me in St. Louis," "Ziegfeld Follies," "The Clock," "Harvey Girls," "Easter Parade," "Words and Music," "Barkleys of Broadway," "On the Town," "Annie Get Your Gun," "Royal Wedding," "Show Boat," "Singin' in the Rain," "Band Wagon," "Kismet," "Brigadoon," and "Invitation to the Dance." His widow and a daughter survive.

GILBERT, BOBBY, 75, vaudeville performer, and for 30 years a film actor, died of hepatitis Sept. 19, 1973 in Hollywood. Surviving are his widow, and a son Alan, a tv producer.

GOMBELL, MINNA, 81, Baltimore-born stage and film actress, died Apr. 14, 1973 in Santa Monica, Cal. Made film debut in 1931 in "Doctors' Wives," followed by over 100 pictures including "Bad Girl," "The Great Waltz," "Hunchback of Notre Dame," "Boom Town," "Mexican Spitfire," "Destiny," "Night Club Girl," "Swingin' on a Rainbow," "Penthouse Rhythm," "That Girl," "The Best Years of Our Lives," "Perilous Holiday," "Last Bandit," and "Pagan Love Song." No survivors reported.

GRABLE, BETTY, 56, St. Louis-born film and stage musical actress, died July 2, 1973 of lung cancer in Santa Monica, Cal. Among the more than 40 films in which she appeared are "The Gay Divorcee," "Down Argentine Way," "Moon over Miami," "A Yank in the R.A.F.," "Song of the Islands," "Springtime in the Rockies," "Million Dollar Legs," "Mother Wore Tights," "Coney Island," "Tin Pan Alley," "Pin Up Girl," "Sweet Rosie O'Grady," "The Dolly Sisters," "The Shocking Miss Pilgrim," "When My Baby Smiles at Me," "How to Marry a Millionaire," "Three for the Show," and her last in 1955 "How to Be Very, Very Popular." She was WW II's most popular pin-up, and became the industry's highest paid star. She was married to and divorced from Jackie Coogan and Harry James. Surviving are two daughters by her second marriage.

GREAZA, WALTER, 76, St. Paul-born film, stage, radio, and tv character actor, died June 1, 1973 in Kew Gardens, NY. Pictures in which he appeared are "13 Rue Madeleine," "Boomerang," "Northside 777," "Street with No Name," "The Great Gatsby," "Larceny," "New Mexico," and "It Happened to Jane." He was a regular on the tv series "Treasury Men," "Edge of Night," and "Sgt. Bilko." No reported survivors.

GREEN, ABEL, 72, editor of Variety for 40 years, died of a heart attack in his NYC home on May 10, 1973. He leaves his wife and two brothers.

HAINES, WILLIAM, 73, Virginia-born film actor, died Dec. 26, 1973 of cancer in Santa Monica, Cal. He retired from movies in the 1930's and became a popular interior decorator. Among his films are "Brown of Harvard," "Sally, Irene and Mary," "Spring Fever," "Alias Jimmy Valentine," "Excess Baggage," "Navy Blues," "Young and Beautiful," "Slide, Kelly, Slide," "Way Out West," "Fast Life," and "Tell It to the Marines." Surviving are two brothers and two sisters.

HARDIE, RUSSELL, 69, film, stage, and tv actor, died July 21, 1973 after a long illness in Clarence, NY. He appeared in "Broadway to Hollywood," "Christopher Bean," "Stage Mother," "Sequoia," "The Band Plays On," "As the Earth Turns," "Pursued," "West Point of the Air," "In Old Kentucky," "Down to the Sea in Ships," "Whistle at Eaton Falls," and "Men in White." He also acted in the tv series "Naked City." Two sisters survive.

HARTMAN, PAUL, 69, film, stage and tv actor, dancer, and comedian, died Oct. 2, 1973 of a heart attack in Los Angeles. After a successful stage career, he went to Hollywood in 1952, and appeared in such films as "45 Fathers," "Inherit the Wind," "Soldier in the Rain," "How to Succeed in Business," "Sunny," "Higher and Higher," "Man on a Tightrope," "The Reluctant Astronaut," and "Luv." He was a favorite on the "Mayberry RFD" tv series. A son survives.

HARVEY, LAURENCE, 45, Lithuanian-born film and stage actor, died of cancer Nov. 25, 1973 in his London home. After over 30 European films, his role in "Room at the Top" brought him to the attention of U.S. audiences, and stardom. His other films include "Romeo and Juliet," "Three Men in a Boat," "Butterfield 8," "The Alamo," "Darling," "Life at the Top," "Magic Christian," "A Dandy in Aspic," and his last, "Night Watch." He leaves his third wife and daughter.

HAWKINS, JACK, 62, British stage and film actor, died of cancer and complications July 18, 1973 in London. He appeared in over 50 films, including "The Lost Chord," "Peg of Old Drury," "Fallen Idol," "The Elusive Pimpernel," "Crash of Silence," "Outpost in Malaya," "Cruel Sea," "Malta Story," "The Intruder," "Land of Fury," "Third Key," "Bridge on the River Kwai," "Ben Hur," "Five Finger Exercise," "Lawrence of Arabia," "Rampage," "Lord Jim," "Masquerade," "The Poppy Is also a Flower," "Great Catherine," "Oh! What a Lovely War," "Waterloo," "Shalako," "Nicholas and Alexandra," "Young Winston," and "Jane Eyre." Surviving are his second wife, former actress Doreen Lawrence, two sons, and a daughter.

HAYAKAWA, SESSUE, 83, Japanese-born film star, died Nov. 23, 1973 in Tokyo of a cerebral thrombosis complicated by pneumonia. In silent films he was one of Hollywood's leading lovers and villains in over 120 productions, and established his own company. In the 1930's his popularity waned and he went to France. In 1949 he returned to the U.S., and eventually to Japan where he became a Zen priest. Among his many films are "Typhoon," "The Cheat," "Yoshiwara," "Macao," "Green Mansions," "Love City," "Swiss Family Robinson," and "Bridge on the River Kwai" for which he received an Academy Award nomination. A son and two daughters survive.

HENNING, PAT, 62, comedian, film and tv actor, died in his sleep Apr. 28, 1973 in Miami Beach, Fla. He had appeared in over 25 movies, including "Man on a Tightrope," "On the Waterfront," and "The Cardinal," and in tv series "Wagon Train," "The Honeymooners," "Flipper," and "Gentle Ben." He received an Emmy for "The Catered Affair." He is survived by his widow.

HOLDEN, FAY, 79, English-born film and stage actress, died of cancer June 23, 1973 in Los Angeles. After a successful 30 year stage career as Gaby Fay, she changed her name and began playing character roles in such films as "Florence Nightingale," "I Married a Doctor," "You're Only Young Once," "Guns of the Pecos," "Test Pilot," "A Family Affair," and as Andy Hardy's mother in 15 of the series, her last in 1958 in "Andy Hardy Comes Homes." A brother survives.

HOLT, TIM, 54, California-born actor, died of cancer Feb. 15, 1973 in Shawnee, Okla., where he was manager of a radio station. Son of star Jack Holt, his film career began at 10, and he appeared in 149 movies. In 1952 he was fifth among the top western actors, and top male star on the RKO lot. His films include "Vanishing Pioneer," "History Is Made at Night," "Renegade Ranger," "Spirit of Culver," "Come on Danger," "West of Tombstone," "His Kind of Woman," "Stagecoach," "My Darling Clementine," "Swiss Family Robinson," "The Magnificant Ambersons," "Hitler's Children," "Treasure of the Sierra Madre," and his last "The Time Machine." He leaves his third wife, two sons, and a daughter.

HUFF, LOUISE, 77, stage and silent film actress, died Aug. 22, 1973 in NYC. She made her film debut in 1914, and among her pictures were "Seventeen," "Great Expectations," "Tom Sawyer," "Disraeli," "The Millionaire Double," and "O You Women." She was the widow of Edwin Stillman, and leaves a son and two daughters.

INGE, WILLIAM, 60, screen writer, and Pulitzer Prize winning playwright, was found dead June 10, 1973 from carbon monoxide poisoning, an apparent suicide, in the garage of his Hollywood Hills home. His play "Picnic" was adapted for films, and he wrote screenplays "All Fall Down," "Splendor in the Grass" for which he received an "Oscar," and "Bus Riley Is Back in Town." He was buried in his native Independence, Kan. A sister survives.

Sessue Hayakawa (1949)

Fay Holden (1949)

Tim Holt (1952)

Raymond Keane (1926)

Cecil Kellaway (1970)

Veronica Lake (1942)

JACOBS, ARTHUR P., 51, producer, died June 27, 1973 of a heart attack in Hollywood. His films for his APJAC Co. include "What a Way to Go," "Dr. Doolittle," "The Chairman," "Planet of the Apes," "Goodbye, Mr. Chips," "Beneath the Planet of the Apes," "Escape from the Planet of the Apes," "Conquest of the Planet of the Apes," "Play It Again, Sam," and "Tom Sawyer." Surviving is his widow, actress Natalie Trundy.

JEANS, URSULA, 66, British screen and stage actress, died Apr. 21, 1973 in London. Among the many films in which she appeared are "Calvacade," "Storm in a Teacup," "Mr. Emanuel," and "The Weaker Sex." She leaves her second husband, actor Roger Livesey.

KATZMAN, SAM, 72, NY-born film producer, died Aug. 4, 1973 in Hollywood. His many credits include "His Private Secretary," "Jungle Jim" series, "Escape from San Quentin," "Last Blitzkreig," "Juke Box Jamboree," "Rock around the Clock," "Twist around the Clock," "Kissin' Cousins," "Harum Scarum," "Your Cheatin' Heart," "Riot on Sunset Strip," "The Love-Ins," and "Angel, Angel, Down We Go." Surviving are his widow, a daughter, and a producer son, Jerry.

KEANE, RAYMOND, 66, Denver-born actor, died Aug. 31, 1973 in Los Angeles. Began his career in 1925, and appeared in such films as "Midnight Sun," "Big Gun," "Meet the Prince," "Lone Eagle," "How to Handle Women," "Magic Garden," "Power of Silence," and "Loose Ankles." He retired from movies and became active in advertising. His widow survives.

KELLAWAY, CECIL, 79, South African-born character actor, died Feb. 28, 1973 in Hollywood. He appeared in over 75 films after going to Hollywood in 1938, including "Everybody's Doing It," "Wuthering Heights," "Intermezzo," "Luck of the Irish," "The Postman Always Rings Twice," "Harvey," "Portrait of Hennie," "Brother Orchid," "I Married a Witch," "Kitty," "Frenchman's Creek," "My Heart Belongs to Daddy," "Star-Spangled Rhythm," "Kim," "Young Bess," "The Cardinal," "Hush, Hush, Sweet Charlotte," and "Guess Who's Coming to Dinner" for which he received an Academy Award nomination. Surviving are his widow, and two sons.

KENNEDY, DOUGLAS, 55, film and tv character actor, died Aug. 10, 1973 in Honolulu. Among his films are "Opened by Mistake," "Those Were the Days," "Way of All Flesh," "Northwest Mounted Police," "Nora Prentiss," "Dark Passage," "Possessed," "Look for the Silver Lining," "Last Train from Bombay," "Torpedo Alley," "Cry Vengeance," and "Strange Lady in Town." He starred in the tv series "Steve Donovan, Western Marshal." He leaves his widow and two daughters.

KORNMAN, MARY, 56, actress, died of cancer June 1, 1973 in Glendale, Cal. For 7 years was female lead in "Our Gang Comedies," followed by "The Boy Friends," "College Humor," "Picture Brides," "Strictly Dynamite," "The Calling of Dan Matthews," "Youth on Parole," "Swing It, Professor," "I Am a Criminal," and "On the Spot." She had been in retirement for 20 years. Her husband survives.

LAKE, VERONICA, 53, a Brooklyn-born boxoffice favorite in the 1940's died of hepatitis July 7, 1973 in Burlington, Vt. Her seductive peekaboo hair style set a fashion in such films as "I Wanted Wings," "Sullivan's Travels," "This Gun for Hire," "Glass Key," "I Married a Witch," "Star-Spangled Rhythm," "So Proudly We Hail," "Hour before Dawn," "Bring on the Girls," "Hold That Blonde," "Out of This World," "Miss Susie Slagle's" "Sainted Sisters," "Saigon," and "Slattery's Hurricane." In recent years, she had been living and acting on stage in England. She was married four times. A son and two daughters survive.

LANDIN, HOPE, 80, Minneapolis-born stage and screen actress, died Feb. 28, 1973 in Hollywood. Her many film credits include "I Remember Mama," "Bridge of San Luis Rey," "Reap the Wild Wind," "Unconquered," "How to Marry a Millionaire," and "The Greatest Story Ever Told." No survivors reported.

LANE, ALLEN "ROCKY", 64, top western star of the 1950's, died Oct. 27, 1973 from a bone marrow disorder in Woodland Hills, Cal. In addition to his many western films, he appeared in "Not Quite Decent," "Forward Pass," and "Conspiracy." He was the voice of "Mr. Ed" in the tv series. Surviving is his mother.

LEE, BRUCE, 32, San Francisco-born Chinese kung fu film actor, died July 20, 1973 of a brain edema in Hong Kong. His movies include "Fist of Fury," and "The Chinese Connection." He also appeared on tv in "Batman" and "Green Hornet" series. His widow survives.

LEE, LILA, 68, New Jersey-born silent screen star and stage actress, died Nov. 13, 1973 of a stroke in Saranac Lake, NY. Among her many films are "Broken Hearts," "Adorable Cheat," "Just Married," "Bit of Heaven," "Black Pearl," "Sacred Flame," "Murder Will Out," "Blood and Sand," "Male and Female," "Unholy Three," "The Gorilla," "Radio Patrol," "False Faces," "War Correspondent," "People's Enemy," "Honky Tonk," "Show of Shows," "Argyle Case," and "Blind Alley." She was married and divorced three times. Her son, writer-actor James Kirkwood, survives.

LERNER, CARL, 61, film editor, died Aug. 26, 1973 in NYC. His credits include "Best Years of Our Lives," "Red River," "Uncle Vanya," "Klute," "The Swimmer," "Requiem for a Heavyweight," "Middle of the Night," "The Fugitive Kind," "The Goddess," and "12 Angry Men." His widow, a son, and a daughter survive.

LORDE, ATHENA, 57, stage, radio, film, and tv actress, died of cancer May 23, 1973 in Van Nuys, Cal. Her movies include "Fuzz," "Hush, Hush, Sweet Charlotte," "Marjorie Morningstar," "Skin Game," "Dr. Death." Surviving are her husband, actor Jim Boles, two daughters, and a son.

LOWE, EDWARD T., 83, screen writer, died Apr. 17, 1973 in his Los Angeles home. He began his career in 1911 and retired in 1946. His prodigious list of screen credits include "Hunchback of Notre Dame," "Broadway," "Tenderloin," "King of Jazz," the Charlie Chan and Bulldog Drummond series, "House of Frankenstein," "Dracula Meets the Wolf Man," "Scattergood Baines," "Tarzan's Desert Mystery," and "Sherlock Holmes." His widow and two daughters survive.

MacDOUGALL, RANALD, 58, screen writer, died Dec. 12, 1973 in Los Angeles. He was a former president of the Screen Writers Guild, and was nominated for an "Oscar" for writing "Mildred Pierce." Other screenplays include "Objective Burma," "Possessed," "June Bride," "Hasty Heart," "Breaking Point," "Secret of the Incas," "Cleopatra," "Jigsaw," and "The Mountain." Surviving are his widow, actress Nanette Fabray, two sons, and two daughters.

MacGOWRAN, JACK, 54, Dublin-born stage and film actor, died Jan. 30, 1973 in NYC, where he was appearing in "The Plough and the Stars." Made his debut in "The Quiet Man," followed by "Tom Jones," "Lord Jim," "Young Cassidy," "Dr. Zhivago," "Cul de Sac," and "King Lear." He leaves his widow and a daughter.

MACREADY, GEORGE, 63, stage and film actor, died July 2, 1973 in Los Angeles. After his first movie "Commandos Strike at Dawn" in 1942, he appeared in 78 others, including "Gilda," "Down to Earth," "Walls Came Tumbling Down," "A Song to Remember," "Counter-attack," "Return of Monte Cristo," "Black Arrow," "Johnny Allegro," "Wilson," "Detective Story," "Desert Fox," "Julius Caesar," "Paths of Glory," "Duffy of San Quentin," "Tora! Tora! Tora!," and "The Abductors." A son and two daughters survive.

MAGNANI, ANNA, 65, died Sept. 26, 1973 from a tumor of the pancreas in Rome. Her film credits include "Friday Theresa," "Open City," "Angelina," "Love," "Miracle," "Volcano," "Golden Coach," "Bellissima," "The Fugitive Kind," "Wild is the Wind," "Secret of Santa Vittoria," and "The Rose Tattoo" for which she received an Academy Award. Surviving is a son.

MARION, FRANCES, 86, screenwriter and former actress, died May 12, 1973 in Los Angeles. She had written over 136 scripts, and won "Oscars" for "The Big House" and "The Champ." She wrote most of the screenplays for Mary Pickford and Rudolph Valentino, and such others as "Camille," "Anna Christie," "Min and Bill," "Dinner at 8," "Stella Dallas," "Rebecca of Sunnybrook Farm," "Scarlet Letter," "Humoresque," "Dark Angel," and "Peg o' My Heart." Two sons survive.

MAYNARD, KEN, 77, Texas-born cowboy hero of over 300 movies, died Mar. 23, 1973 in Woodland Hills, Cal. First galloped onto the screen in 1923, and for 20 years was a top boxoffice star. He was the first cowboy to sing on film. His films include "Red Raiders," "Songs of the Saddle," "Parade of the West," "Branded Men," "$50,000 Reward," "Janice Meredith," "King of the Arena," "Fiddlin' Buckaroo," "Strawberry Roan," and his last in 1969 "Bigfoot." No survivors reported.

MELCHIOR, LAURITZ, 82, Danish-born great Wagnerian tenor, and screen actor, died Mar. 18, 1973 following an emergency operation in Santa Monica, Cal. His films include "When Hell Broke Loose," "Live Fast Die Young," "Angry Red Planet," "Case of Patty Smith," "Robinson Crusoe on Mars," "Time Travellers," "Ambush Bay," "Planet of the Vampires," "Thrill of Romance," "Two Sisters from Boston," "This Time for Keeps," "Luxury Liner," and "The Stars Are Singing." He was married three times, and leaves a son and daughter. Interment was in Copenhagen.

Lila Lee (1932)

Anna Magnani (1955)

Lauritz Melchior (1947)

J. Carrol Naish (1955)

Michael O'Shea (1944)

Katina Paxinou (1947)

MIDDLETON, GUY, 65, British actor, died July 30, 1973 in his home near London. Some of his better known roles were in "Happiest Days of Your Life," "No Place for Jennifer," "Laughter in Paradise," "Marry Me," "Young Wives' Tale," and "Adventure for Two." No reported survivors.

MONROE, VAUGHN, 62, singer and bandleader, died May 21, 1973 after an operation in Stuart, Fla. He was featured in such films as "Meet the People," "Carnegie Hall," "Singing Guns," and "Toughest Man in Arizona." His widow and two daughters survive.

MORELAND, MANTAN, 72, Louisiana-born comedian, died Sept. 28, 1973 in Hollywood. He had appeared in 310 films, and is probably best remembered for his role as the pop-eyed chauffeur to Charlie Chan. He had also appeared on tv in "The Bill Cosby Show." No reported survivors.

MORRISON, GEORGE "PETE," 82, who appeared in over 200 silent western movies, died Feb. 5, 1973 in Golden, Colo. Two sons survive.

NAISH, J. CARROL, 73, Ny-born stage, screen, and tv actor, died Jan. 24, 1973 in La Jolla, Cal. He was a master of dialects and appeared in over 250 pictures, including "Hatchet Man," "Her Jungle Love," "Capt. Blood," "Beau Geste," "A Medal for Benny" for which he received an Academy Award nomination, "The Southerner," "Humoresque," "Joan of Arc," "Toast of New Orleans," "Annie Get Your Gun," "Hit the Deck," "New York Confidential," "Rage at Dawn," "Violent Saturday," "Desert Sands," and "The Young Don't Cry." He was star of the tv series "Life with Luigi." Surviving are his widow and a daughter.

NIBLO, FRED, JR., 70, screenwriter, died Feb. 18, 1973 in Encino, Cal. Among his films are "Fighting 69th," "City Streets," "Penitentiary," "East of the River," "Hell's Kitchen," "Find the Witness," "Nine Lives Are not Enough," and "Father's Son." He leaves his widow, a son, and two daughters.

O'SHEA, MICHAEL, 67, stage, film, and tv actor, died Dec. 4, 1973 of a heart attack in Dallas, Tex. His screen debut in 1943 in "Eve of St. Mark," was followed by over 100 roles in such films as "Lady of Burlesque," "Captain China," "Fixed Bayonets," "Jack London," "Violence," "A Latin in Manhattan," "Man from Frisco," "Circumstantial Evidence," "Bloodhounds of Broadway," and "Something for the Boys." He played in the tv series "It's a Great Life" for two years. He leaves his widow, actress Virginia Mayo, and a daughter.

PAXINOU, KATINA, 72, screen and stage actress, died of cancer Feb. 22, 1973 in her native Athens, Greece. Her film debut in 1943 in "For Whom the Bell Tolls" won her an "Oscar," and she subsequently appeared in "Confidential Agent," "Mourning Becomes Electra," "Prince of Foxes," and "Rocco and His Brothers." Surviving are her husband, actor-director Alexis Minotis, and a daughter.

PERCY, EILEEN, 72, Irish-born silent film star, died July 29, 1973 in Beverly Hills, Cal. Among her many films are "Burnt Fingers," "Backstage," "Twelve Miles Out," "Spring Fever," "Telling the World," "Broadway Hoofer," and "The Flirt." She retired in 1927. Surviving is her second husband, songwriter Harry Ruby, and a son.

PRICE, DENNIS, 58, British stage and screen actor, died Oct. 6, 1973 in Guernsey, Channel Islands. Among the impressive list of his films are "Caravan," "Canterbury Tale," "Tunes of Glory," "The Millionairess," "Kind Hearts and Coronets," "Hungry Hill," "Dear Murderer," "The Intruder," "Naked Truth," "School for Scoundrels," "Victim," "Wonderful Life," "Horror of Frankenstein," and "Twins of Evil." Two daughters survive.

RANDOLPH, ISABEL, 83, stage, film, radio, and tv actress, died Jan. 11, 1973 in Burbank, Cal. Her screen roles included westerns with Gene Autry and Roy Rogers, "On Their Own," "Yesterday's Heroes," and "Look Who's Laughing." She appeared on tv as Dick Van Dyke's mother in his first series. She leaves two daughters.

REEVES, THEODORE, 62, playwright and screenwriter, died Mar. 18, 1973 of a heart attack in his Hollywood home. His best known films are "National Velvet," "I Walk Alone," "Last Train from Chungking," "Devotion," "The Storm," "Blossoms of Broadway," "The Doctor and the Girl," and "Bernadine." His widow survives.

REID, CARL BENTON, 79, stage and screen actor, died Mar. 16, 1973 in his Hollywood home. He moved to Hollywood in 1943 and appeared in many films, including "Little Foxes," "Tennessee Johnson," "North Star," "A Lonely Place," "The Great Caruso," "Will Rogers Story," "Smuggler's Gold," "The Egyptian," "Carbine Williams," "Left Hand of God," "Porkchop Hill," and his last "Madame X" in 1966. He had a continuing role in tv's "Burke's Law." Surviving are his widow, former actress Hazel Harrison, and a daughter.

ROBINSON, EDWARD G., 79, Rumanian-born film and stage character actor, died of cancer Jan. 26, 1973 in Hollywood. He made his film debut in 1924 in "The Bright Shawl," followed by 100 other pictures, including "The Racket," "They Knew What They Wanted," "Little Caesar," "Dr. Ehrlich and the Magic Bullet," "House of Strangers," "Red House," "The Idol," "Five Star Final," "Little Giant," "Man with Two Faces," "Kid Gallahad," "Amazing Dr. Clitterhouse," "Confessions of a Nazi Spy," "Brother Orchid," "Sea Wolf," "Unholy Partners," "Tales of Manhattan," "Flesh and Fantasy," "Woman in the Window," "Double Indemnity," "Our Vines Have Tender Grapes," "All My Sons," "Key Largo," "Ten Commandments," "A Hole in the Head," "Song of Norway," and his last "Soylent Green." He leaves his second wife, and a son.

RYAN, IRENE, 70, Texas-born vaudeville, radio, stage, film, and tv acress, died Apr. 26, 1973 in Santa Monica, Cal. Her greatest fame came as the pipe-smoking Granny Clampett in the nine season tv series "Beverly Hillbillies." Her first husband died in 1955, and her second marriage ended in divorce in 1960.

RYAN, ROBERT, 63, Chicago-born versatile stage and screen actor, died of cancer July 11, 1973 in NYC. He made his screen debut in 1943 in "Bombadier," subsequently appearing in over 90 other films, including "The Sky's the Limit," "The Set-Up," "Crossfire," "Tender Comrade," "Marine Raiders," "Berlin Express," "Boy with Green Hair," "The Racket," "Clash by Night," "Naked Spur," "Escape to Burma," "Odds against Tomorrow," "Bad Day at Black Rock," "Lonelyhearts," "King of Kings," "Billy Budd," "Battle of the Bulge," "The Wild Bunch," "The Iceman Cometh," and his last "Executive Action." He leaves two sons and a daughter.

SANDS, DIANA, 39, stage and film actress, died Sept. 21, 1973 of cancer in NYC. Her first screen role was in "A Raisin in the Sun," followed by "Four Boys and a Gun," "An Affair of the Skin," "Georgia, Georgia," "The Landlord," "Doctor's Wives," and her last, "Honeybaby, Honeybaby." She was married and divorced twice. Surviving are her mother, a brother, and a sister.

SEDGWICK, JOSIE, 75, silent picture actress, died of a stroke Apr. 30, 1973 in Santa Monica, Cal. In addition to being one of the popular western leading ladies, she also appeared in straight roles. Surviving is her sister, actress Eileen Sedgwick.

SIODMAK, ROBERT, 72, Tennessee-born director and producer, died Mar. 10, 1973 of a heart attack in Switzerland where he had been living for 18 years. Among his noted films are "Phantom Lady," "The Tempest," "Hatred," "Fly by Night," "The Suspect," "Strange Affair of Uncle Harry," "Spiral Staircase," "Dark Mirror," "The Killers," "The Devil Strikes at Night," "Escape from East Berlin," and his last "Custer of the West." Two brothers survive.

SMITH, ART, 73, stage and screen character actor, died Feb. 24, 1973 of a heart attack in West Babylon, NY. Included among his films are "Native Land," "South Sea Sinner," "Red, Hot and Blue," and "Brute Force." He is survived by one son.

STOSSEL, LUDWIG, 89, character actor in more than 50 films, died Jan. 29, 1973 in Hollywood. His movies include "House of Dracula," "Jennie," "Pride of the Yankees," "Cloak and Dagger," "Song of Love," "Somebody Loves Me," "Merry Widow," "Call Me Madam," "The Sun Shines Bright," "Geraldine," "Beginning of the End." His greatest fame came from his "Little old winemaker-Me" tv commercial. His widow survives.

STRANGE, GLENN, 74, screen actor, died Sept. 20, 1973 of cancer in Los Angeles. He had appeared in over 300 films, including many westerns, "House of Frankenstein," "House of Dracula," "Sea of Grass," "Red Badge of Courage," "Action in the North Atlantic," "Red River," and "The Cardinal." For 11 years he was the bartender, Sam, in the "Gunsmoke" tv series. He is survived by his widow, and a daughter.

Edward G. Robinson (1963)

Robert Ryan (1968)

Diana Sands (1965)

Nick Stuart (1928)

Albert Eddie Sutherland (1924)

Constance Talmadge (1925)

Ernest Truex (1951)

STUART, NICK, 69, Rumanian-born actor and band leader, died of cancer Apr. 7, 1973 in Biloxi, Miss. He appeared in over 50 films including "River Pirate," "News Parade," "Girls Gone Wild," "Joy Street," "Chasing through Europe," "Why Leave Home," "Swing High," "Honeymoon Zeppelin," "Campus Crushes," "Goodbye Legs," "Hello Television," "Police Call," "High School Hero," "Why Sailors Go Wrong." He gave up his band in 1961 and opened a men's store in Biloxi. Surviving are his second wife, and a daughter.

SUTHERLAND, ALBERT EDDIE, 76, English-born retired director, died Dec. 31, 1973 in Palm Springs, Cal. Began his career as a Keystone Kop, then joined Charlie Chaplin's staff. Among his film credits are "Comin' Through," "Burning Up," "Old Army Game," "Love's Greatest Mistake," "Tillie's Punctured Romance," "Number Please," "Dance of Life," "Saturday Night Kid," "Sky Devils," "International House, "Mississippi," "Diamond Jim," and "Follow the Boys." He also worked on tv's "Big Town" and "Mr. and Mrs. North." No reported survivors.

TALMADGE, CONSTANCE, 73, Brooklyn-born silent film star, died Nov. 23, 1973 in Los Angeles. Her most notable films were "Intolerance," "Scandal," "The Honeymoon," "Up the Road with Sally," "A Pair of Silk Stockings," "Sauce for the Goose," "Tempermental Wife," "Virtuous Vamp," "Perfect Woman," "Polly of the Follies," "Divorcee," "East Is West," "Dulcy," "Her Sister from Paris," and "Venus." She did not extend her career into talking pictures. She was the sister of Norma and Natalie Talmadge, who also starred in films. Her fourth husband died in 1964.

TERHUNE, MAX, 82, actor and sound effects man, died June 5, 1973 of a heart attack and stroke in Cottonwood, Ariz. He appeared in numerous westerns, and in "Giant," "Rawhide," "King and Four Queens," "Jim Thorpe, All American." A son survives.

TINDALL, LOREN, 52, stage and screen actor, and piano virtuoso at 4, died May 10, 1973 of a heart attack in Hollywood. He had appeared in "Over 21," "Good News," "Miss Grant Takes Richmond," and "Wait Till the Clouds Roll By," among others. Surviving are two brothers and three sisters.

TRUEX, ERNEST, 83, versatile stage, film and tv actor, died June 26, 1973 in Fallbrook, Cal. His film credits include "Good Little Devil," "Artie," "Caprice," "Whistling in the Dark," "Warrior's Husband," "Adventures of Marco Polo," "Start Cheering," "Bachelor Mother," "Lillian Russell," "Christmas in July," "Life with Blondie," "Always Together," "Girl from Manhattan," and "Twilight for the Gods." He leaves his third wife, former actress Sylvia Field, and three sons.

INDEX